Roxbury
Place-Name Stories

Advance Praise from Roxbury, Conn. Notables

"Green had the desire, perseverance, and inquisitiveness to pursue what is going to be a lasting treasure for our community. Insights into the nuggets that make up Roxbury's heritage make this a quick and pleasurable read. Thank you for being an inquiring mind and a treasure. The benefit is all ours."

Barbara Henry, First Selectman

"This is a most extraordinary *vade mecum*, compiling all that is remarkable, memorable, and lovely about our little town. For those who have lived here all their lives and for those just getting to know the place, Green captures the essence of Roxbury in ways that inform and amuse. She paints a living portrait of Roxbury's many charms and offers a vibrant picture of the features that give a town character and personality."

Steven Schinke, President, Roxbury Land Trust

"Green has woven a fascinating picture of Roxbury in her investigation of the place names of the town. She has done exhaustive research into the origins of the names of its roads, watercourses, districts, buildings, and even some distinctive rocks. This is not an easy task in a small rural town, where much of its history is in the oral tradition.

Delving into town records, printed sources, unpublished manuscripts, and the memories of older residents, she has developed a clear panorama of Roxbury where the white settlers first arrived in the 18th century. …Countless families passed through Roxbury on their way north and west. Some left only their names on locations in the town, like the Green Mountain Boys—Ethan Allen, Seth Warner, and Remember Baker."

Timothy Field Beard, FASG & Town Historian

"Green has crafted a delightful history of Roxbury, truly a 'must read' for all residents. It will be an important addition to our local history collection."

Valerie G. Annis, Director, Minor Memorial Library

Roxbury
Place-Name Stories:
facts, folklore, fibs

JEANNINE GREEN

iUniverse, Inc.
New York   Bloomington

Roxbury Place-Name Stories:
facts, folklore, fibs

iUniverse books may be ordered through booksellers or by contacting:

iUniverse
1663 Liberty Drive
Bloomington, IN 47403
www.iuniverse.com
1-800-Authors (1-800-288-4677)

Because of the dynamic nature of the Internet, any Web addresses or links contained in this book may have changed since publication and may no longer be valid. The views expressed in this work are solely those of the author and do not necessarily reflect the views of the publisher, and the publisher hereby disclaims any responsibility for them.

Cover Design: Billy Steers

ISBN: 978-1-4401-8694-3 (sc)
ISBN: 978-1-4401-8692-9 (dj)
ISBN: 978-1-4401-8693-6 (ebk)

Printed in the United States of America

iUniverse rev. date: 12/23/2009

To
Elinor Peterson Hurlbut and
Helen Hathaway Frisbie
for their inspiration and encouragement

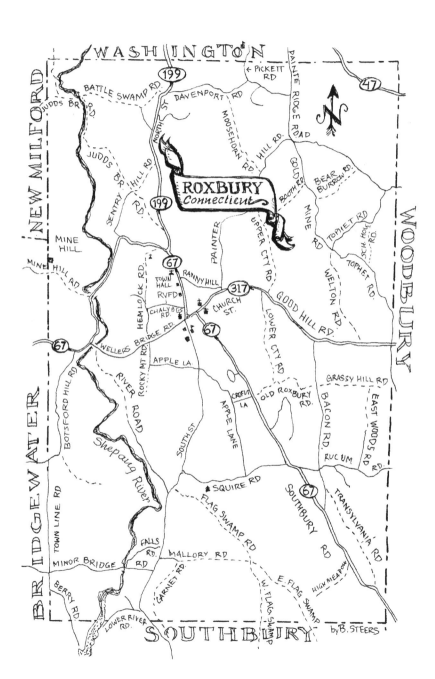

Table of Contents

Acknowledgments

The inspiration for this book came from Cynthia Newby, member of the Board of Directors of the Minor Memorial Library and I thank her for suggesting it. Writing a book is a humbling experience because one depends on others to share their time and expertise. Friends and strangers alike, whose names appear in the text and endnotes, contributed to this work in large and small ways and I thank them all. Many called with tips, arranged contacts, and never doubted I would complete this work.

First, my sincere thanks to Roxbury Town Clerk Peter Hurlbut who guided me through public records, told me stories not in the record books, and answered all of my seemingly ridiculous requests. I shudder to think what First Selectman Barbara Henry and members of her staff, Kim Baron, Christine Giordano, Judy Moker, and Linda Bertaccini must have thought about some of my questions, but they always responded with good cheer.

My thanks to the Minor Memorial Library staff who went beyond the call of duty. Without Library Director Valerie G. Annis' introduction to the "maroon books" of newspaper clippings, I would have been lost. Betty Synnestvedt exhibited a special talent for finding books behind books, untitled books, and unpublished manuscripts. Silky Berger merits a special bow for finding material from around the state and the Library of Congress.

I am grateful to the librarians, curators, and trustees who unlocked cases, threaded reels of microfilm, and gave over keys to climate-controlled rooms. I thank them all at the Gunn Library, Litchfield Historical Society, New Milford Library, New York Public Library Map Room, South Britain Library, Southbury Library, and Woodbury Library.

Many cheerleaders helped me cross the finish line. Sadly, some friends could not finish with me. To all I am grateful: Jerry Allford, Martha Baldwin, Lorie Barber, Jim Burr, Deborah Donnelly, Toby Goldfarb, Carolyn Goodrich, Frank Harland, Joyce Hornbecker, Betty Hurlbut, Jim Hurlbut, Jonathan Hurlbut, Colby Kalisher, Judith Kelly, Paul and Jean Leppert, Martha Matheu, Paul Milikin, Patricia O'Connor, Susan Payne, Steve Pisni, Jeannette Puglio, Paula Reichardt, Peggy Richards, David and Kathy Ryerson, Steven Schinke, Gina Shield, Dr. Simon Sobo, Billy and Julie Steers, and Marie Swanson.

I cherish the time Helen Frisbie and Elinor Hurlbut, the most youthful seniors I know, have spent with me. They told stories and opened up their legendary files of news clippings, photos, and old postcards. Thank you for keeping all that paper!

I will be forever grateful to my sister, Dolly Shivers, who was enthusiastic from the beginning, talked me through difficult times, and offered advice that helped make this a better book—all while working at a demanding job. Finally, a message to my perpetually cheerful brother, Jim Shivers, I finally have an answer. The answer is, yes—the book is finished. Thank you for asking.

To my friend Isabel Cymerman who endured it all with infinite patience, no amount of thanks will be enough. Her willingness to keep our dogs Sandy and Koko fed, watered, and pooped, while I pounded on the PC, made the writing that much easier.

Introduction

W hen I began to research this local history, I hoped for a cache of old letters hidden somewhere under a Roxbury rock. Like a detective, I wanted to reach into a crammed drawer and find faded letters and diaries that would reveal clues to Roxbury's origins. I longed for tales that would untangle Roxbury's roots and describe the people whose names were posted all over town. Perhaps someone would remember a trunk in an attic. Being an experienced librarian, a director of global systems for a Fortune 500 company, and a systems consultant to many other corporations, I knew miracles were unlikely to happen and serious research would be required.

I read local histories, wrote letters, sent e-mail messages, made telephone calls, and held interviews, all in search of stories. Little gems that arrived in the mail, came over the Internet, or found their way into conversations are scattered like nuggets throughout this work.

Most place-name books are about countries, states, or large cities, and are often alphabetical lists of names with facts about counties, towns, post offices, and streets. This book is different because it traces the origin of place-names in Roxbury, Connecticut, a small town in Litchfield County. It is not a scholarly work, but rather a book filled with informative, interesting, and fun stories about place-names bestowed by early settlers, later immigrants, and newcomers.

Each group left their imprint when they chose a name. Their selections provide insight into the life of the people who lived here, evoke memories of earlier times, signal what was valued in the past, and suggest what we treasure today. Their preferences also offer clues about what was in the minds of the namers.

When the first settlers arrived in the 1600s, they were isolated—far from any shore, far from any large town, far from their native England. They were primarily farmers who settled on land owned by Indians and Roxbury was a part of present-day Woodbury. At that time, Woodbury was the Pomperaug Plantation and Roxbury was Shepaug. The two names had much in common. Both were Indian names of nearby rivers. The Pomperaug River flowed through Woodbury and the Shepaug River defined the plantation's western border.

Shepaug, a Mohegan word meaning rocky water, is one of the few Indian names to survive in Roxbury.[1] The name Shepaug is an abbreviation of Mashapaug, meaning large standing water, according to R. A. Douglas-Lithgow in *Native American Place Names of Connecticut*. Early documents recorded Shippauge, Shippaug, and Sheepaug before settling on Shepaug and referred to Roxbury as Rocksbury and Roxberry.[2]

Roxbury followed a pattern of development typical of many Connecticut towns—settlement, ecclesiastical society, town. Originally, as Shepaug, it was a part of the Woodbury settlement and then as Roxbury, it became an ecclesiastical society and finally, an incorporated town. It developed this way by permission of the Connecticut General Court that also ordered its name.[3]

The Massachusetts General Court established the pattern for naming New England towns and rarely deviated from its rules.

Settlements retained their Indian names. When they became ecclesiastical societies and towns, they were given English names. The court chose the name and gave no reason for its choice of name. Names were "by order of the court."[4]

Roxburians had no influence on naming their ecclesiastical society or their town. After naming the Shippauge settlement and laying out the boundaries for the ecclesiastical society, the Connecticut General Court in 1743 granted that Shippauge "shall be called and known by the name of Roxbury."[5] Anyone who has tried to clear land, plow a field, or dig a garden has no doubt that this town is riddled with rocks and deserves the name authorities bestowed on it. The suffix *bury* signifies a fort or a dwelling-place. Thus, Roxbury was a fort or dwelling place among the rocks. The court kept the name Roxbury when it permitted the town to incorporate in 1796.

Just the same, its name origin is curious. Records are unclear, but the name may originate from another rocky place. When officials named Roxbury, Massachusetts, they broke with tradition, abandoned their rules about christening towns with English village names, and allowed a purely descriptive name to enter the landscape.[6] Perhaps because men on the Connecticut General Court had a genealogical connection to Massachusetts and no doubt knew of this town's rocky terrain, they were inclined to bestow the same name.[7]

The court may have mandated town names, but locals made the decisions about the little names. For example, townsmen needed to distinguish one stream from another and one hill from another. They discarded Indian names in favor of more familiar English words. Inevitably, patterns of naming emerged that exist today. For example, Mineral Springs Brook, Grassy Hill, and Clover Knoll were descriptive. Locals named places for unforgettable incidents they had witnessed. A real or imagined battle by a stream became Battle Swamp. A sighting of panthers roaming the hills became Panther Hill. When the first adventurers arrived they named Good Hill—an attractive, inspiring name. But they chose more ominous labels when they named Tophet and Hellgate—names that suggested darkness and danger.[8]

Over the centuries, each group left its imprint by changing, discarding, and adding names. Immigrants who came to work in the mines, in the quarries, at the hat shops, and on the railroad left their imprint. City folks who came looking for quiet have left their mark on this small village. Some place-names have remained for centuries; others have survived a few years and then passed into oblivion. This work is a collection of stories about those names.

No doubt, the town clerks and probate judges in Woodbury and Roxbury wanted to hide every time I arrived with laptop, notebooks, a camera, piles of pens, and pages of questions. I parked myself at their tables and pored over land records, town-meeting minutes, annual reports, vital records, probate files, and old maps. Libraries, historical societies, and museums were gold mines of old newspapers, genealogies, cemetery records, maps, censuses, and church records. With caution, I also turned to cyberspace.

I traveled every road—slowly—to the annoyance of tailgaters and speeders who preferred to whiz past historic homes, old barns, and green fields. I ventured onto private roads. It seemed important to measure, understand special features, and grasp what a road might have looked like as an Indian trail or a cow path in the days before they had a name. I lurked in cemeteries, hunted headstones, visited churches, hiked preserves, hung over the sides of bridges, and stared into brooks and streams to get a feel for what stories might be hiding beyond the cold facts found in documents. I studied family trees of early settlers when I found them. I looked for trees and plants in places where names suggested they would be growing. I imagined wild animals roaming through places with names like Moosehorn Brook, Bear Borough, and Wildcat Mountain. In other words, I poked and peeped into places I dare not mention.

When it came to organizing the mounds of information I had gathered, simplicity ruled, and so I arranged the book into chapters with descriptive titles. The first chapter gives a brief sketch of the town's history; the second contains forgotten names and names no longer commonly used. Each subsequent chapter contains stories about the origin of present-day names in places such as cemeteries, bridges, waterways, preserves, parks, churches, and roads. Each place-name is alphabetical within a chapter.

Every place-name has a story—some short, some long. Sometimes I could not determine the origin of a place-name, so a few sentences will have to suffice until someone provides more information. A name may appear three or four times with slight variations and each has its own story. For example, Flag Swamp, Flag Swamp Road, East Flag Swamp Road, and West Flag Swamp Road are four stories. Where the name is a surname the story may be a capsule genealogy. Some name origins may have begun as facts, but over years of retelling have become folklore—they too are included.

For readers who want to explore further, I added endnotes and a source list. Frequently, I uncovered more than one source about a name. If so, endnotes will lead you to them. A detailed index follows the source list. I have undoubtedly been guilty of errors about the origin of some place-names and welcome corrections.

This collection of nearly three hundred stories is about place-names dredged up from the past and used in the present:

curious, amusing, and sometimes convoluted tales that are part of Roxbury's rich history. Sometimes stories explain the names and sometimes they don't.

It is nonfiction, although some of the stories about witches, hermits, slaves, lost children, and other tales may be fiction. It not only includes facts but also contains fallacies and fibs that have occasionally turned history into folklore.

This project has taken longer than expected, but has been from start to finish a labor of love. If you learn more than you ever wanted to know about the intricacies of the federal census, the vagaries and variations in name spellings, and the trivia that makes the study of place-name origins addictive, I make no apologies. Whimsy was often my guide.

1 A Glimpse of the Past

Roxbury is a rural New England town of approximately 2,000 people nestled in the hills of northwestern Connecticut. This 27.4 square-mile rectangle is about six and a half miles long north to south and four miles wide east to west. It is a picture postcard village known for its rocky terrain. Its highest peak soars over 1000 feet at its northeast corner on Painter Hill and its lowest valley dips to 250 feet at its southwestern corner in the Shepaug valley. The Shepaug River, broken by whitewater, waterfalls, and boulders, defines its western border as it tumbles south into Lake Lillinonah, a dammed portion of the Housatonic River. Woodbury lies across hills to the east.

Like most of Connecticut's 169 towns, Roxbury developed from settlement, to ecclesiastical society, to incorporated town. Woodbury, its parent town, settled in 1673 under the name Pomperaug Plantation.

When religious differences got out of hand in Stratford, the Connecticut General Court

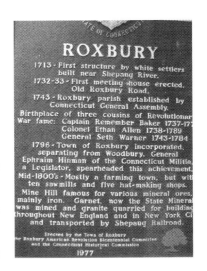

ROXBURY

1713 - First structure by white settlers built near Shepaug River.
1732-33 - First meeting house erected, Old Roxbury Road.
1743 - Roxbury parish established by Connecticut General Assembly.
Birthplace of three cousins of Revolutionary War fame: Captain Remember Baker 1737-177 Colonel Ethan Allen 1738-1789 General Seth Warner 1743-1784
1796 - Town of Roxbury incorporated, separating from Woodbury. General Ephraim Hinman of the Connecticut Militia, a Legislator, spearheaded this achievement.
Mid-1800's - Mostly a farming town, but wit ten sawmills and five hat-making shops. Mine Hill famous for various mineral ores, mainly iron. Garnet, now the State Minera was mined and granite quarried for building throughout New England and in New York Ci and transported by Shepaug Railroad.

Erected by the Town of Roxbury he Roxbury American Revolution Bicentennial Committee and the Connecticut Historical Commission

1977

ordered Capt. John Minor to lead the Rev. Zachariah Walker and fifteen men to follow the Pootatuck (Housatonic) River about sixty miles north. Once there, they were told to purchase land from the Pootatuck Indians and to settle a new plantation. The band of adventurers had detailed instructions about what rivers to follow, where to head north, when to turn east or west.

With map in hand, the venturesome settlers trekked through the wilderness and followed the Pootatuck River until they saw another river that flowed from the north and joined the Pootatuck River. It was the Pomperaug River, but the pioneers thought it was too small to be the one they were looking for, so they continued west and found the Shepaug River. Even though the men thought this river also looked small, they followed it north to present-day Mine Hill. The men were lost and exhausted but forged ahead. They turned east, arrived at Good Hill, looked down into the Pomperaug Valley, and knew their search had ended.

The court had selected Capt. John Minor to lead the settlers because he was fluent in Indian languages and could negotiate with the Indians to acquire land. In total, he negotiated six land purchases with the Pootatuck Indians. The second one, known as the Shepaug Purchase, was dated March 17, 1685-1686 and included about two-thirds of the present town of Roxbury. The sixth, or Confirmatory Purchase, was signed May 28, 1706 and included all former grants and purchases and a large tract of land that became the northern part of Roxbury.

Historian William Cothren explained that records of the first deeds were made over a hundred years after the settlement. It is likely that the second and sixth purchases were also recorded long after they were signed. Cothren assured us that Woodbury's settlers came upon these lands in a fair, honest, and legitimate fashion. However, he made no mention of the payment for the second and sixth purchases. He points out that the price of land bought from the Indians was not very high. He concluded that the Indians did not value their land highly. Settlers had paid for earlier purchases with a gray homespun coat, a hatchet, and a little powder and lead.[1]

Settlers came prepared with a code of laws called the Fundamental Articles that directed them about how to pay the Indians. The Articles also provided instructions on how to allocate land and grant home lots to each family. The laws commanded them to settle around a center as protection against the Indians. It guided them on how to hire ministers, build churches, and organize schools. With these strict rules from the court, the settlers began the hard work of clearing the land, building homes, and creating the Pomperaug Plantation.[2]

As the population grew, families settled farther away from the center. No one surveyed the western lands in the Shepaug Purchase until 1712 and the following year a man named Joseph Hurlbut became the first to settle that land; others soon followed. Unlike the Pomperaug Plantation, the Shepaug settlement was scattered and had no town center.

In those days, there was no separation of church and state, but there was a rule that applied to every person in a settlement. They absolutely had to attend worship; no excuse was accepted. The rule presented problems for Shepaug settlers who attended church in Woodbury and still paid taxes to it. The Woodbury meetinghouse was miles away, and worshippers from Shepaug had to travel on foot and horseback, a long and arduous trip, especially in winter. They soon tired of trekking over two ranges of hills at 800-foot elevations over rocky terrain to attend worship six or eight miles away. Worship however, was compulsory.

In desperation, the settlers petitioned the court for permission to hire a minister for the winter months, but it was not until 1732 that the court allowed them to build a meetinghouse closer to where they lived, and a town center began to form. Settlers continued to petition the court, this time for permission to establish their own ecclesiastical society. The court refused petition after petition until 1743, when it finally granted permission to the Shepaug settlers to establish their own society and be relieved from paying taxes to Woodbury.[3]

Fifty-three years would pass before Roxbury became an incorporated town. Meanwhile, the American Revolution broke out and Roxbury's Green Mountain Boys—Seth Warner, Remember Baker, Jr. and Ethan Allen—became heroes of that war. Finally, in 1796 Roxbury became one of twenty-two post-Revolutionary Connecticut towns

Between 1713, when Hurlbut arrived, and 1796 when the town incorporated, men like Asahel Bacon, Judge Nathan Smith,

COL. SETH WARNER MONUMENT, Roxbury, Conn.

and Phineas Smith from Woodbury, and Gen. Ephraim Hinman from Southbury had moved in, built elegant homes, established businesses, and begun to practice their professions. These men were wealthy, creative, and optimistic about Roxbury's future.

They were prepared to invest in and grow this town, and others wanted to live where they lived. A new town center began to form when the Congregational and Episcopal Churches built edifices along present-day Church Street and Wellers Bridge Road.

Roxbury was primarily an agricultural community in those days, and though these men were merchants, lawyers, and businessmen, they were also farmers. In the early nineteenth century, nearly half the town's one thousand people were farmers. They were self-sufficient with a strong internal economy. Families and small businesses provided the necessities of food, clothing, and shelter.

The town flourished in the first decades of the nineteenth century. Artisans and small manufacturing supported a stable population. Millers ground flour from grain, shoemakers made shoes and repaired saddles, fullers and weavers prepared cloth, tanners cured leather, blacksmiths made nails and horseshoes, and coopers made barrels to store and ship goods.

Mine Hill, one of the first stops Stratford settlers made in their search for the Pomperaug River, became a major employer. From 1750 to 1850 and again after 1900, men harvested silver and iron ores, mined garnets, silica, and quarried granite. A village named Chalybes supported the miners and quarrymen with boarding houses, a post office, general and hardware stores. Mining was a well-paying industry, and quarrying prospered nearly forty years and continues today. The rich and powerful fought over ownership rights to the hill.

The Oxford Turnpike, now Route 67, ran between Roxbury and New Milford. The turnpike connected this town to larger markets and was instrumental in the growth of the hatting industry. Homes of leading hat manufacturing families like Lathrop, Squire, and Hurlbut still stand. The hat fabricating and hat assembly industry survived from about 1820 to 1865, but the small shops were no match for the mechanized hat manufacturing system in nearby Danbury.

The Civil War broke out and disrupted lives in a state where over 50,000 were killed, wounded, or missing. This town lost few men, but incurred a war debt that took years to pay off. After the Civil War, the Industrial Revolution was in full swing, but Roxburians were slow to change and reluctant to plunge into manufacturing and new technologies. The Shepaug Railroad is an example. Fundamentalists saw it as the work of the Devil and farmers worried it would damage cattle and buildings. The population at large feared strangers and city slickers would move into town. Nevertheless, regular trains started running shortly after New Year's Day 1872. But it was too late; the mines had stopped producing and the heavy ore shipments the railroad expected never materialized. In addition, the panic of 1873 swept the country and dashed all hope for industrial or tourism industries to develop along the railroad route.[4]

A little hope appeared on the horizon—tobacco. In January 1878, the *Woodbury Reporter* noted that Roxbury had produced upwards of $30,000 worth of tobacco during the previous season. Robert Keeler employed thirty men to sort and pack tobacco; Eli N. Bradley hired extra hands; others reported planting fifteen acres, and many farmers grew three to five acres. The tobacco was a fine quality used to wrap cigars, not the shade-grown tobacco seen in other parts of the state. Even though keeping a crop in good shape was a lot of work, tobacco proved to be a lucrative business.[5]

Other industries did not fare so well. By World War I, mining and quarrying had almost disappeared. Chalybes, also known as Roxbury Station, became a ghost town. Workers left town and boardinghouses closed. In time, the village itself vanished. In 1920, only 647 people lived in Roxbury and only 122 farms remained. Half the farmers were in dairy production; the rest were general farmers. In the new century, tobacco prices fell, and the few remaining farmers started beef and dairy farms. Nathan T. Beardsley raised Red Devon oxen and was one of the more successful farmers.

Before World War I and during the Great Depression, people looked for places to escape the hustle and bustle of big cities. Roxbury's landscape was unspoiled, beautiful, and near the city. Outsiders arrived and bought up old farms for summer retreats and retirement homes.

Between 1910 and 1960, the population was less than one-thousand. By 1930, most farms were gone, and the population dwindled to 553 people. After World War II, highways improved, and people with automobiles were on the move. Artists, sculptors, authors, playwrights, and actors from the stage and screen who wanted second homes and privacy moved to Roxbury. Mystery writer Ellery Queen and actress Sylvia Sydney bought homes in the town center. Sculptor Alexander Calder moved to Painter Hill; playwright Arthur Miller and his wives actress Marilyn Monroe and photographer Inge Morath lived nearby. Authors William and Rose Styron settled in another part of town. Actors Walter Matthau and Richard Widmark and author Frank McCourt settled in the northwestern part of town. Most of these personalities are gone now, but others still find privacy and refuge here.

This is still a part-time and full-time country refuge for high-profile and well-to-do residents who enjoy the privacy, quiet, and rural beauty that playwright A. R. Gurney described as the feel of a nineteenth century farm village.[6] Still, the town has changed from being an agrarian community. The town's population is the highest it has ever been in its history, yet less than a handful of farms remain in Roxbury. Maple Bank Farm is one that has survived and is the oldest operating farm in Connecticut.

One reason Roxbury has retained its bucolic beauty is that early generations left the landscape unspoiled, and throughout the twentieth century additional steps have been taken to preserve its beauty. For example, the town introduced strict zoning laws in 1932, the Roxbury Land Trust was established in 1970 to preserve undeveloped land, and in 1997 the town adopted a Scenic Road Ordinance

As a result, visitors passing though will see white picket fences, stone walls, and streets with mature maples and oaks. There are no sidewalks, no stoplights, and no supermarkets. People congregate at the one school, four churches, a public tennis court, a restaurant, a gas station, a market/deli, three museums, a library, a senior center, a land trust office, a town pond, a post office, a fire station, a transfer station, a town hall, and numerous parks, gardens, and nature preserves.

A Board of Selectmen presides over a town meeting form of government, and volunteers who serve on commissions do much of the work of the community. Locals protect their rural surroundings, support their community, and embrace its rich past. Its historic homes are all private homes cared for by owners who cherish their history; none have become commercial establishments.

Generations of residents have left their mark on the land, many in the form of place-names. Over a century passed before Roxbury could untangle itself from Woodbury. By then, Pomperaug Plantation settlers had already bestowed many names, but new industries, growth, and unexpected events required new names. In this twenty-first century, townsmen still add place-names to the landscape of this now prosperous and prestigious community. Read on for the stories behind those names.

2 Gone But Not Forgotten

*N*ow you see it; now you don't. Officials like to rename, renumber, and discontinue roads and highways. Post offices and villages vanish. Even immovable objects like hills, fields, and rocks disappear from memory, and folks forget names that were once memorable. Discontinued, vanished, and forgotten—a gloomy picture, if you think about it.

But cheer up; we're here to remember stories of places and names dredged up from the past. The following curious, amusing, and sometimes convoluted tales were all part of Roxbury's rich history. Sometimes they explain the names; sometimes they don't.

Baker Plains. John Baker's name is not in *Who's Who*, but he played a critical role in Roxbury's history. In 1746, when Roxbury's first church was bursting at the seams with parishioners, John Baker petitioned the Connecticut General Assembly to allow the society of Roxberry to build its second meetinghouse. This level stretch of land half a mile north of Christ Church, where his family settled, bears his name.[1]

Bishop Avenue. The name may be from Miles Bishop who, in 1813, served in the State House of Representatives in the Connecticut General Assembly. His descendants were farmers in Roxbury through the mid-twentieth century. The *New Milford Gazette*, April 7, 1899 cited the avenue's name when it announced that someone had moved from Bishop Avenue into the house vacated by Thomas Spargo.[2]

Booth Hill. Richard Booth (b. 1607) emigrated from England and settled in Stratford in 1640. His descendants included Ebenezer Booth, an early member of the Congregational Church and Ely Booth (1775-1854), whose son, Hervey Minor Booth, became a prominent Roxbury philanthropist.[3]

Bradley Street. Student Jeremiah Decker wrote in 1864 that the Seth Warner Monument was at the corner of Main and Bradley Streets. Four years earlier, when census takers counted Roxbury's population, thirty Bradleys lived in Roxbury, enough to merit a street named for them.[4]

Brian Tierney Lane. This lane leads to a preserve on Squire Road that honors Brian Edward Tierney (1948-1968), a Roxbury soldier killed in South Vietnam.

The land trust provided evidence of the glacial activity in the area. Some geologists believe that the deep gullies that run through it and the enormous boulders perched on the ledges and hills are evidence of Noah's flood. They believe that a huge upheaval in the Arctic Ocean sent floodwaters rushing across New England, dropping boulders and rocks in its wake.[5]

Wooden steps and footbridges lead through trails that twist along Jacks Brook to the Cascades waterfall. Other trails wind through hemlock forests, stands of beech trees, and rows of mountain laurel. Still others meander through hay fields. Climb the steep slope above the Cascades, head southeast, and you will see one of the town's most notable trees, called the "Lightning Tree." Enjoy a walk under the cathedral ceiling formed by the fallen branches.[6]

Bull Meadow. Need a quick $700? William Stuart, a notorious counterfeiter, claimed he put $700 of good money and

$700 of bad money in a jug and stashed the jug in a ledge on the north side of Bull Meadow. To look for Stuart's loot, nose around the meadow on the west side of the Shepaug River below Wellers Bridge. The moniker may be from bulls that grazed in the field or from what locals thought of Stuart's story.[7]

Burwell Tavern. Though unconfirmed, legend has it that in 1785 a man named Burwell built the tavern on the corner of Church Street and Southbury Road. Today, the private home, known as the Burwell Tavern-Thomas House, also honors the Thomas family who held the property for a hundre years.[8]

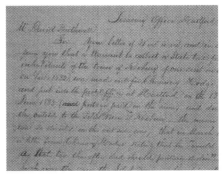

It's unlikely we'll ever know who built the roadhouse since public records are silent on the matter, but we do know that Burwell and Brothwell were variations of the surname. For example, in September 1788, notices were posted throughout the area to settle Benedict Burwell's estate.[9]

From 1790 through 1830, Joseph F. Brothwell lived in Woodbury, and in 1832, Cyrus Brothwell's heirs mortgaged his property. Brothwell descendants lived there until the 1880s and any one of them could have built Burwell Tavern.[10]

On the other hand, David Brothwell's father might have built the tavern. David Brothwell (1792-1838) was an entrepreneur and representative to the state legislature, and in 1828, he was the only person in town licensed to sell liquors and wines.[11]

He not only sold liquor but also sold Dr. Brandreth's Vegetable Universal Pills that claimed to remove all impurities in the blood, improve circulation, and cure everything from measles, fever, and small pox to sore eyes and enlarged glands. At two shillings a pack, the pills were so popular that during 1836-1837, Dr. Brandreth ran bi-weekly ads in the *Connecticut Courant* to warn customers about false ads, phony agents, and counterfeit pills.

Camp Mel. A dot on a 1955 U. S. Geological Survey map pinpointed the camp a mile and a quarter east of Roxbury Falls. Even though snow covered the ground, I went looking for the camp, and ran into Russell Dirienzo, selectman and award-winning chair of the Inland-Wetlands Commission. When I asked Dirienzo about the camp, he pointed toward Southbury, said that Mel was a recluse who lived in the woods and that people called his place Mel's camp. I was captivated, but unconvinced.

Local realtor Russell Poteet said that Camp Mel was a Boy Scout camp and longtime resident Lois Hodges said she never heard of the camp, but would ask her brother. Sure enough, Bill Platt, a lifelong resident of Southbury, confirmed that long ago his family sold a piece of land in Roxbury near the fire tower behind the Southbury Training School. Platt said the Boy Scouts planned to build a camp there but never did.

I thought maybe remnants of a camp still existed, so when the snow melted, I again headed for the hills behind the fire tower, but found no camp. I'm certain, though, that Mel was lurking in the woods staring at me.

Castle Street. In its early days, other names for this street were Castle Road, Lower Road, and East Street. Most locals, however, called it Castle Street for over 150 years. It included present-day Squire Road and Rucum Road and was part of the road from South Britain to New Milford.[12] The street name is from the many Castle family property owners who built homes here the early to mid-1800s; three historic Castle family homes still stand on Rucum Road.[13]

When Clayton B. Squire (1881-1978) was ninety-six years old, he told an interviewer for a local history that there was a lot of controversy over renaming Castle Street. People wanted to keep the name Castle because it was one of Roxbury's oldest families. If there was controversy, one would expect to find it in town minutes or annual reports, but I have found nothing, so cannot date when the name changed. According to Squire, it was thought that no one named Castle still lived in town at the time. In *Roxbury Remembered*, the author mentioned that Norman Hurlbut kept a 1923 newspaper clipping of the last will and testament of Celia A. Castle that showed that someone by that family name did live here.[14]

Cattail. These rampant wetland plants with hundreds of tiny flowers stuck on top of tall brown spikes stand like gigantic cigars on a stick and once covered a small piece of land opposite the Congregational Church.[15]

Center Hill. The origin of the name is lost, however, according to one account, counterfeiters stashed their booty on Center Hill in a cave called Gamaliel's Den located west of Moosehorn Brook.[16]

Chalybes. Dr. Horace Bushnell (1802-1876) gave the name Chalybes to a small mining village in Roxbury, but the name caused a bit of a stir.

On February 16, 1867, the *Hartford Daily Courant* announced that a new post office called Kalibs opened at Mine Hill. The name appeared to have been a problem and on July 25, 1873, the same newspaper wrote that letters addressed to the post office had borne eighteen incorrect names and added that the Litchfield *Enquirer* thought the plainer name Roxbury Station would be acceptable.

The *Enquirer* must have carried some influence because from 1875 until 1918, the name was Roxbury Station. Later, that office closed, and a Roxbury post office that had been open since 1820 delivered all the mail.

Christian Street. Curiously, in 1864, Jeremah Decker wrote that he lived at 101 Christian Street, now called South Street, even though, as far as we know, addresses had no numbers then.[17] I found no record for the name origin, and found no surname Christian in any Roxbury censuses. The U. S. Geological Survey, however, printed the street name on its maps in 1949 and 1955, and Malcolm Bray Realtor printed it in 1973 on a promotional map.

Community Hall. When a minister from Christ Church held services on Sunday evenings, miners and quarrymen gathered to worship at the hall near Roxbury Station. One newspaper account reported that George Washington, a colored preacher from another town, held services there for a week at the mission.[18]

Confirmatory Purchase. John Minor, of the Pomperaug Plantation, negotiated this sixth and last purchase with the Indians on May 28, 1706. It was the only recorded deed signed by English and Indian women. The deed allowed the Indians to retain the Pootatuck Reservation that contained their principal village. It also included a large tract of land that became the northern part of Roxbury.[19]

Cream Puffs. Tempers soared, fists flew, and bloody noses gushed when toughs from Roxbury Station called boys from Roxbury Center "Creampuffs with cow dung on their heels."[20] It all happened on Sundays when the boys battled it out on a baseball field near Wellers Bridge. According to Peter Hurlbut, town clerk, the "softies" had equally cheeky names for their opponents; see River Rats below.

Crescent Lodge No. 243. Every Friday night, at least from 1886 through 1889, esteemed citizens—Hodge, Castle, Squire, Minor, Leavenworth, Sanford, Pons, and Bradley—met at the town hall. They dressed in full regalia, saluted, marched around an altar, read stories, and sang to celebrate abstinence. During the prior decade, the Woodbury Reporter carried regular announcements of

temperance meetings and celebrations, and on March 14, 1878 it promoted a "necktie sociable" to celebrate the Good Templars' seventh anniversary. All Good Templars' members performed the dressing, marching, saluting ritual. Roxburians Frank and Albrt Pierce attended temperance lectures in Woodbury and may have attended the anniversary party.[21]

By early 1886, some Roxburians joined the International Organization of Good Templars and formed Crescent Lodge No. 243 and by January 1887, forty-eight people were members, thirty "brothers" and eighteen "sisters."[22] The prior summer, members held a peaches and ice cream fundraiser to conquer the evils of distilled spirits and moral decay spreading across the globe. That same day, their fellow citizens looked to the heavens for pleasure—possibly with a tankard of ale in hand—and enjoyed a rare eclipse of the sun.[23]

Crows Nest Rock. An 1826 deed signed by Asahel Bacon and Elnathan Mitchels signed a deed in 1826 that transferred land near Crows Nest Rock, so called, in the southwest part of Roxbury, south of the bridge and west of the Shepaug River. The description clearly distinguishes the location from Raven Rock in the northwest part of town on the east side of the river.[24]

East Street. Today, we know it as Squire Road, formerly Castle Street. According to longtime resident Bud Squire, his father always called it East Street. Squire added that Merwin Bronson's wife had a blue-blooded fit when the street name was changed to Squire Road—so angry that she had her address listed in the phone book as Jack's Brook.[25]

Fields, The. Roxbury land records identified it as a large flat mass of ground between Sentry Hill and Judds Bridge.[26]

Fire Tower Lane. Resident Marian Skedgell said that when the State owned this lane on Painter Hill, now part of a private driveway, the State mowed it and kept it clear for a fire tower. She recalled what a treat it was to climb to the top. From atop the tower, she could see Long Island Sound some forty miles away.[27] The fire tower is gone now, but on a hot summer day in 2005, Skedgell and I scrambled through poison ivy and brambles to find the tower's concrete foundation; it too had vanished.

Frisbie Road. Frisbie was a household name in the 1920s when Mrs. Frisbie's Pies became a national craze, but she did not name this road. The name is from 1795 when Edward Frisbie built his home there. His descendant Harmon Frisbie, inherited the property and later converted the Old Frisbie Place, into a rooming house for quarrymen at Mine Hill.[28]

Over the years, folks no longer needed this short stretch of road, so in 1980 the town discontinued part of it and in 1998 discontinued the entire length. Maybe rumors of a misadventure kept folks away. No Frisbie was involved, but a tenant was.

The Mannerings were tenants at the Old Frisbie Place and William Whiteman, a hired hand from England, lived with them. All was quiet until the *New Milford Gazette* splashed a headline that read: "Was It Murder?" A photograph of Jane and Edward Mannering, decked out in formal clothes, their dog at Edward's feet, topped the two-column story. A photographer had snapped the couple's picture Tuesday, February 15, 1893. Four days later, Edward Mannering was dead.

Jane Mannering immediately became the prime suspect in a case that had the potential to become one of the most famous criminal cases in Connecticut history. The question was, had Jane murdered her husband with strychnine? If so, did she do it alone, did William help her, or did Edward, a hard-drinking man, poison himself by mistake? Gossipers whispered that the Mannering's marriage was an unhappy one and that Jane was much too fond of William.

Word about the case spread and people came from all around to gawk; crowds packed the Roxbury Town Hall as Justice Cyrus E. Prindle began hearings. David Barnes' house became the holding pen for the accused, but after preliminary hearings and numerous delays, the trial moved to the superior court in Litchfield.

Details of the story came out. Edward had been drinking heavily for two or three days and on Saturday, he took salt and saltpeter to help him sober up. At 8 o'clock Sunday morning, as usual, William filled a pail with kitchen scraps and went out to feed the pigs. Edward joined him, even though he felt sick.

By the time Edward got back to the house, he was in agony. His body shook, his neck was stiff, and his teeth clenched. His wife gave him a cup of coffee with a little gin in it while William ran to his neighbor for help. When he returned, Edward Mannering was dead.

Witnesses said that Jane often complained about her husband's drinking and cruelty. She had once told George Hurlburt, a prominent Roxbury merchant, that she hoped her husband would be dead when she got home. A storekeeper testified that both Mannerings bought strychnine to poison foxes that were killing their turkeys. Yet, all witnesses testified to Jane's good character.

William swore that when he went to feed the pigs again Sunday evening, two pigs were lying down. They had eaten the day's leftovers, cried in pain, and didn't want to be touched. They squealed and made noise all night. The next morning, both pigs were dead.

A doctor testified that he found strychnine in a box of Royal Baking powder in a kitchen cabinet. The attending physician, the Medical Examiner, and the Coroner all testified; attorneys on both sides made elaborate arguments.

The jury deliberated for two hours; the verdict, "Not guilty." The applause was so loud it shook the courthouse and Jane Mannering fainted. Later, someone erected an unadorned headstone in the Center Cemetery with the simple inscription, Edwin Mannering.[29]

Glenacres School. Michael Martin, with degrees from Columbia, Harvard, and Yale did most of his teaching in Europe. Between 1928 and 1933, he taught in the largest private school in Germany, but as Hitler came to power, he left Germany. In September 1933, Martin opened this boarding school on Chalybes Road.

Glenacres School was open to girls and boys during its first two years, but later became a boys' school for students aged ten-to-sixteen-years old. Martin was interested in teaching gifted students and focused the curriculum on the sciences. A fourteen-page brochure described the school as

an "ideal environment for the physical and mental development of a small group of boys." Black and white photos depicted an environment typical of private schools of the day—boys in jackets and ties—attending math class, leaning over microscopes, and balancing easels on their knees during art class on the lawn.

Martin opened the school in the Rev. Zephaniah Swift House, built about 1795, and remodeled the barn for classrooms. Current owners have said that the upstairs attic has small cubicles that may have been a dormitory.

By all accounts, the school was a success and some of the boys who attended went on to Phillips Exeter, St. Paul's, and Groton academies. In June 1939, when Glenacres had its largest registration, Martin closed the school. He told a local newspaper that he wanted to prepare himself to teach religion and would study at the Episcopal school in Cambridge, Massachusetts to prepare himself for that endeavor.[30]

Goat Rock. Land records in 1808 and 1828 described land near Goat Rock as being on Mine Hill and near the town line with New Milford. How the name came about is anyone's guess. Droves of cattle and swine and flocks of sheep may have wandered in the hills, but no records tell us whether goats roamed this rock. Maybe locals thought the shape of this rock reminded them of a goat.[31]

Granite Hill. Granite quarries at Mine Hill produced stone to build churches, part of New York City's 59th Street Bridge, the Brooklyn Bridge, and Grand Central Station. Companies still lease land and quarry stone on this hill.

Great Meadow. It must have been a broad sweep of cleared land or open field spread across the landscape to earn the laudatory name Great Meadow. In the 1700s, it referred to a flat stretch of land north of Roxbury Station in the area once known as Upper Farms.[32]

Halfway House. Stagecoach passengers stopped here for food and rest after a rough ride and this mid-point or "halfway" house was on the route between Stamford and Hartford. Today, it is a private home on River Road.[33]

Hellgate Falls. Folks who lived here in the eighteenth century knew this demonic name. For all we know it may have been a wildly popular place. Regretfully, history books are silent about the origin of the name. Were folks frightened of the powerful falls and gigantic boulders? Did demons rise from the falls? Did Indians ambush white men or cast a spell on them in this place? Was there a tunnel under the falls that led to Hades? Did a local zealot believe evil spirits or the devil lived here? No legends or tales have been told about this name; however, if you insist on locating Hellgate Falls, read on.

These directions are a little out-of-date, but no others exist. If you want to find the falls, you'll have to follow them. A deed dated April 22, 1799 to measure and survey John Atwell's land named this place. His land was west of the road that went from Major Ephraim Hinman's to Warners Mill and on the east side of Rocky Mountain. From there, go past numerous heaps of stones and a white oak bush west of Abiathan Squire's dwelling, then pass more heaps of stone and turn south to a spot of muddy land. You've arrived at Hellgate Falls.[34]

Hoop Hole Road. Each spring, men climbed Hoop Pole Hill to cut black ash and hickory saplings, called hop poles or hoop poles. They cut the poles into six-foot lengths, soaked them in water, pounded them with a mallet, and split them into strips. Barrel makers, known as coopers, pounded the strips again so they would be soft enough to wrap around barrels, casks, and kegs to hold the staves together. When the strips dried, they were said to be as strong as iron.[35]

Maps named the hill Hoopole, Hooppole, Hoop Pole, and Hoop Hole until 1995 when the U. S. Board of Geographic Names put a stop to the confusion and declared it Hoop Hole Hill. No matter the spelling, playwright Arthur Miller lived on the road and said it was dangerous. He wrote a letter to ask the town to close the road because people were using it to come onto his property without permission. Even worse, they set up camp, hunted, and lit fires making it unsafe for his family. On January 21, 1999, the town closed the road.[36]

Josiahs Hill. The name honored Dr. Josiah R. Eastman (1771–1861), Roxbury's only resident physician for nearly thirty-four years. Today, the name is Booth Hill. Dr. Eastman followed his father's example and became a physician. When he earned his license in 1793, he planned to open a practice in East Haven, but scarlet fever was raging in Roxbury, so he returned to his birthplace.

Dr. Eastman was a member of the Congregational Church, held several local offices, and practiced medicine in nearby towns. In 1813, he became famous for developing a successful treatment for an epidemic fever that swept across lower Litchfield County and killed twenty-two people in Roxbury.[37]

Leatherman. The Leatherman was a frightful looking character who wandered the back roads of New York and Connecticut for thirty years, always dressed from head to toe in leather. He never begged, yet families along his route fed him.

He was a precise man who traveled the New England countryside on a rigid, predictable schedule from 1858 to 1889. People knew exactly when to expect him, and some have said that every thirty-four days he stopped at their house, always at the same time of day.

His real name was Jules Bourglay, and if the stories about him are true, he was a lonely Frenchman who suffered from unrequited love. For nearly three decades, he trudged through heat, rain, drought, and bitter New England winters. The press reported his passage through Roxbury on Wednesday, June 16, 1886.[38]

He was a tired and lonely man in his sixties when the blizzard of 1888 paralyzed the northeast. The heavy snow delayed the Leatherman by four days. Somehow, he struggled through that bitterly cold winter, but the combination of his age, hard life, and harsh weather finally took its toll. He fell ill and died March 24, 1889 in a cave near Ossining, New York—an 1814 French prayer book was in his breast pocket.[39]

Little Field. Though records are unclear, this field on North Street is probably the same parcel of land that Lewis Rumsey sold to Asahel Bacon in 1789. Locals know it as Rumsey Meadow.[40]

Look Out Rock. Stagecoaches wended their way through Brookfield, crossed the Housatonic River, turned onto Baker Road, and forded the Shepaug River before they stopped at a halfway house for passengers to rest.

According to legend, Indians hid behind the rock on the banks of the river, watching and waiting, ready to raid weary stagecoach passengers. Locals believe that Indian relics and arrowheads found in fields near the rocky ledge are proof that the story is true.[41]

Lower Farms. About 1715, Henry Castle settled in the plains above Roxbury Falls in what became known as Lower Farms. The name was given to distinguish this settlement from one called Upper Farms farther north on the Shepaug River.[42]

Main Street. In 1864, present-day Wellers Bridge Road and Church Street were , together, known as Main Street, according to references in a letter written to the *Roxbury Gazette*.[43] It was the most important road between Roxbury and Woodbury and Roxbury and New Milford.

Metcalf Road. During the Great Depression, Rowe (a. k. a. Raoul) B. Metcalf (1900-1965), bought most of the land around Judds Bridge to create a diary farm. At one time, he had a herd of three hundred cows and owned fifteen farms that spanned 2,300 acres in Roxbury.

Metcalf was a gamesman and experimenter who shared a common goal with the state of Connecticut. Both wanted more birds in the environment for hunters. Quail were scarce and raising grouse in captivity was a problem, but Metcalf knew of a bird closely related to the ruffled grouse. It was the Chukar partridge—a bird from India. In 1934, the state gave Metcalf permission to release Chukar partridges into the wild to test whether they would survive. If his experiment succeeded, the State agreed to release Chukar partridges on public hunting grounds. Today, the *Connecticut Hunting and Trapping Guide* includes Chukar partridges—the daily limit is two; the season limit is ten.

Part of Metcalf's property was sold after his death, and in the 1980s, Arthur L. Carter, former publisher of *The Litchfield County Times,* bought the remaining property. In August 1980, the town discontinued Metcalf Road.[44]

Molasses Hollow. A dip in the land south of Tophet Road filled up with molasses when a barrel fell off an ox-cart, and someone tagged the sunken sticky mess Molasses Hollow.[45]

Moose Horn Hill. Moose horns were scattered all over the place—clinging to the hill, jammed between rocks, swimming in a brook—now we're stuck with a naming mistake. Here's how things got muddled.

Moose have antlers; sheep have horns. Antlers are temporary; horns are permanent. Antlers have branches; horns do not. Males have antlers; males and females have horns. Well, the last is only partially true—it's easy to be confused. For example, reindeer are exceptions to the male antler rule; Santa Claus' reindeer may not all be male.

Moosebeat. Moose are big. The average adult can weigh up to 1,000 pounds and stand six feet at the shoulders. These members of the deer family are the largest wild animal in North America. Where the place-name Moosebeat originated is unknown. Maybe someone heard moose beating the ground with their hooves—perhaps sparring an opponent. Moose are not friendly; a threatened moose will kick and stomp until the threat stops moving.[46]

Land records first mentioned this name in a deed dated May 5, 1802; another reference called it Moose Beat Lot and described it as a stretch of land in the valley to the east of Painter Hill. It has been said that this was a place where moose wintered, but is now a place entirely forgotten by this generation.[47]

Moosehorn Hollow. About 1700, Cornelius Hurlbut and his brothers launched Roxbury's first business venture when they built a sawmill at Moosehorn Hollow. Why Moose Horn is the hill and Moosehorn is the hollow is anyone's guess.[48]

Munnacommock. On Sunday, March 17, 1686, nine men who represented the Pootatucks set their marks on the deed known as the Shepaug Purchase. Munnacommock was the Indian name for the land east of the Shepaug River that comprised two-thirds of Roxbury and the northwest boundary of Southbury.[49]

Old Generation Road. Though the road is gone, a plan for it lies rolled up in the vaults of the town hall. The March 1942 survey map showed the proposed layout of Old Generation Road. It was projected to be forty-feet-wide, and it was to replace an old highway on Vera Q. Ayers' property. On the long, narrow map, a line depicting Old Generation Road meandered between Route 199, north of

Judds Bridge Road, down Painter Hill Road, and through Toplands Farm until it twisted down the hill to the town center.

Old Roxbury Days. This country festival began in 1972 when the Roxbury Volunteer Fire Department wanted to raise money for a new firehouse. The three-day event had crafts exhibits, a country store that sold ice cream and penny candy, a flea market, an antique cars display, and exhibits of antique tools and farm machinery. Horse shows, drum and bugle corps, chicken barbecues, and horse-drawn carriage rides were part of the festival. For six years, there were no Old Roxbury Days. Then the Roxbury Historical Society revived the event, and their barn became the centerpiece with displays of antique tools, a one-horse sleigh, antique tractors, and old wagons. Old Roxbury Days ended July 25, 1998.[50]

Old Tophet Road. On March 29, 2003, the town discontinued Old Tophet Road from its intersection with Good Hill Road to the Lilly Preserve parking lot. The biblical origin is the same as Tophet Road. See the chapter on roads for the scoop on this devilish place.

Ore Mountain. Today, called Rocky Mountain, the mound is a mile south of the town center. Its name origin is unknown and no records show mining at that location.[51]

Orton Post Office. In 1900, this temporary post office operated at Roxbury Falls and handled mail for workers at the silica mill and garnet mines.[52] The name origin is unknown, though the surname Orton was among those in early Woodbury and Roxbury. By the twentieth century, no Ortons lived in Roxbury, though families with that name did live in New Milford.

Oxford Turnpike. Virginia was home to the nation's first turnpike company, chartered in 1785, and ten years later a Roxbury visionary joined the turnpike revolution. Phineas Smith

(1759-1839) believed that a road between Roxbury and Oxford would benefit the town's economy. His turnpike brought hat making and other small commerce to Roxbury and paid investors a whopping 12 percent return.[53] See the story of Southbury Road for more on the Oxford Turnpike.

Paquabaug. Also called Munnacommock, a 1659 map identified it as an island in the Shepaug River.[54]

Paradise Valley. Miners and quarrymen stayed at Bridget Berry's boarding house in Paradise Valley, another name for the Shepaug Valley near Minor Bridge."[55]

Pine Cobble. A local historian called the rounded mound, a "queer little hill." Cobble was a prominent place-name in western New England and was a widespread English dialect word for a rounded hill. The origin of the word has been disputed, but is probably English and akin to the word cobblestone, a naturally rounded stone.[56] This cobble rose northeast of Mine Hill near an old mill on the Shepaug River. Town meeting minutes referred to it as a parcel of land in the western part of Roxbury, a little south of Roxbury Station.[57]

Pulpit Rock. For centuries, Pulpit Rock was a staging area for calls to arms, appeals for bravery, and prayers for peace. You will find the lone, jagged rock nestled among trees on the banks of the Shepaug River on Baker Road south of Hodge Park. According to one account, it dates back to a time when Algonquin Indians lived in the Shepaug Valley.[58]

From this rostrum, Indian chiefs counseled their followers, roused them to wage war, and encouraged them to be brave. Legend had it that John Eliot (1604-1690), apostle to the Indians, preached the gospel of peace from this pulpit.[59]

In the summer of 1942, America was at war with no peace in sight, and America's troops needed support. People gathered at Pulpit Rock to raise emergency war funds. At a garden club fund-raising event, folks paid to enter the contests with names like: Victory Garden Bouquet, Choice Flowers in August, and United Nations.[60]

River Rats. The teams battled it out on a field near Wellers Bridge—River Rats against Cream Puffs. According to Peter Hurlbut, River Rats were a local baseball team and a favorite nickname for boys from Roxbury station. [61]

Roswell Ransom Tavern. Capt. Roswell Ransom's tavern, built about 1740, was a lively place and a property that changed hands repeatedly until the Christ Church bought it in 1846 and turned it into a rectory. All celebrations ended, however, when a company of militia congregated at Ransom's tavern for training on October 31, 1787. At four o'clock in the afternoon, a shot rang out, and a man was dead. David Downs's father had gone to the tavern to ask an officer to excuse his son from the General Training scheduled for the next day in Southbury.

When he arrived, soldiers were milling about, laughing, and talking about the next day's events. Men named Hitchcock and Hurlbut were admiring Hurlbut's gun. Hitchcock asked if the gun was a good one, and asked if it was loaded. Hurlbut said the gun was empty and told Hitchcock to try it. Hitchcock picked up the gun, pulled the trigger, and in an instant, forty-five-year-old David Downs was dead. He left a wife and six children. A news reporter warned people to be more cautious, but wrote nothing more about the tragedy. No doubt, military training days continued at the tavern that Ransom operated for nine more years.[62]

Roswell Ransom faced more tragedy. Six years after the shooting, a fire swept through his Woodbury general store and pork house causing extensive damage.[63] Maybe he became discouraged, or maybe officials only granted tavern licenses to residents, but in 1796, he moved his family to New Haven—no reason given.[64]

Route 67A. The number is gone, and the name has changed. Today, it's Old Roxbury Road, but from 1960 to 1963, the number Route 67A was Clapboard Road (now SR 867) between Routes 67 and 133 in Bridgewater.[65]

Route 131. Have a stash of old maps stuffed in a drawer? If one is pre-1932, don't use it to plan a trip on Route 131 or you'll end up in Sherman. On New Year's Day 1932, officials scrapped the highway numbering system begun in the 1920s and concocted a new scheme, fondly known to road aficionados as the Great Renumbering. That same year, Route 131 became a Roxbury highway that included North and South Streets and ended near Roxbury Falls.

In 1935, it became Route 199. That same year the state numbered a new Route 131 in Thompson and connected it to already existing Massachusetts 131. It remains that way today.[66]

Roxbury Creamery. When the Shepaug Railway trains stopped at Roxbury Station, hundreds of bottles of milk were loaded onto the railroad cars. Farmers hitched up their wagons, loaded them with milk cans, and drove to the creamery where the milk was processed, bottled, and shipped by rail to New York City and other cities and towns.[67]

Roxbury Hollow. Stage drivers made their run through this hollow when they carried passengers and mail between towns. It was a quiet, secluded place near Botsford Hill until the Shepaug Railroad screamed through with its noisy engines and clanking wheels.

After the postal service in Washington, D. C. failed to deliver service in rural areas, stagecoach drivers took over and Roxbury's Walter Thomas often drove his stage through the hollow. He began, in 1888, to drive the stage from New Milford to Roxbury, stopping at farmhouses where he dropped mail into a small wooden box on a post.[68]

Roxbury Station. Formerly called Chalybes, this post office delivered mail until 1918 when it closed. A post office in the town center that had operated since 1820 took over delivering all mail. See the story above about Chalybes for more details.

Rumsey Meadow. When the government counted the population in 1790, at least one, possibly two, Rumsey families lived in Woodbury. The number depends on how you decipher the enumerator's scrawl. Nathan Rumsey's household included two free white males sixteen or over and one free white female. David Rumsey's, or David Ramsey's, household included two free white males sixteen or over, three free white males under sixteen and two free white females. The census scribbler provided no more information, though a 1789 deed noted that a Lewis Rumsey had sold a parcel of land, and the 1800 federal census counted Benjamin Rumsey in Roxbury.[69]

Not long ago, someone familiar with local history posted a sign marked Rumsey Meadow in a field on North Street near Moosehorn Hollow. The sign is gone now.

Sanfords Hill. Four generations of Sanfords, sometimes spelled Sandford, held properties at 28 and 40 Wellers Bridge Road and both properties remained in the family for over a century.

Stephen Sanford (1769-1848) moved to Roxbury in 1795 and built a home at 40 Wellers Bridge Road. Upon his death, the property passed to his son, and though we know little about Stephen Sanford, his family and friends thought enough of him to dedicate a stained-glass window memorial in his name at Roxbury's Christ Church.

His son Stephen Sanford Jr. (1808-1888) had been living on Tophet Road with his wife and seven children, but two years after his father's death, he sold his home and moved his family to Wellers Bridge Road to care for his mother. Stephen Sanford Jr. continued a New England tradition when he built a home at 26 Wellers Bridge Road for his son, Charles Sanford (1841-1917). Charles inherited his grandfather's home and retained it until 1908 when he sold it out of the Sanford family. His oldest son inherited #28 and lived there until the mid-1900s.[70]

Shady Side. When the Thomas family owned the former Burwell Tavern, wide boughs hung like curtains, shielding the place from the sun, thus prompting the name.[71]

Shepaug Purchase. Nine carefully drawn circles and squiggles settled the matter. For the second time, the Pootatucks had sold their land to the English. The March 17, 1686 transaction, known as the Shepaug Purchase, comprised two-thirds of the present town of Roxbury and part of Southbury.

Shepaug is an Indian word meaning "rocky river" and the Shepaug River along Roxbury's western border is the only Indian place-name in Roxbury.[72]

Silent Valley. The origin of the name is unknown and the lane has disappeared, but the private unpaved path off Sentry Hill appeared on a 1994 Rand-McNally Litchfield County map and on a 1998 list of private roads compiled by the selectman's office.

Stiles Mountain. David Judson Stiles (b. 1783) left his father's home in Southbury and built a home in Roxbury on present-day Tamarack Road. Stiles was a farmer and shrewd businessman who saw potential commercial value in investing in Mine Hill and spent thirty-two years clearing title to that land.

By the mid-1800s, David J. Stiles owned most of the mining rights to the hill, though some claimed he was not the owner. He hired the best lawyers, like Woodbury's William Cothren, who called the legal battle a "tiger fight." After thirty years of litigation, the courts finally confirmed that Stiles was the rightful owner. People who knew Stiles' daughters said they lived in grand style and "blossomed out" in a rash of new gowns after the sale of the hill.[73]

Trowbridge Mill. John Trowbridge (1752-1807) came to Roxbury in 1793 and built a mill on Fenn Brook. His sons continued the mill operation after his death and expanded it by building a foundry across the brook on nearby North Street. They made wagons and ox carts at the foundry and some people believe that because arrowheads have been found on the property, Indians may have used the site.[74]

Upper Farms. The level land adjoining the Shepaug River near Fort Shepaug was known as the Upper Farms to distinguish it from another area known as Lower Farms.[75]

Warners Mill. Warners Mill was a section of town named after Dr. Ebenezer Warner, grandfather of Revolutionary hero, Seth Warner. A school district and a factory bore the family name. A one-room schoolhouse stood near the corner of River Road and South Street in Warners Mill District No. 5, and the Warner & Company Hat Factory, that operated from 1750-1875, was two miles south of the town center. Another three-story mill and factory at Warners Mill, on Jacks Brook, caught fire early one morning in 1885 and burned to the ground.[76]

West Street. The directional name pinpointed its location west of Roxbury, but over time, it became Wellers Bridge Road.

Peek at the *Bicentennial Celebration Calendar 1996-97* for November to see an undated photo of this street when it was a wide, dusty boulevard.

Westbury. Shepaug townsmen, fed up with trekking six miles to worship, had managed to gain permission from the general court to hire a preacher in the winter months but that was not enough. Worshippers wanted their own ecclesiastical society, separate from Woodbury.

The small group realized they were too small to stand on their own, so they made common cause with families in New Milford and Washington. Specifically, they wanted the western boundary of Roxbury to include part of New Milford and the northern boundary to include part of the North Purchase. Furthermore, townsmen wanted the eastern border moved two and a half miles west of the Woodbury church.

Together, in 1732, the group petitioned the general assembly to form the parish of Westbury. The court denied the petition, so the Shepaug families decided to petition alone, but again authorities refused them. Finally, in 1743, the court awarded them a parish of their own and named it Roxbury. The name Westbury was already taken; the court had given it to a town known today as Watertown.[77]

Wheeler Avenue. In 1864, in a letter to the press, a student said that Benjamin S. Preston's dry goods store was at the corner of Main Street and Wheeler Avenue. His description is confusing though, since Preston's store was at the corner of present-day Church Street and Southbury Road. It is, therefore, difficult to know which road the student was referring to as Wheeler Avenue.

Wheeler families were in Roxbury from the early 1800s, and in 1810, Joseph Wheeler told census takers that eleven people lived in his household. Enumerators listed only the name of the head of household and the number of people in the household, and they grouped people by age and sex. They recorded no information about where Joseph lived or what he did for a living. Since his was the only Wheeler family in Roxbury, it is likely that this avenue was named for him or his ancestors.

In 1882, Garry Wheeler was a licensed auctioneer in Roxbury, though no local census listed his name. By 1870, two Wheeler families lived here; both were farming families.[78]

Wildcat Rock. Also called Wildcat Mountain, it was southwest of Rucum Hill. Wildcats roamed the area, though we don't know what kind of feline they were—bobcats, panthers, lynx, or other feral felines.[79]

3 Water, Water Everywhere

Waterways course through Roxbury. Some are large expanses of wetlands that Roxbury's Inland-Wetlands Commission works diligently to protect. Others are small meandering brooks that flow mile upon mile through town like Jacks Brook, Fenn Brook, and Pierce Brook.

While the era of water-powered mills is a largely forgotten chapter of our history, Roxbury's early settlers welcomed the brooks, rivers, and other waterways needed to generate energy for their mills. Water was essential to saw wood into lumber, grind grain into flour, and power tools that fullers needed to finish cloth. A good water supply was vital to the survival of the town and some historians have even suggested that inhabitants moved to the present center in search of water. Today, anyone who walks through town soon becomes aware of how much water flows through it.

English settlers had no guidelines about what to name waterways, so they tended to use familiar names, such as names of property owners, plants, animals, and memorable events. Names of many waterways appear on small green signs that pop-up at unexpected moments as you drive through town.

Alder Swamp. Alder plants are members of the birch family often found near wetlands. When settlers went in search of water, they found it where the alders grew and settled a new town center in that place and gave it the name Alder Swamp. In 1923, one resident noticed that the bushes still grew on the northern end of the monument green.[1]

Battle Swamp Brook. If you're baffled by the name, you're not alone. Take, for example, the "battle" versus "bottle" dispute that has lasted for centuries. One would have expected historian William Cothren to offer proof of his claim in 1854 and again in 1874 that the name was Bottle Swamp Brook. Alas, he did not.

When Helen Humphrey entered the fray nearly a hundred years later, she insisted that Battle Swamp Brook was correct because Indians fought there. Unfortunately, she provided no evidence about why or when they scuffled.[2]

Finally, someone had evidence. Former teacher and resident Helen Frisbie said that her family found a sign penned Bottle Swamp, but thought the sign was a misspelling. On the other hand, her son, Peter Frisbie, artist, teacher, and former resident said that Bottle Swamp was the correct name. Roxbury teachers taught students that the swamp was shaped like a bottle.

Tenuous evidence, yes, but did you notice that no one mentioned the water words—Battle Swamp, Battle Swamp Creek, or Battle Swamp Brook? Scientists would probably quibble over whether the water is a swamp, a creek, or a brook, whereas regular folks would plunge ahead and call it Bottle Swamp, Bottle Swamp Creek, and other names.

Beaver Pond. The name is from the little critters that have splashed in the Shepaug River for over two-hundred years, and according to Peter Hurlbut, if they had a mind to, they could flood the town center. You'll find their watery playground, sometimes called Beaver Hole, north of Minor Bridge Road.[3]

Browns Brook. The stream flows from Paradise Valley and crosses the town line between Southbury and Roxbury. The name origin is probably from the Brown family in Southbury, that also gave the name to Brown Street. Roxbury's Brown family lived on River Road where Mrs. Brown had a soap factory.[4]

Or, the name may be from Mr. Brown who may have been the hermit known as the Bee Man, an old silica worker who stayed after the mines failed. He lived among a crowd of beehives tucked away in the hills near Paradise Valley. The hermit wasn't entirely alone though. During the summer, children liked to visit the beehives, taste the honey, and listen to the Bee Man play his fiddle and passersby who heard his music said no ordinary musician could play such sweet melodies.[5]

Camp Brook. The brook bends southeast from Bridgewater until it meets the Shepaug River. In earlier days, it meandered through Sheldon Camp's (1814-97) farm, no doubt delighting his ten children. As it sloshed downhill it gathered momentum and became a channel of rushing water with enough force to power Camp's sawmill.[6]

Cross Brook. The name could refer to something in the shape of a cross or it could be a surname. In the words of one directory, though, the name is from the fact that the brook crosses a town line.[7]

Fenn Brook. This brook, named for the Fenn family, tumbles down Sentry Hill to the town center, flows under the Hurlbut Bridge, and meanders through properties along Church Street. Two brothers, William Aaron Fenn (1817-1868) and Aaron William Fenn (1815-1886) both rose to eminence in Roxbury— one as a physician and probate judge, the other as a soldier.

We know little about Dr. Aaron W. Fenn, though he lived in Roxbury and served as probate judge from 1845-1849. Dr. Fenn and his wife adopted his brother's daughter and raised her in their home on Chalybes Road. Unfortunate circumstances of war meant the brothers might have fought against each other—one as a Confederate soldier, the other as a Union soldier.

William A. Fenn worked as a saddle and carriage maker in Eufaula, Alabama, but when the Civil War broke out, he and his family were unable to escape to the north. As a result, Fenn was drafted as a Private into the Eufaula Light Artillery. He was a prisoner of war until his unit surrendered at Meridian, Mississippi on May 10, 1865. Fenn returned to Roxbury where he died three years later.

The war was over, but times were still tense and even though his body was buried in the Center Cemetery, townsmen were wary of the Confederate soldier and forbade his family to place a flag on his gravesite. Finally, ninety-four years after his death, on Memorial Day 1962, Roxburians held a parade in his honor. The Governor of Connecticut and the President of the United States both sent letters of commendation and the Stars and Bars of the Confederate flag finally decorated his grave.[8] Today, Private William Aaron Fenn and Dr. Aaron William Fenn rest side-by-side in Roxbury's Center Cemetery.

Flag Swamp. Sometimes spelled flagg, flagge, or flegge, the water flows mostly in Southbury between Bronson Mountain and Wildcat Mountain.[9] In spring, the narrow sword-like leaves of the Yellow Flag (*Iris pseudacorus)* flutter in the breeze. Many residents believe the word *flag* is a surname or refers to the flower. Flag is indeed a surname, but according to Town Historian Timothy Beard, no family with that name lived in Roxbury.[10]

The *Oxford English Dictionary* defines flag as a type of plant with a bladed leaf that grows in moist places. As currently used, the word denotes a member of the genus *Iris*, especially the *Iris pseudacorus*, but its earlier meaning applied to any reeds or rushes. For those interested in how the word changed over time, the dictionary illustrates its changing usage from 1387 to 1873. For more the name origin, see Flag Swamp Road.

Hedgehog Swamp. If you believe one historian's tall tale, the name is from a fight between a canine and porcupine in the wetlands east of Warners Mill.[11]

Jacks Brook. The brook begins in Tophet Hollow, flows through Pulford Swamp, and tumbles into the Shepaug River. It is the only place in Roxbury named for a slave. Jack may never have existed, but if he did, he would have lived in the 1600s or earlier and died before 1693, the year the name Jacks Brook first appeared in Woodbury records.[12]

With no other records available, we must rely on historian Cothren's undocumented tale written over 150 years after Jack's death. According to Cothren, Jack was an African slave who lived a sad life and died a tragic death. Was he writing about a real person or passing along a bit of folklore? In either case, others have embellished the story.

Jack was an unhappy man who longed for his native Africa, and some thoughtless person told him that when he died he would return to his beloved Guinea. Jack believed the cruel story, grew despondent, and committed suicide. His body was buried near the highway southwest of Pulford's Swamp. Years later, someone found an ancient stone sculpture shaped like a human figure and believed it was an African God. People were suspicious and immediately concluded it had belonged to Jack. They were so afraid the icon would corrupt them that they hid it deep inside a well where it could never be found.[13]

Lake Lauriat. Lake Lauriat lies between South Street and Southbury Road and seemingly grows larger by the minute thanks to eager beavers. The name is a memorial to Denise Lauriat, a devoted wife, mother, and friend to all who knew her. She was also a realtor whose generous assistance to one developer led him to request that the lake be named in her honor, and in the 1990s it was officially named Lake Lauriat.

Before property around the lake was developed, the lake took on the name of the nearest homeowner. Two favorite names were Senior Pond and Lee's Pond.[14]

In 1942, to save fuel, schools closed for a month. Resident Ernie Finch Sr., a student then, recalled skating on Senior Pond every day that January. The pond was named for homeowner John L. Senior. When mystery writer Manfred Lee, a. k. a. Ellery Queen, lived near the pond, neighbor Bud Squire and his friends peddled their bikes to Lee's Pond to skate with Ellery Queen's kids.[15]

Lendeveg Brook. The 1874 F. W. Beers *County Atlas of Litchfield, Connecticut* showed this brook flowing near Battle Swamp Brook.[16] Maps named it Lenevig Brook, but public documents recorded the German surname as Lendeveg, Lendevig, and Lendveg. This brook was named for Roxbury farmer George W. Lendeveg (b.abt 1843), son of Frederick Lendeveg, a saddler in Fairfield during the 1850s and '60s.[17]

On September 27, 1862, at age nineteen, George W. Lendeveg joined the volunteer militia in New York City and enlisted as a Corporal on the Union side. Two months later, he enlisted with Company C, 165th Infantry Regiment New York, but the military discharged him nine days later. George he left the United States, though we don't know when because shipping lines did not keep records of departures from this country. On March 8, 1869, however, when the wooden side-wheeled steamer, the *Rising Star*, sailed from Aspinwall (Panama) and docked in New York City, twenty-seven-year-old George Lendeveg stepped ashore.[18]

By age thirty-seven, Lendeveg had moved to Roxbury, and between 1880 and 1906, he bought and sold many properties. In the early 1890s, Lendeveg served as town auditor, booth tender, and assessor and was a farmer who owned extensive property in the Judds Bridge area.[19]

Little Jacks Brook. A common naming convention has been to give the branch of a large body of water its diminutive name. That is probably the case here, where this name refers to a branch of Jacks Brook Another possibility exists, though. If you read the story about Jacks Brook, you'll notice that no information has surfaced about his family or even if he had a family. We are left to wonder—does this name refer to a branch of Jacks Brook or does it suggest that Jack had a son? This brook begins at Lake Lauriat, flows south into Jacks Brook, and merges with the Shepaug River near High Bridge Road.

Mineral Spring Brook. The name is from the minerals found and mined in Roxbury. As early as 1724, according to *Time and the Land,* someone noticed outcrops of mineral veins cutting across Mine Hill, and owners of the hill damned Mineral Spring Brook to create a permanent water supply. The water is a yellowish-orange color from its high iron and sulphur content.[20]

Mohawk Brook. The brook is north of the Weller Cemetery. No Mohawks lived in Roxbury, but they did live in New York State and occasionally drifted into the western part of Connecticut to intimidate the Pequots.[21]

Moosehorn Brook. The brook glides down Moose Horn Hill, gushes down Painter Hill, and drains into the Shepaug River. Tradition has it that the name, spelled as one word, came from moose horns found in the area.[22]

Pierce Brook. William Pierce was a hard-working farmer who, in the 1800s, bought property along this stream that runs under South Street near the town line with Southbury. His children and grandchildren farmed the land for decades, but only his granddaughter wrote about her days on the family farm.

As children, Ella Pierce (1840-1912) and her sister and brothers probably played in Pierce Brook, but at seventeen, while her father and brothers tended the farm, Ella occupied herself with school, chores, and romance. She also started a diary.[23]

At bedtime on New Year's Day 1877, she began to pen her thoughts and intimate feelings in a tiny black book—her resentment when a teacher called her "cheeky," her sadness when she and Robert Camp ended their flirtation, and her horror at the frightful scenes she witnessed between her brother Albert and his wife.

She wrote that her brothers Frank, Albert, and George built houses, sheared sheep, cleaned rye, mended wagons, stripped tobacco, and went to temperance meetings while she sewed, ironed, played croquet, picked berries, baked pies, and went to prayer meetings. Ella also wrote about familiar events, for example, Frank's dental visits to fill nineteen cavities resulting in $36 worth of gold and cement.

Ella Pierce's diary was one of the few personal writings I unearthed during my research and I found the naïve, honest reflections of a teen-age girl living in Roxbury in the second half of the nineteenth century enchanting. The one-hundred-fifty-three- year-old Litchfield Historical Society is keeper of Ella's 132-year-old diary.

Pulford Swamp. In old England, if you met a man named Baker you knew he probably baked bread all day. In ancient Woodbury and Roxbury, if you met a man named Pulford or Fulford you knew he probably pounded cloth all day.

About Roxbury's Abel Pulford, we know a few facts—he bought property in Roxbury in 1799, stayed twenty years, and then moved to `Southbury.[24] No notes, letters, or diaries remain to tell us what he did all day. Abel was probably a relative of Abraham Fulford however, and we do know how Abraham spent his time.

Abraham Fulford possessed skills so indispensable that, to entice him to stay, Woodbury townsmen offered him ten acres of land and in January 1700, Abraham Fulford became Woodbury's first fuller or clothier. His job was to process cloth, usually wool, for people to sew. He scoured wool to get the dirt out and then fulled it to make it bulky. Abraham went to his fulling mill to clean, comb, weave, hang, shrink, beat, and pound. That is what he did all day.

Quarry Hill Brook. The only mention I found of the name was an item in an 1893 newspaper that invited people to visit Quarry Hill Brook to view maidenhair ferns. Go east, it directed, past Castle Street. At the brook, walk another five or ten minutes until you see an abundance of maidenhair ferns.[25]

River Road Pond. The town leases, from the Roxbury Land Trust, a ten-acre parcel with a watering hole where humans, canines, and catfish splash around in the two and one-half-acre swimming hole on the banks of the Shepaug River while hikers, dog walkers, and wild creatures romp in the surrounding woods.[26]

Roxbury Brook. The federal government paid one-hundred percent of the cost to repair this brook when 1975 fall floods severely damaged it.[27] Follow the brook's journey through town as it spills down Painter Hill, meanders along the north side of Church Street, and tumbles over rocks where it joins Fenn Brook under east of the Hurlbut Bridge.

It's possible that Roxbury Brook is incorrectly named, is located somewhere else, or doesn't exist, even though a 1955 map shows it flowing east of the Hurlbut Bridge. Mapmakers are sometimes wrong. They don't live in town, they rely on pictures from the air, and they repeat information from earlier maps.

Talk to Peter Hurlbut whose family has been here for generations and he'll tell you that he doesn't know Roxbury Brook and that his farm is on Fenn Brook, just east of the Hurlbut Bridge.[28]

Roxbury Falls. During November 1853, a great freshet caused the river at Roxbury Falls to rise to twenty-five feet, four feet higher than ever before.[29] In those days, the river cut through rocks wedged so tightly together that water forced its way out in great gusts hundreds of feet above the riverbed.

Then the Shepaug Railroad builders came along. They cut down trees and blasted rocks, then hurled both into the river, all to build a railroad bed. They were happy. They had denuded forests, defaced cliffs, calmed river waters, and transformed gushing falls into a trickle. They had destroyed the natural beauty of the area.[30]

The railroad didn't last long and the damage was done, but some old timers still remember enjoying Roxbury Falls long after the railroad closed. Jackie Dooley, now in her eighties, recalled when she and her brothers and sisters went skinny-dipping near the falls. She was quick to add that they kept their swimming suits nearby in case someone was looking at them. Dooley added that things have changed, and the falls aren't so wild anymore because railroad workers moved the rocks.

Resident Mary Weaver recalled Arthur Miller and Marilyn Monroe swimming at Roxbury Falls and was in awe of how Miss Monroe could climb down the rocks in high-heeled shoes.[31]

Second Hill Brook. This brook begins as a small pond in Bridgewater west of Mine Hill, twists and turns for miles downhill, crosses the town line, and tumbles into the Shepaug River below Wellers Bridge.

Shepaug River. The Native American name, spelled Chippaug, Sheepaug, Shippauge, and Shepaug, honors an early Bantam chief and means "rocky river" or "rocky waters."[32] The river flows south from Warren and merges with the Bantam River. It continues along Roxbury's western border until it meets Lake Lillinonah in Southbury.

Impress your friends with a few statistics about the rocky river. It flows through eleven Connecticut towns; its watershed area covers 150 square miles; it drops twenty to thirty feet per mile, the steepest of any river in the state.[33] As for the number of rocks, you'll have to count them yourself.

Tamarack Swamp. The swamp lies south of Sentry Hill Road and is named for the tamarack or larch tree, a kind of pine tree with reddish-brown bark and blue-green needles. The word is derived from Canadian French *tamarac,* assumed to be of Algonquin origin.

Transylvania Brook. This stream begins north of Rucum Road and flows south through Roxbury, Woodbury, and Southbury. The prefix *trans* is from the Latin meaning "beyond," "across," or "through," and the Latin word *sylvan* provides the meaning, "woods" or "forest."

Transylvania is a region in central Romania, formerly part of Hungary. The online Romania Tourist Office Web site referred to a Medieval Latin document dating from 1075 as *Ultra Silvam*. *Ultra* means 'beyond' or "on the far side of ..." and *Sylva* means "woods or forest." Presumably, then, settlers who were familiar with Latin saw the brook as flowing beyond, through, or on the other side of the forest.[34]

Turrill Brook. Turrill, Turill, Terrill, Turrell, Tarrill, Tyrell and Tyrrel are all spellings of the surname given to the brook that flows through Roxbury and Southbury crossing town and county lines. In 1673, Stratford resident Roger Terrill (d. 1722) signed the Fundamental Articles for the settlement of Woodbury, though no records indicated whether he ever lived there.[35] Censuses for 1790 and later listed his descendants in Woodbury and Roxbury.

One was farmer and carpenter Thomas Turill (1804-1882) and his family who lived near Lower River Road in 1850.[36] According to a survey of historical homes, his house remained in his family until 1930.[37] He was buried in the Squire Road Cemetery.

Another descendant Oliver Tyrrell (1829-1899) was a stubborn man. He supported building the Shepaug Railroad yet when it came time for him to give up fifty feet of his land south of Roxbury Falls for railroad tracks he refused.[38]

Yet another descendant, twenty-eight year-old Stephen Tyrrell (1822-1875), lived in New Milford and worked as a hatter. When the hat-making industry faltered, he became a farm laborer and later built a house at 198 River Road.[39] In his forties, Tyrrell served in the Civil War under Capt. Cyrus E. Prindle, and was a naïve and stubborn soldier. In Winchester, Virginia, when Tyrrell was on picket duty, fellow soldiers on the front lines warned him the Rebels were coming. They told him to run; he insisted saw nothing to run from, and stood stock-still.

Before he knew what happened, Stephen Tyrrell was a prisoner in the notorious Andersonville prison where 13,000 Union soldiers died, mostly of diseases caused by overcrowding and starvation. He was one of the few men who survived long enough to return home. Stephen Tyrrell died a pauper on Valentine's Day, 1875. A headstone in the Squire Road Cemetery bears his name and Company D, Thirteenth Regiment, Connecticut Infantry. No mention was made of his confinement in Andersonville prison.[40]

Watering Hole. You'll find it on Southbury Road near the town line. Some call it the Springs; others call it the Watering Hole. Some believe the water is clean, pure, blessed; others believe it's filthy, foul, polluted. Nevertheless, believers in both camps lug empty bottles across narrow planks on a muddy path to filch free water.[41]

4 Bridges Over Rushing Waters

Ask most locals where Jacks Brook Bridge or Moosehorn Bridge are and they probably can't tell you—these bridges are small, barely noticeable in the landscape. Ask directions to Judds Bridge, Wellers Bridge, or Minor Bridge and most locals can direct you, but no sign will tell you when you get there. It's as if the town has a tradition of not naming bridges.

Other bridges blend into the landscape. They are boardwalks meant for hikers. For example, three wooden footpaths zigzag through the Brien E. Tierney Preserve, one hovers over the earth at the Natalie White Preserve, and another leads to a wildlife viewing station at the Van Deusen Preserve. No one knows why, and probably no one has noticed, but for nearly three centuries, Roxbury's bridges were unnamed. Then, in the twenty-first century, a stonemason engraved "Hurlbut Bridge 2003" in large letters on a structure near the town center, giving the oldest name in town to its newest bridge.

Botsford Hill Bridge. No sign gives its name, so you might want to call it the Second Hill Brook Bridge for the stream that runs under it. It's is not much longer than a car length, has low stone sides, and crosses the brook near the intersection of Botsford Hill and Baker Roads.

Hurlbut Bridge. This is the only bridge in town with a name carved on it and if locals called it anything; they called it Fenn Brook Bridge—at least until it was rebuilt and renamed. First Selectman Barbara Henry noticed that no road, park, or monument bore the name of Roxbury's founding family and in 2003, she and the board of selectmen took legislative action to name this bridge in their honor.[1]

Men worked for months building the sturdy bridge. They were not building a wooden footpath or a delicate New England covered bridge, but a structure for fast-moving cars on their way to who-knows-where. They built the bridge with heavy stones and high walls to last, as the Hurlbuts have, for generations.

If Roxbury had a "First Family," it would be the Hurlbuts. Their ancestors reach back to 1713 when Joseph Hurlbut rode into the wilderness, cleared a parcel of land, and built the new settlement's first house. For three centuries, his descendants have plowed the land, kept the books, enriched the community, and preserved his memory.

The Hurlbuts have been justices of the peace, probate judges, fire chiefs, soldiers, deacons, wartime aircraft spotters, tree wardens, and farmers. They have been active in the historical society, PTA, Grange, Senior Center, and Shepaug Club. They have volunteered as fire and ambulance responders and been town clerk for as long as anyone can remember.[2] For the last 120 years, if you talked with a town clerk, you spoke with a Hurlbut—and still do. That public office has passed from father to son, husband to wife, mother to son, and father to son in a straight line.

Henry S. Hurlbut (1834-1910) was town clerk from 1872 until his death. His son Norman Henry Hurlbut (1879-1957) succeeded him and served for forty-five years.[3] Political affiliation never mattered to the family or the voters, so when the town elected Norman Hurlbut's son Alden B. Hurlbut (1911-1998), everyone was pleased. He was a Democrat and his wife was a Republican. Beginning in 1957, Alden B. Hurlbut served as town clerk for twenty years with his wife, Elinor Peterson Hurlbut, as his assistant.

In those days, Alden and Elinor had no office and no office hours; instead they conducted the town's business at their dining room table. Alden worked on the farm all day and Elinor tended to the household and raised three children. In addition, they responded to the stream of people who knocked on their farmhouse door at all hours of the day and night to ask for a hunting or fishing license, a marriage license, or a title search.

While Alden and Elinor worked mostly at home, sometimes they trekked across town to help people who wanted to see public records. For example, if someone needed to do a title search, Elinor picked up her son Jonathan, walked the half-mile to the tiny brick hall of records, and with babe in arms, directed the title searcher to land records. Later, records were stored in the town hall, and even though space was tight, at least the Hurlbuts could move town business from their dining room table to an office.

In spite of constant interruptions at home and having to lug papers across town, Alden and Elinor had fun. Though much of the job was drudgery, celebrities added spice to the job. In November 1958, Alden registered actress Marilyn Monroe (then Marilyn Miller) to vote, and one day Elinor invited a stranger into her living room and later learned that the unexpected visitor was actor Dustin Hoffman. He wanted a marriage license. Celebrities, townspeople, and family alike all rapped on the Hurlbut's front door. Even Elinor's niece Cathy Hurlbut had to knock on the farmhouse door to get her marriage license.[4]

After Alden retired in December 1977, both political parties endorsed Elinor for town clerk. Imagine how proud Alden would have been to attend the 2007 celebration to honor his wife's fifty years of service in the town clerk's office.

Today Henry S. Hurlbut's great-grandson holds that office and his great-great-grandson is assistant town clerk. Alden and Elinor's son Peter Hurlbut learned the job at the dining room table, and when his turn came, he followed his mother's example, registered Republican, and became town clerk on January 6, 1986. Jim Hurlbut, Peter's son, apprenticed during summers and holidays and in 2008, accepted the position of assistant town clerk.

Lewis Elmer Hurlbut (1909-1992), Alden's brother, focused on his family, farm, and community. Like his grandfather, father, and brother, Lewis loved nature and was an environmentalist before "green" became popular. He devoted his life to his wife, Ethel Frost Hurlbut, and their eight children. In addition to managing a large farm and operating a farm stand, he was director of the Roxbury Land Trust, and a member of both the Planning and Zoning Commissions. Like his father, who wrote a local history, Lewis wrote *Roxbury Remembered* about the town he loved. With his friend Frederick Ungeheuer, Lewis wrote the book based on memories of the Hurlbut family and interviews with townspeople.

His farm is the only farm in Connecticut that has been in continuous operation since the 1700s. An item in the August 27, 1986 *News Times* reported that Maple Bank Farm once covered 150 acres, has been home to nine generations of Hurlbuts, and started with a six-acre land grant from an English King.

Hurlbut's daughter, Cathy, and her husband, Howard Bronson, own and operate Maple Bank Farm that was once a few vegetables in a cart. Now it is an extensive farm stand with fruits, vegetables, flowers, homemade pastries. And it has a shop that sells food goodies and skeins of fine wool from sheep raised on the farm. The Bronsons also raise corn and other crops on a fifty-seven-acre tract at the southern end of Baker Road near Mine Hill Preserve. That farmland preserves deep, rock-free topsoil along the banks of the Shepaug River.

Lewis Hurlbut instilled in his daughter a love of farming and a passion for trees. Hurlbut grafted thousands of trees in his lifetime, served as tree warden, and was an ardent conservationist. He planted and replaced trees along roads, in nature preserves, and near public buildings. In his honor, a tree nursery was planted behind the Minor Memorial Library and trees from that nursery have been planted in parks and public lands throughout town. Hurlbut loved one tree in particular, though he did not plant it. The grand white oak, known as the Memorabilia Tree, on North Street was a mere sprout when his ancestors settled here nearly three centuries ago.

Judds Bridge. In 1979, selectmen referred to this bridge, then seventy-six years old, as a historic landmark. The old wooden bridge was unsafe, but finally, after years of negotiation the federal government agreed to restore it. Major repairs turned it into the steel structure that today spans the Shepaug River and is safe for emergency vehicles, snowplows and school buses.[5]

The name is from Daniel Judd (1782-1870) and Lewis Judd (b. 1823), wealthy farmers who lived nearby. The Judd name has lived on, though other names have been associated with this bridge. Some still call it Rowe Bridge, named for Rowe B. Metcalf (1900-1965), a wealthy man who bought thousands of acres during the Great Depression to create a dairy farm.[6] Today, Arthur L. Carter, former publisher of *The Litchfield County Times* owns and operates a large dairy farm on the property he purchased from Metcalf's family.

Little Jacks Brook Bridge. Even though a small green sign says Jacks Brook, the water that flows under this bridge is Little Jacks Brook. This bridge is a low stone structure on South Street near the intersection with High Bridge Road.

Minor Bridge. Descendants of Englishman Thomas Minor (1608-1690) lent their name to this bridge and the road leading to it. Twenty-four families with his surname, spelled Miner, lived in Woodbury in 1790; it was the most prevalent family name in that town.

The bridge spans the Shepaug River near Falls Road and is a brawny structure with high iron railings that stretch across thick concrete foundations on both sides. Clearly, the structure intends to outlast any ranting and ravings of rushing water. When the river rises, the temptation to jump in for a swim is so overwhelming the town posted a sign with red letters on a white background, No Jumping off Bridge by Order of Selectmen. While the bridge stands firmly in the landscape, the sign has disappeared.

Moosehorn Brook Bridge. This low, moss-covered stone bridge is at the entrance of a preserve one-half mile northwest of Sentry Hill Road on Judds Bridge Road. The brook that flows under it joins the Shepaug River. Lendeveg was an earlier name for the brook and the bridge; see Lendeveg Brook for the story of that name.[7]

River Road Bridge. At a bend in the river, waterfalls hurl white water under this recent-ly reconstructed bridge with its solid concrete base and towering wood railings. It re-places a bridge that formerly crossed farther upstream on High Bridge Road.

Roxbury Station Bridge. The unofficial name is from its location near the former railroad station where the Shepaug Railroad picked up passengers, delivered mail, and shipped milk to distant markets.

The hope was that the bridge would withstand the rumble and rattle of the train, but like all bridges across the Shepaug River, this one has required repeated repairs over the years. Since 1990, the bridge has a solid concrete base topped with metal reinforcements.

Wellers Bridge. The name honors the Weller families who lived nearby, but for over two hundred years, the bridge has been a problem. It has fallen down, been torn down, and has washed away. When Daniel Weller (1728-1816) dedicated the bridge on a fine autumn day in 1799, a crowd gathered to hear him speak. He may have been a shy man or unused to speaking in public because he hesitated and could hardly get the words out. Nevertheless, he began, "Friends and fellow citizens, one year ago this beam was a tree in yonder forest." Embarrassed, he stammered and had to begin again, "Friends and fellow citizens, one year ago this beam was a tree in yonder forest—and I wish to God it was there now." The crowds cheered, howled and were no doubt relieved that Weller had only a few words to say, because as soon as he finished speaking, they rushed to the nearest tavern.[8]

Fifteen years later, one of Daniel Weller's relatives, Samuel Weller (1764-1816), either enjoyed too much partying or was looking for a fight. In any case, he and his friends went out one night and tore the bridge down. Attorney Isaac Leavenworth filed charges, the state's attorney got involved, and the town refused to pay to fix the bridge.

Wellers Bridge kept falling down, and sometimes a family feud got the job done; other times a flood would do it, like the November 13, 1853 torrent that swept away nearly every bridge in town.[9] The floodwaters receded, the riverbed dried out, and men packed the base of the newly rebuilt bridge with stones. Surely, it would hold. The river was low then, and people crossing the river found only enough water to "wet their wagon wheels." It was 1881 and the worst drought in a generation.[10]

In early July 1886, the bridge fell down again. Neither a flood, nor a drought brought it down. Some thought it was the oxen; others thought the stones did it. In any case, a strong pair of oxen carrying a heavy load of stones plunged into the river. The oxen swam to safety; the stones sank, and the town rebuilt Wellers Bridge.[11]

Even when the bridge was not falling down, it was a dangerous place. Consider a line in the September 1916 report that noted the town paid a veterinarian five dollars for "examination of cow alleged to be hurt by bridge."[12]

Notwithstanding Mother Nature, family feuds, and cattle, it took the U. S. Army and the state of Connecticut to rebuild this bridge. After the 1955 floods washed it away, the United States Army took over and built a temporary crossing, then turned it over to the state. Two years later, Connecticut built a two-lane bridge upstream from the temporary one, then turned Wellers Bridge and its problems back to the town.[13]

5 Cemeteries, Memorials, Quiet Places

eading Roxbury headstones is like paging through a family album of farmers, tradesmen, educators, soldiers, civic leaders, merchants, miners, quarrymen, and others who settled this town. To find names of Roxburians who died before 1743, look to the parent town of Woodbury, because the court did not permit Roxbury to have its own burial ground until it became a separate ecclesiastical parish. Even so, it was not until 1745 that the first burial took place in a public cemetery in Roxbury.

A reporter for the *New Milford Gazette* wrote, in 1894, that the town center had many cemeteries. They were probably family plots, since it was common practice for each family to have its own burial ground.[1] Human nature being what it is, throughout Roxbury's history people have inscribed names on gravestones, plaques, benches, and boulders to honor fallen heroes, officials, benefactors, family, and friends.

You will find memorials tucked away in unexpected places— under trees, in parks, in preserves, and other places that quietly and unobtrusively pay tribute to those we want to honor and remember. Mostly, you'll look down in search of names. For one, though, you'll need to look up—the twenty-one feet tall granite obelisk on the town green honors the Revolutionary hero Seth Warner.

Beardsley-Leavenworth Cemetery. Englishman Thomas Leavenworth (d.1683) was among Roxbury's original property owners. He and John Leavenworth owned so much land near Good Hill and Grassy Hill that the area was known as the Leavenworth neighborhood. This cemetery, named for the Leavenworth family who owned property on Tophet Road, was a small family burial ground. One local historian referred to it as Lord's Hill, though no records tell us why. No matter the name, it has disappeared.[2]

In *Roxbury Remembered*, Lewis Hurlbut said that when property owners began to plow the fields, his father, Norman Hurlbut, moved the headstones up to the stone walls near the road. He did not say when the markers were moved or what happened to them after the move.[3]

The headstone hunt was on—I wanted to find out what happened. I compared early maps and concluded that the burial ground probably vanished sometime between 1934 and 1945, even though two residents recalled seeing the headstones in the field as late as 1996. I sought the help of an expert, someone familiar with local history. Former resident Barbara Jean Mathews is a professional genealogist with six generations of family buried in the Center Cemetery—just the person to help. We exchanged e-mail messages and though she was at a loss as to why the burial ground vanished, she supplied detailed information.

Mathews wrote that Levi L. Gleason had recorded the exact spelling from each stone in this cemetery in the order in which they were standing. She sent me a copy of Gleason's list of names, birth and death dates, and ages on the headstones that were standing in the cemetery on October 24, 1934.[4]

In addition to Gleason's list, I found a faded typed manuscript held together in a worn loose-leaf, three-ringed binder tucked away on the shelves of the Gunn Memorial Library. It was a list of tombstone inscriptions compiled in October 1910 by Edward and Helen Boyd. The Boyd's counted seven headstones lying on a stone wall north of C. A. Isham's house on the east side of the highway.[5]

The two lists contained different information. The most prominent name on both lists was Capt. David Leavenworth (1738-1820). Leavenworth was Captain of the Fourth Company, 13th Regiment of the Colony of Connecticut in the Revolutionary War.[6] Forty-two men from his company fought in the "Danbury Alarm," twenty-six of his men saved the post at Peekskill, New York, and others did battle in Norwalk.[7] In 1910, the Boyds recorded, one headstone for the Captain's first wife, Olive Hunt Leavenworth, whereas twenty-four years later, Gleason noted two headstones with her name.

Both lists included Martin Leavenworth (1785-1813), Sheldon Leavenworth, and Abigail Beardsley.[8] The Boyds also recorded a footstone with the initials E. L. and a headstone for Morse (1764-1852), the Captain's son and Martin Leavenworth's father. Gleason's list contained neither.

That should have ended my research on the vanished burial ground, but when I asked locals about it, I heard disturbing stories. Jim Green, former manager of the Transfer Station, said a property owner discarded the gravestones. He knew nothing about what happened to the graves, but said the headstones were moved to the front of the property near a stone wall, confirming the Boyds' findings, and the story that Norman Hurlbut had moved them.

James Martin, longtime resident and employee of the Town Garage, repeated Green's story and recalled that, as a boy, he and his friends placed American flags on the headstones every Veteran's Day. The property owner got annoyed and each year removed the flags. One year the headstones were gone; the owner told the boys that the headstones had been vandalized.

Martin and his friends were skeptical and angry and went back for years to place a flag where the headstones had been. Finally, they stopped because someone kept removing the flags.[9]

Green and Martin were talking about the 1940s and '50s. Bud Squire said that when he was a boy he saw the headstones standing.[10] Resident Mary Jonker moved to Roxbury in 1993 and remembered seeing the headstones along the stone wall.[11] Longtime resident Marie Swanson confirmed Mary Jonker's recollection that the stones were leaning against the wall in the northeast corner of a field on Tophet Road as late as about 1996.[12] Others told of people who kept the stones as memorabilia, but no one knew what happened to the graves. Like so many others in New England, the Beardsley-Leavenworth family burial has disappeared.

Center Cemetery. This burial ground opened in 1816 with a deed from General Ephraim Hinman, and over the years, others deeded more land until it is now Roxbury's largest burial ground. Various groups have cared for it, but maintenance was not their top priority, so it fell to neglect, until 1860, when the Roxbury Cemetery Association took over with its strong leadership,

strictly enforced by-laws, and careful record keeping. It has now cared for the burial grounds for nearly 150 years.[13]

Caretaking is one thing, but solving mysteries is another, and the association has had its share of detective work, especially when it comes to thefts. At least three thefts remain unsolved. Some years ago, a thief carted off a huge fountain near the center of the grounds. The association's members were astounded as to how anyone could have stolen the heavy structure, but vowed to replace it. An anonymous donor learned of the disappearance and gave a gift of another fountain. The thieves are still at large.

The second snatch was more curious; it remained a secret for years because no one knew anything was missing. In 2006, a North Street resident reported that he found thirteen tombstones under his porch. The Roxbury Cemetery Association collected the stones and set them in three orderly rows behind the military monument at the front of the Center Cemetery. When Peter Hurlbut told me the story, curiosity got the better of me. I wanted to find out where the stones came from. Two inscriptions had faded beyond recognition, but after a day of sleuthing, I found the names that belonged to the stones and discovered that they had been stolen from the Squire and Center Cemeteries. Someday the association will return them to their rightful places, but it's doubtful the thief will ever be found.

A third mystery emerged when Town Garage Manager Ernie "Butch" Finch Jr. pointed to a headstone someone had abandoned outside his office door. He didn't know who left it or where it came from. A top corner was missing and the year of death was unclear—1838 or 1858. With a little snooping, I was able to identify that the inscription on the stone was for Raphael Flowers who died October 26, 1853 at age seventy-nine. One day, no doubt, the association will return it to the Center Cemetery where it belongs.[14]

Two headstones in the Center Cemetery bear mentioning. One is for a child; the other is for a soldier. Charlotte Sanford, daughter of Stephen and Sarah Sanford, died January 19, 1813 at age sixteen. We have no information about her, other than that she was the first person buried in this cemetery.[15]

A soldier's marker memorializes Charles Seneca Durbin (1821-1906), a Civil War Veteran, recipient of the Distinguished Service Cross, and the only known black veteran buried in this cemetery.

For clarity, I will refer to him as Durling, since that was the name on his marriage certificate. The labyrinth of first and last names in Durbin's records, however, made for intriguing research challenges, since I found no birth certificate or document with his signature to confirm his correct name.

Let's begin with the census. Census takers stopped by homes, spoke with the head of household or another adult in the family, and recorded what they were told. In Durbin's case, census takers wrote his Christian name as Charles and Charles S., so it is likely that Durbin called himself Charles.

One might expect military records to be more accurate since an interviewer spoke directly to the individual or the person himself filled out a form. In Durling's case, his military records gave his first name as Seneca, with no middle initial or middle name.

As for his surname, census takers scribbled several variations. If you search for him, look for Derling, Durbin, Durlin, Dearling, and Durling. Other public records were no more accurate. For example, the military enlisted Durlin, his bride married Charles Seneca Durling, and a realtor sold property to Derling. A doctor wrote Durling on his death certificate, and immediately below the doctor's words, the undertaker wrote Durlin. And someone, presumably a family member or someone who knew him, ordered Seneca Durbin carved on his headstone.[16]

He lived in Coventry when he enlisted on January 12, 1864 as a Private with the United States Colored Troops and served with the Union side. He joined Company B, Thirty-first Infantry Regiment UC and was discharged on May 23, 1865.

After the war, Durling worked as a laborer in Newtown. He later moved to Roxbury, and on March 11, 1884, married Maria Nickols Potter. Both were in their forties; she was a widow, he a widower. The Rev. David E. Jones performed the ceremony in the Congregational Church. Where the couple lived during their first two years of marriage is unknown, but in September 1886, Durbin acquired property from George B. Crofut near the corner of Bacon and Rucum Roads, on present-day Transylvania Road.[17]

After Durling died at age eighty-five, his wife, Maria, and nine others in the household remained in Roxbury for four years and then moved to Brookfield. In later years, some family members returned to Roxbury. Two women claimed his military pension. One listed herself as his wife; the other listed herself as his widow, though neither lies with him in Roxbury's Center Cemtery.[18]

Christ Church Columbarium. This tranquil setting located between the church and the rectory was completed and dedicated on June 22, 1997. The circular structure is a hollow wall built of fieldstone with a slate-topped cover. One hundred and twenty chambers are con-

tained within the wall, each prepared to accept the remains of a loved one. A simple brass memorial plate identifies the deceased in each burial site.

In 2003, the church built a Memory Garden in the columbarium. It is composed of pavers with a granite-cross motif in the center, and each memorial brick displays the name of a loved one interred in a different location. An endowment fund ensures the upkeep of the columbarium and Memory Garden in perpetuity.[19]

Great Oak Cemetery. A reporter described the solitary 380-year-old white oak, nicknamed the Memorabilia Tree, at the entrance to this cemetery as being of Paul Bunyan proportions. In 1673, settlers may have passed near the sprout on their way to Pomperaug Plantation after crossing the Shepaug River. Fortunately, no one trampled on it, so it grew into a majestic landmark treasured by Roxbury residents as if it were a descendant of one of the original settlers.[20]

The Roxbury Cemetery Association purchased this twenty-five-acre burial ground in 1997 from Tara Associates. As of 2009, about a dozen headstones stand in the town's newest cemetery. The earliest death date on a headstone is April 17, 1991 for ninety-year-old Frank L. Allen, but the first burial was Ella Secor who died April 9, 2001, leaving a puzzle for future generations to ponder.[21]

Old Burial Ground. This historic burial ground, also called Old Roxbury Cemetery and Old Cemetery, is a small roadside graveyard on a low hill. In the 1700s, Roxbury's first churches stood next to it and Samuel Blakeley's (1669-1758) was the oldest headstone inscription.

In 1784, Seth Warner was laid to rest in this ground on Old Roxbury Road, but seventy-four years later, his remains were moved to a monument on the town green. This hallowed ground was also the resting place of the Reverend Thomas Canfield, first minister of the Congregational Church, who died January 16, 1795 at seventy-five.[22] The last burial was in 1832, seventy-four years after it opened.

The views south and west from the graveyard were more remarkable in earlier days. You could almost inhale the smoke from trains traveling across New York and New England, and some said you could see all the way to Brewster, New York. To the east, worshippers could see the long oval elevation of Good Hill with its farmhouses and rich farmland.[23]

Weather and time have taken a toll on the soft-stone markers. Many are unreadable, making it impossible to know all the souls buried here. A low stone wall and metal fences enclose the cemetery. Behind the burial ground, a stone pulpit was built in 1965 to celebrate the bicentennial of the first Christ Church. For decades, brambles hid the pulpit until the fall of 2006 when Dr. Paul Elwell uncovered it.

Tracey Andrews, who lives nearby, recalled the days when she was a girl and visited here. She could read the headstones then, remembered that many had the same death date, and wondered whether people died that year from a plague or other epidemic.[24]

Saint Patrick's Cemetery. This one-hundred-year-old cemetery is owned and maintained by Saint Patrick's Roman Catholic Church and is the only cemetery in town with a name sign. The oldest grave is dated 1912. Catholics from Roxbury were buried in New Milford's St. Francis Xavier Cemetery before someone donated land for this burial ground. A narrow curved drive separates this cemetery from the Weller Cemetery on Hemlock Road.[25]

Seth Warner Monument. The monument honors Colonel Seth Warner (1743-1784), military hero of Ticonderoga, leader of the Green Mountain Boys, son of Dr. Benjamin Warner, and grandson of Dr. Ebenezer Warner, one of Roxbury's earliest settlers.[26]

The Colonel was over six feet tall, a courageous and commanding man, considered by Gen. Washington to be among his most daring and trustworthy officers. Though Warner fought in sixteen battles in the northern colonies, he died at home the day after Christmas, 1784. No doubt, his family was proud of his military service, but the hero's death created a terrible burden for them because he had spent most of his money in the war. When he died, his family was destitute.

His family had two worries—one was lack of money; the other was that someone would steal the Colonel's body. In those days, the law allowed creditors to claim a body, so thirty men were ordered to stand guard outside his home. The militia followed the funeral procession to the Old Burial Ground, fired a volley over his grave, then left.[27]

His remains rested there for seventy-four years, until 1858, when the town built a monument in his honor and reburied his remains beneath the obelisk on the town green. The Colonel's coffin was cherry wood with a heart-shaped silver plate on top held down with silver nails. He wore an ornament on his sword belt, but a mystery arose about his sword. His daughter, Abigail Meacham, wrote a letter to the committee in charge of the burial at the monument. She wrote, "In regard to the sword I can only say that I saw it lying on the coffin during the services. I do not recollect whether it was buried with him or not; it is my impression that it was."[28]

In 1976, 200 years after Vermont promoted Warner to brigadier general, the Connecticut legislature named him an honorary major general in its militia. The reason his new rank was honorary, as recommended by the attorney general, was to block his descendants from suing for back pay. One Roxbury resident was not satisfied and pressed the federal government to recognize the fallen hero. On January 19, 1995, two hundred and eleven years after a gunshot from an Indian sniper ended Col. Warner's military career, a Connecticut congressman read a speech about Warner into the Congressional Record.[29]

Squire Road Cemetery. Castle Street Cemetery, Old South Cemetery, and Lower Cemetery were all names of the burial ground.[30]

Burials were particularly difficult in earlier days. For example, Joseph Castle was buried in 1864 and thirty years later, a reporter for the *New Milford Gazette* wrote about his funeral, saying, that Castle's burial took place shortly after a severe snowstorm and the casket was first carried on a sled to the burial ground. The snow was so deep that the pallbearers had to wear snowshoes and carry the coffin by hand.[31]

The Castle Street Cemetery once had an arch hung over the entrance heralding the family name, but the arch disappeared and a decorative fence was built around the one-acre plot. The fence is a marvel in design and carpentry, with thirty-three sections, each representing one year of Christ's life on Earth. Elongated diamond-shaped wooden slats across each section discourage evil spirits from entering the cemetery and lingering around the graves.[32]

About 1900, Henry Bronson designed that fence and Clayton B. Squire built it of native pine when he worked at Bronson's sawmill. In an interview when he was ninety-six, Squire said he had painted the fence every couple of years since he built it and planned to paint a little each day in the coming summer.[33]

Painting the fence had become a family tradition and after Clayton died in 1978, his son Bud Squire and granddaughter Connie Squire Hunter continued the tradition. Though many of the headstones have faded and fallen with the passage of time, the fence remains fresh and new. Some headstones are crisp and clear, glistening like the fence, though others, like the 1745 stone for Martha Warner, are illegible. The cemetery is full now; the last burials were in the mid-1960s.

Weller Cemetery. This second oldest cemetery in Roxbury contains the graves of sixteen Wellers, including Thomas Weller (1680-1751) and his family. Its former name was North Cemetery, and since it was established before Roxbury was incorporated, deeds to the property are in Woodbury.[34]

No one had mapped the location of graves or the number of graves in this burial ground, until 2005-2006, when Eagle Scout Kevin Falconer, decided to change all that. Kevin's interest in genealogy led him to create a permanent record of the names and dates of all the people buried here. He and his friends marked off the boundaries, carefully rubbed and recorded information from headstones, and counted nearly two hundred graves.[35]

In an interview with the *Republic-American* (Waterbury, Conn), Falconer said that starting in the 1800s, gravestones faced east, to the sunrise and toward a new day. The backs of headstones faced west, to darkness and the devil. He assured his interviewer that all the headstones in the Weller Cemetery faced east.[36]

Memorials and Commemorations. Tokens of remembrance—trees, benches, markers, plaques, carvings—are placed around town to honor and celebrate people still living as well as loved ones who are gone. The Contemplation Garden and the Christ Church Memory Garden are only two examples of places to look for memorials.

A sundial from the Friends of the Roxbury Library memorializes William James Walker III, their friend, founder and past president. A small bronze plaque at the foot of a young maple tree behind Christ Church notes the passing of Charles Frisbie; another in the Everett B. Hurlburt Community Park peaks out from the foot of a boulder in memory of a child, Callen Matthew Frohne.

A sturdy granite bench in front of the Roxbury Museum displays the name of Deborah B. Donnelly, a respected journalist, valued friend, and recorder of local history. Nearby, the Roxbury Republican Town Committee erected a bench in memory of Robert J. Eipper for his long service. A memorial bench at the Battle Swamp Preserve commemorates David H. Knutson, former president of the Roxbury Land Trust. On Judds Bridge Road, overlooking the Shepaug River, Allen S. Hurlburt's name is carved into a large boulder in remembrance of his thirty years as first selectman. A metal marker atop a redwood bench near the falls in the Tierney Preserve reads, "In Memory of Richard Rose." Small memorials in front of the firehouse remember Gilberto Cartegena, Scott Gary Adams, and all who have served the Roxbury Volunteer Fire Department.

Other symbols honor those who have made special contributions. One is the grove of trees dedicated to Elinor Hurlbut next to the town hall and the Lewis Hurlbut tree nursery behind the Minor Memorial Library. A small brass plaque under a nearby tree reads, "In honor of Dorothy Diebold friend, benefactor and neighbor on her 100th birthday, 2/3/2005, with thanks and congratulations from the residents of Roxbury." At Mine Hill, plaques honor past presidents Wilbur "Bill" Shook and Larry Kershnar and Mildred A. Erwin, a past director of the Roxbury Land Trust and former Roxbury probate judge, as well as Elaine Beglan, wife of David Beglan, a former director.

6 Parks and Gardens

Parks and gardens are scattered around town—picnic and pocket parks along the banks of the Shepaug River, a community park and tennis courts near the town center, a town park and pond on River Road. Most are restricted to Roxbury residents. Many are named for their benefactors; others are named for their location. Roxbury is a gardening town and though most gardens are on private property and only occasionally opened to the public, one that is open all year round is the Contemplation Garden.

Chase Park. The name honors Rodney Chase who was associated with the Chase Brass Company in Waterbury. His heirs donated the six-acre parcel near Falls Road in 1965 and designated it a public park.[1]

Contemplation Garden. What could be more luxurious than to have your own outdoor reading room surrounded by shrubs, tall wispy trees, and a blue-sky ceiling? Minor Memorial Library patrons have it all in the Contemplation Garden that opened in July 2004 to mark the library's tenth anniversary. Roxbury's David Gardener designed this retreat on the north side of the library with a border of low shrubs and a double row of European hornbeam trees. James and Mary Weaver provided seed money to create the garden dedicated to Dr. Mary McIntyre, a doctor in Roxbury in the early 1900s. Dr. McIntyre's children, grandchildren, and great-grandchildren still live in town.

Memorial benches, each carved with the name of a loved one, are set among the trees and a meandering walkway links the garden to the front of the library. Among those remembered are: Cecelia W. B. Bébel who taught Mary and Steven Schinke to love books, music, people, and life; Lillian Golden (1911-2004) for her love of family and her love of reading, and Alfred (Poppy) Bevilaque, husband, father, and grandfather who remains forever in the hearts of his family.

Trees also stand as memorials. An engraved three-by-five-inch marker at the foot of each tree names a loved one. One inscription celebrates "our grandchildren," Dina and Jacob Anbinder, Noah and Rebecca Baron and Madeline and Steven Anbinder. A marker for Michael Zaslow, is inscribed, "We shall not cease from exploration," a quote from T. S. Eliot's *Four Quartets*. One inscription reads simply, James and Mary Weaver.

Everett B. Hurlburt Community Park. Locals know this park as the Hurlburt Park or Apple Lane Park. Everett B. Hurlburt

(1863-1971 contributed funds for this playground and for community tennis courts, an addition to the Hodge Memorial Library, an ambulance, and trees for the Booth Free School. At thirty-three, in 1896, he and the Rev. Walter Downes Humphrey started Roxbury's first public library. Hurlburt was a generous benefactor and astute businessman. He joined the J. B. Williams Company, a cosmetics firm in Glastonbury, where he introduced Aqua Velva after-shave lotion and later became president of the company.[2]

For over thirty years, crowds have gathered for the annual Pickin' and Fiddlin' contest run by the Roxbury Volunteer Fire Department and Ambulance Association. Contestants come to strum banjos and stomp to blue grass music drawing crowds that squeeze into Hurlburt Park and now outnumber the entire population of Roxbury.

The annual fall Tractor Parade, for residents only, is another crowd-pleaser sponsored by the Recreation Commission. Families line the street to catch candies tossed from tractors of all shapes, sizes, and vintages that parade through town to celebrate Roxbury's agricultural past. Folks follow the decorated machines to Hurlburt Park to take a closer look at the agricultural equipment used in earlier days, enjoy country music, exchange stories about Roxbury's rural past, feast on barbecue, place bets at a cow-paddy raffle, and applaud children competing in the tractor-pull event.

People who contribute their time and talent to community projects often go unrecognized, but not in Roxbury. Every summer the first selectman holds a Volunteers' Picnic in the Hurlburt Park pavilion to honor those who have contributed to the town. But folks don't have to wait for annual events. The park is a daily beehive of activity with joggers, dog walkers, basketball and softball players, and children on jungle gyms. Picnickers find shade under the covered pavilion, and runners from all over New England gather on Saturday mornings to compete in the Roxbury Road Race Series sponsored by the Roxbury Recreation Commission and hikers follow the marked Shepaug Trail along the park's edge.

Hodge Park. This tiny gem, a gift from Charles W. Hodge (1856-1936), son of Colonel Albert L. Hodge, lies along the banks of the Shepaug River north of Roxbury Station. The narrow strip of land was an oasis on the riverbank, a place for families to picnic, but over time, it became an eyesore, littered with brush and trash. In 1996, resident Conrad Hade made cleaning the little roadside park his pet project. Thanks to his efforts,

families now flock to the peaceful spot to lunch, cookout, or relax on benches and watch the river roll by.[3]

River Road Town Park. It's not Coney Island, but it's got a pond, a sandy beach, hiking trails, and the Shepaug River. During the summer, swimmers, picnickers, day campers, and beachcombers flock to the pond. Hikers and dog walkers are attracted to the wide trails through the woods and over the Volunteers' Bridge to an old railroad bed and other preserves. Anglers are enticed by the excellent catch-and-release trout fishing and tubers enjoy the fast-moving white water in the river.

Roxbury Falls Park. Everett B. Hurlburt donated funds to clear, maintain, and add picnic tables, and on September 30, 1963, officials named it for the rushing white waters that tumble over the rocks in the Shepaug River.[4]

Sherman Park. The Connecticut Light and Power Company owned the property near Lake Lillinonah and at a special town meeting, July 13, 1957, town officials gained authorization to purchase the land for a town park. Drs. Robert and Ruth Sherman donated the $1,340 needed to buy the fourteen-acre property at the end of Lower Falls Road.[5]

7 Places to Worship and Rest

In the 1800s, the sound of church bells filled the air and called people to worship. The Methodist, Congregational, and Episcopal Churches all had bell towers that seemed to touch the sky. Most worshippers loved hearing the bells calling them to services.[1]

Some people, however, felt there were too many bells—at least too many in one place. For example, Roxbury Hollow worshippers didn't like the bell clanging one bit; it reminded them of how far away they were from the town center. They contacted the *New Milford Gazette* with their complaints. "We want a church," the swarm shrieked. It was a disgrace—there were too many churches in the center—four in the town center and none in their neighborhood. The crowd wanted a fight and warned the newspaper to stay out it.

The people in the hollow cried that they were two and a half miles from Roxbury Center, were poor and had no teams of horses to take them to worship. Furthermore, even though they were church members, many rarely attended services since they had no transportation and resented having to hold evening services in private homes. Even worse, during the summer, heathens moved into the area and were not about to travel two or three miles to church. Rumor was that people would come down to the hollow to see a man drunk and hear more profanity in a day than they heard in a year in the town center.

The message was clear—folks in Roxbury Hollow needed their own church, but not a new one! It would be preposterous to build a new church when there were already too many. They had a plan—move one of the churches from the town center, and they knew exactly which church to move. Not the Catholic Church—most people in the hollow were Protestant. Not the Methodist Church—people who worshipped there lived near the church. "The Congregational Church," they cried, "certainly had better stay where it is." That left only the Episcopal Church.

The Episcopal Church had the closest affinity to people in the hollow, they argued, and it had the most attendees from the hollow. In fact, it would be a gain, not a loss, for the church to "come amongst us." Non-Episcopalians in the hollow agreed that they would rather attend a nearby Episcopal Church than travel miles to their own.

In their view, Roxbury Hollow was the "heart of the town" and if the Episcopal Church moved there, it would establish the area as an Episcopalian enclave. Furthermore, the argument went, it was time for the Congregationalists and Methodists to consider forming a "union church." In the opinion of the crowd, moving the Episcopal Church to their side of town and uniting the Congregationalists and Methodists, constituted a reasonable, desirable, and practicable proposal.[2]

Despite the clamor, churches in the town center stayed where they were, but the Episcopal Church made one concession. Their minister, after preaching a morning service in the center, would travel to Roxbury Hollow and preach a sermon at the Community Hall in the afternoon.

Eventually, churches in Roxbury did move, but not from their locations. For example, the Episcopal Church on Wellers Bridge Road faced east and then was turned to face south. The Congregationalists didn't move their church; they moved their chapel. The Methodist Church disappeared and the Roman Catholic Church changed its entrance from facing the street to facing a parking lot. Here are the stories of the town's churches that have come, gone, moved, and newly arrived.

Baptist Church. In 1790, Roxbury Baptists were part of a congregation in South Britain. As people from surrounding towns left that church, Roxbury Baptists formed their own organization.[3] They leased property on North Street from Henry Hurlbut in an area that became a school district known as Baptist District No. 7 and on December 30, 1800, parishioners voted to build a twenty-five by thirty-foot church near Benjamin Rumsey's property on North Street.[4]

The seventy-member congregation selected the Rev. Fuller in 1803 and forty-one more joined after he was ordained as minister. Nevertheless, things didn't go well. Some people signed up as members, but didn't attend worship or support the ministry. Church members, in 1809, told the scoundrels who refused to attend services that they were no longer welcome in the Baptist Church and handed them over to the Presbyterians.

By the early 1820s, the Baptist Church had almost no members and in 1825, their church became a schoolhouse with the agreement that worshippers could still hold services in it. By 1876, only two church members were still living; both were ninety years old.[5]

Christ Church. The Episcopal parish in Roxbury, established in 1740, was the oldest Episcopal parish in Litchfield County.[6] It may have begun even earlier, when Joseph Weller, David and

Isaac Castle, Nathan Squire, and Titus Beach agreed to organize an Episcopal congregation and to meet at a private home in the southern part of town near the old town center.

In 1740, the Rev. John Beach of Newtown organized the Episcopal Society of Roxbury. He was a missionary priest with the Church of England who served in the colonies under the Society for the Propagation of the Gospel in Foreign Parts and was under the jurisdiction of the bishop of London. He and several other clergy in the area were converts from Congregationalism, and in fact, the Rev. John Beach had been the Congregational minister in Newtown.[7]

In 1807, the Episcopalians built a second edifice—the one they worship in today. It faced the town green and stood between a schoolhouse and a tavern with a row of horse sheds behind the church. A road ran north between this church and Capt. Ransom's tavern, and for years, perhaps to protect parishioners from screaming students and wandering merrymakers, a picket fence surrounded the church.[8] In 1841, this church took the name Christ Church.

The Episcopalians also liked to move buildings and in 1861, parishioners remodeled this building and turned it to face south.[9] Later the road was moved, the schoolhouse became the parish house, and the tavern became the rectory.

Artifacts such as hand-wrought decorative ironwork by Frank Collins, a local blacksmith, pictures imported from Europe, and stained-glass windows accentuate the church. The stained-glass windows line both sides of the nave, let in light above the altar, and adorn both sides of the entrance. Sometime in the 1880s, people began to donate memorial windows and today, eight stained-glass windows beautify this church. One was dedicated to Deacon Amos Squire, a Deacon in the Congregational Church. His wife, an Episcopalian, dedicated the window in her husband's memory. Hotel owner William (Bill) Seward and his sister Julia dedicated a window in memory of their parents.[10] Other memorial windows include one in memory of Stephen Sandford, a faithful member of the church and one to the Rev. George Louis Foote, called to rest November 11, 1863. At the entrance, a roll of honor lists names of fallen soldiers of our nation's wars.

During its bicentennial celebration in 1940, the Rev. Robert B. Day, rector of Christ Church, joined ministers from three states, town officials, and a large congregation to celebrate the founding of their faith in Litchfield County. Celebrants placed a tablet marking the location of the first church. It reads, "Near this monument stood the first Episcopal Church to be erected in this district, 1763 A. D...."[11]

Early church records have been lost leaving questions about the exact date and location of the first Episcopal Church. A letter dated 1764 noted that there was a "pretty church, neatly finished" on the hill near the old graveyard.[12] The church and its foundation are now gone and it would seem impossible to find the exact location of the original buildings, but some have tried.

One who tried was the Venerable Lewis N. Tillson, a rector from Litchfield, who in 1965 joined the Roxbury Episcopalians to celebrate the 225th anniversary of their parish. During preparations, he discovered the remains of the foundations of the earlier churches, and with the help of townsmen, built the commemorative stone altar that stands at the southwest corner of the Old Burial Ground. He concluded that the church was built in the 1740s, earlier than the accepted date of 1763. In addition, the Rev. Tillson concluded that the location was indeed at the junction of Old Roxbury Road and Lower Country Road.[13]

Christ Church Parish House. Built in 1835, this parish house was the Center School until the church purchased it in 1942. An addition was built in 1958, and in 1990, named in honor of the Diebold family who generously donated to its restoration at the time of the 250th anniversary celebration of Christ Church.[14]

A portrait hangs in the parish house to celebrate the Rev. Robert B. Day, rector from 1933 to 1950, who was a World War I veteran, a talented musician, and an active member of this community. A young local artist and parishioner recognized his service and painted the Rev. Day's portrait. As a student in 1941, Ariane Beigneux won a Pulitzer Prize and in 2006, she received a Lifetime Achievement Award from the Connecticut Society of Portrait Artists. Today, she lives in Norwalk and specializes in painting children's portrait.[15]

Christ Church Rectory. More than eight people owned the property before the Rev. George Foote sold it to the church. This Greek Revival-style house, built about 1740, was a private home and a colonial tavern before it became the rectory for the Christ Episcopal Church in 1846.[16] The rectory became a center of learning and scholarship when the Rev. George Foote taught school in the basement. Students met to take advance classes beyond the arithmetic, geography, history, and English taught in regular schools.

Parishioners cherish stories of animals that lived in and wandered through church properties—the rectory, church, and parish house. One oft-told tale is of a rector's cat that was cooped up in the rectory during services so it couldn't wander into the church, walk up to the pulpit, and listen to the sermon from the rector's shoulder.

Another tale is about the Rev. Bruce Shipman's dog, Beulah, who attended services. A black lab of indeterminate parentage, Beulah not only attended worship, quietly listened to sermons, but also played the part of a black sheep in the Christmas pageant. Not to be outdone, Leo, the Rev. John Miller's golden retriever, frequently attended services and also participated in plowing and planting a community garden at the Senior Center. Leo considered himself a full-fledged member of the church and resident of the North Street rectory.

Helen Humphrey, wife of a former rector, died in 1949. The day before the funeral, family came to pay their last respects and found a skunk standing guard at the top of the church steps. A stalemate ensued—the casket was inside, the family was outside, and in between, the skunk stood like a priest in a black and white fur coat. A textbook "fight or flight" situation was in play. Flight won—the skunk strolled down the road uninterested in hearing the final dirge.[17]

Congregational Chapel. Church and state were not separate in the mid-1800s, so when church members needed a place to educate their children, they built a chapel. In 1843, congregants agreed to allow the church to pay Nathan R. Smith to build it in the corner of the meadow adjoining his garden. The chapel, a diminutive version of the church, was thirty-six-feet long by thirty-two-feet wide, with a four-foot portico entrance and with pillars to match the main building. It was a school until 1903, but congregants still held meetings, prayers, and other activities there.[18]

In time, the chapel was too small for the growing membership and too small for Sunday school. In the late fifties, however, when talk of building an addition to the church began, some people protested. They felt the proposed wing, to be built on the east side of the church where horse sheds had stood thirty years before, would destroy the beauty of the building. After considerable debate and court actions, in 1959, members scrapped that plan and reached a compromise. The church would buy property to the west and agree not to build on the east side for at least fifteen years.[19]

Congregants got restless and decided to sell the chapel as a museum. They offered to sell it for one dollar to the town, provided the church received full market compensation for the value of the building and the land. The town refused the offer, so, in 1989, the church moved the chapel from its original location at 18 Church Street and attached it to the eastern end of the meetinghouse.[20]

Congregational Church. The early history of the Congregational Church parallels the history of Roxbury. Both began when,

because of religious conflict, the Connecticut General Court ordered a minister and his followers to leave Stratford and settle a new plantation at Pomperaug. As Pomperaug grew and worshippers moved farther away from its center, worshippers requested a church closer to their homes. Their numerous appeals finally paid off in 1743 when the general assembly granted them the right to their own ecclesiastical society and named it Roxbury.

Five months after the society was established, Capt. John Baker approached the Rev. Thomas Canfield, a twenty-four-year-old graduate of Yale, to become its first minister. By all accounts, Capt. Baker and the selection committee made a fine choice because the Rev. Canfield served for fifty-one years until his death in 1795. The reverend, his wife, and his daughter lay side by side in the burial ground on Old Roxbury Road.

Throughout his tenure, the reverend carefully recorded the details of his life in tiny script in a six-by-three and one-half inch diary. He noted every interview and meeting with the selection committee. He kept daily records of his congregants noting the names of those he baptized, those he married, and those who died. He recorded the names of Negros and Indians who were congregants in his church.

Lest anyone doubt the Rev. Thomas Canfield's integrity, he left a record of his expenses for his mare, molasses, a cask, and bushels of wheat seed. His journal noted that he paid less than one pound each for a toll on a bridge, a shoe on his mare's hind foot, a half pound of tea, and a sacramental contribution. He meticulously listed the titles and price of each book in his library of Latin, Greek, and French dictionaries, books on devotional life, concordances, and the Bible. Only Ralph Erskine's *Gospel Sonnets,* a best-seller in its day, indicated that the minister had time for leisurely reading.[21]

Leisure was hardly on the Reverend's mind, though. Trouble was already brewing. When the Rev. Canfield arrived in 1744, the congregation numbered twenty-seven people and had already built a meetinghouse about a dozen years previously. But the congregation was growing and needed more space. The general assembly agreed, but when a committee selected the site for the new church, worshippers were disappointed. They refused to build; they demanded that another committee select a location, and in October 1745, the second committee recommended the same location as the first. Church members were again disappointed, but proceeded to build and in 1746, they had a new place. It was forty-four feet south of the first meetinghouse.[22]

By 1792-93, members discussed building another meetinghouse and again, they disagreed about where it should be located. At least one man in the congregation became impatient with their dilly-dallying. General Ephraim Hinman, an eccentric but powerful man, grew more and more edgy, but he knew how to get a decision. While the congregation looked on in horror, he brandished a stone hammer and destroyed all the seats in the church. Parishioners were flabbergasted, but finally, on December 6, 1794, the congregation voted and Gen. Hinman got the decision he wanted.[23]

The plan was to build the meetinghouse at a heap of stones in Daniel Hinman's meadow eleven rods north of David Hammond's shop. It would be sixty-feet long and forty-five-feet wide and would cost about $5,000 dollars. The foundation would be from Mine Hill, the building would have light, and the steeple would resemble the one in Southbury. The third meetinghouse in Roxbury opened in 1796 near Gen. Hinman's house.

In 1876, Minot Leroy Beardsley, the town historian, recalled that it had a lofty spire and two stone horse-blocks where parishioners could hitch their horses and wagons. The galleries were so far above the ground floor that boys up in the pews could "meditate mischief" without being disturbed. One person said the barn-like structure had a steeple that reached 130 feet into the air. It creaked and groaned when the wind blew hard and it was so loud you could barely hear the pastor. People worried that it would come down during the middle of a service and decided to have it taken down before someone got hurt.[24]

The creaky steeple didn't fall easily, though. The congregation chose Nathan Beardsley, Minot Leroy Beardsley's father, to gather a team of men to take it down. The men bought a new hay rope, tied it to the steeple, and tried to pull it down, but the steeple wouldn't budge, so they cut the four posts at the foundation, pulled again, and the steeple toppled with a roar. The timid flock was in shock when the steeple fell, but Beardsley had other worries. He had lost a good rope; the new rope was so badly cut it was ruined and a good hay rope was expensive and not easy to replace.[25]

It was not enough for parishioners to be upset about the steeple falling; they also worried about seating arrangements. Taxes and seating arrangements went hand-in-hand. The church needed people to pay taxes to support the church, but some folks weren't paying, and a bit of diplomacy was required to keep the peace. They appointed "seaters to dignify the meeting," a holdover from the Stratford church that had declared that persons over sixty-years old should be considered honorary members, even if they hadn't paid their taxes. Widows had reserved pews in front. Other arrangements assigned young men to sit on the east side and young women to sit on the west side. Married men, married women, bachelors, and maidens were assigned seats in different sections of the church.[26]

All the rules kept this restless bunch on their toes for about forty years. Then, they were ready to move again. This time, Gen. Hinman wasn't there to guide the still-cautious crowd. They wanted to move only fifteen rods from the old church, less than a city block, and wanted the front of the church to line up with the houses along the road.

Therefore, the fourth edifice was built in 1838 and stands today. Controversy arose again, not over a move, but over a stove. People wanted to sell the old stove and raise money to buy a new one. At the same time, the stove issue was raging, the congregation voted to hire the Rev. Austin Isham (1813-1901) for Sabbaths, with the stipulation that he would not be hired until a new stove was installed. Four years later, the church built sheds and stalls next door for horses. Apparently, sheds and stalls were not as controversial as stoves.[27]

A more serious concern than heating and horses emerged in the mid-twentieth century though. The population was a shrinking. Churches banded together to survive and this one was no exception. In 1940, it became a yoked church with Bridgewater. One reason was that, like many small Connecticut towns, Roxbury's population had fallen dramatically—from 1,210 in 1810 to 660 in 1949.

In the early 1950s and again in 1962, the church merged with the Evangelical and Reform Churches to become the United Church of Christ. By 1965, Roxbury's population had returned to what it was 150 years before, and the church no longer needed to join others to survive.

Under the leadership of the Rev. David Peters and with enthusiastic support of his congregation, the 1980s saw more change to the physical structure of the church. The chapel was moved to the east side of the main building, and an addition was built to connect the two. A new parish house was dedicated in 1990, and the Rev. Peters directed an interior and exterior renovation of the meetinghouse in time to celebrate 250 years as a separate ecclesiastical society.[28]

Congregational Parsonage. The church has owned two parsonages in its history. For a time, ministers built or owned their own homes, but after the Rev. Austin Isham retired, the church society decided to build a parsonage.

The first one, built in 1883, was at 16 Church Street and is a private home today. Nearly forty-five years after the church was built, Mrs. Nathan R. Smith donated land for its first parsonage. The Rev. David Evan Jones was pastor then, and he supervised the building project at a cost of about $2,000. The Rev. Jones was the first minister to live in the parsonage. As pastor from 1871 to 1886, he became one of the church's longest serving ministers.

The second and present parsonage at 28 Church Street was originally a private home, built in 1842 by James Leavenworth (b. 1815). Several people owned the property before Charles Beardsley (1807-1888), who built the Congregational Church, bought it. The home passed down through his family until the church bought it.[29]

A later minister, the Rev. John Jones Vaughan arrived from England and lived with his young wife in the parsonage when he began his two-year tenure in 1893. The couple enjoyed a walk in the open air and did so no matter what the weather. One observer suggested that Americans should adopt this English custom because they confined themselves indoors, did not exercise, and were sickly as a result.[30]

Several ministers have lived in the parsonage that, in 1996, was totally renovated. Today, the Rev. David Peters and his family live in the James Leavenworth House. The Rev. Peters has been pastor of this church for over twenty years and life on Church Street has changed since the Rev. Vaughan offered his advice. In the Rev. Vaughn's day, when the reverend went for a walk, perhaps wildlife in the area had lots of room to roam and didn't bother stopping off at the parsonage, but the Rev. Peters' family are cautious when they step into the open air.

A local reporter wrote, that while one bear made an early morning visit to the local veterinarian, it was another bear—smaller, with tags in both ears—hung around the Congregational Church. This bear also arrived in the early morning hours to snatch bird food.

The Rev. David Peters watched from his window as the bear ripped down the bird feeders, tipped over a can of bird seed, and settled down to breakfast. Then, it came back, probably for dessert. Before dawn, still ravenous, it woke up the Peters' family. But it was too early—the bird food was gone—the bear was out of luck.[31]

Methodist Episcopal Church and Parsonage. Congregational Church records indicated that some Roxburians, like Gideon Booth and William Warner, left that church as early as 1817 to become Methodists. The Methodist Church did not fully organize, though until 1847, under the leadership of the Rev. George B. Way.

Just before the Civil War, the question of slavery divided Protestants and several abolitionists, who were Congregationalists, left that faith to join the Methodist Episcopal Church. Fifty-five members formed the original congregation, and prominent men like Colonel George Hurlburt and Stephen Sanford were among those who joined the Methodists.[32]

The congregation struggled to keep the church going. Members occasionally met in private homes, and sometimes met in a building owned by Sheldon Leavenworth. It had been a wagon shop and had an upstairs meeting room, where people met until they built their own church in 1867.[33] The building, with its tall steeple, fit snugly between the hall of records and the old town hall.[34] Historians have questioned the actual date of when the tall steeple appeared on the landscape.

In 1864, a student wrote that the Methodist Church had been "erected within the last two years." Lewis Hurlbut believed that the student was referring to the wagon shop where Methodists met before the church was built, though he acknowledged that it would have been difficult for the student to mistake a meeting room above a wagon shop for a church. Hurlbut concluded that the split in the church began before the Civil War and it is more likely that members built the church before the end of the war.[35]

In 1890s, the Rev. Julius Nelson preached at the small church and probably lived in the parsonage across the street. He achieved fame among his fellow preachers across the United States for his meager salary of $250. Nevertheless, in 1894, he agreed to return to Roxbury and preach another year.[36]

The Rev. William E. Stone chose not to live in the parsonage, even though he had a long journey to get to church. During very bad weather, he was often the only person who made it. To encourage attendance, he announced an "Everybody to Church" day. A tidbit in the press reported that the pastor had traveled ten miles from New Milford through snowdrifts to get to church. Even with some bare ground and good sleighing, it took him nearly three hours. He was "taxed severely," but was glad he made it.[37]

The reverend made every effort to get to services because, though his congregation lived near the church, it was poor and struggled to keep the church going. As people died or moved away, its membership dwindled and after 1935, worship services ceased. The parsonage became a private home, and by 1940, the church was demolished and its steeple disappeared from the landscape.[38]

Sabba-Day House. A small plaque on Old Roxbury Road tells us that a Sabba-Day House, also known as a noon-house, was near the town's first churches. It was a simple wooden shack where worshippers met between morning and afternoon services. It had a chimney at one end, a horse shed at the other end, and smelled to high heaven, but was the only refuge on a cold winter day.

Neighbors met in the noon-house to catch up on the news, snack between services, and gossip. They huddled around the fireplace to keep warm because churches had no heat and the little foot stoves people carried were hardly enough to keep warm in an icy cold meetinghouse. Worshippers built a fire and cooked their noonday meal of cold pie, pork, peas, and donuts they had packed in their saddlebags.[39]

The plaque on Old Roxbury Road doesn't mention whether the Congregational and Episcopal Churches shared a noon-house.[40] When the churches moved to the town center, worshippers no longer need a Sabba-Day House. Folks could do their nooning in a nearby residence or in a local tavern where women and children could eat their lunch by a roaring fire in the parlor and men could drink flip and eat gingerbread in the barroom.

Saint Patrick's Roman Catholic Church. For decades, visiting priests held Mass in Roxbury's Town Hall, in the Methodist Church, or in a hallway over Tyrrell's general store at Roxbury Station. For thirteen years worshippers met in Michael Pickett Sr.'s home.[41]

That all changed on Sunday July 4, 1886 when the Roman Catholic Church opened its doors for the first time. The 125 worshippers were mostly Irish immigrants who had come a decade earlier to work on the railroad and in the stone quarries and later became farmers. Stained-glass windows bear many of their names. Since its beginnings, the church has been a mission church because it would be difficult for 150 to 200 families to support the church alone. Until about 1900, it was a mission of St. Francis Xavier Parish in New Milford, and today the 125-year-old Our Lady of Perpetual Help Church in Washington is the mother parish.[42]

Until the 1950s, this church had a spire and bell tower and the entrance faced the Congregational Church across the road. After fire or hurricane damage, depending on which source you believe, renovators removed the spire and bell tower and built a covered porch with the entrance facing west. During the reconstruction, the bell that hung in the steeple was lost and hasn't been found since.[43]

Shepaug Valley Bible Church. Word of mouth about Harry Ong's Bible study group spread until it grew so large that he arranged with First Selectman Ed Went to rent space in the town hall. Today, fifty-five people meet in the town hall, but as of Father's Day, 1996, this church has a full-time pastor.

When Ong was in search of a pastor for the growing congregation, he contacted his friend the Rev. Michael Phillips who had recently returned to this country after years of performing missionary work in Spain. The Rev. Phillips serves on numerous committees in the community, like the Council on Aging, and ministers to parishioners every Sunday. During the week, church members hold Bible study groups in private homes throughout Litchfield and New Haven Counties. The church purchased the former Mabel Bernhardt Smith's house on South Street in November 2004. It is home to the Rev. Phillips and his family and a meeting place to conduct church business.[44]

The non-denominational, multi-cultural congregation believes in the doctrine of the Baptist Church and upholds conservative interpretations of the Bible. The congregation provides refreshments at the town's annual Christmas tree lighting ceremony, holds tag sales to support the Roxbury Relief Fund, participates in annual luminary lightings, and donates 15 percent of its income to missions in Cambodia, Spain, Thailand and Africa.[45]

8 Roxbury Land Trust – Preserving a Necklace of Green

When *Voices* journalist John Addyman wrote about Roxbury's nature preserves, he coined the phrase "necklace of green." It was not a box of coins in a secret cave, not a cache of bank notes in a vault, nor a hoard of jewels or precious metals. He was writing about the treasure surrounding Roxbury people. They drive through it, walk its meadows, fish its rivers, and hunt its forests. He was writing about gifts of land.[1]

Addyman described how acre by acre, the Roxbury Land Trust (RLT) acquired hundreds of acres of land to preserve the town's rural character, whose history began with farms and farmland. His article focused on three farms totaling eight hundred acres— Orzech Family Farm, Gavel Family Farm, and Good Hill Farm Preserves. The crown jewels Addyman described are part of the over three thousand acres the RLT protects—about 16 percent of all the land in Roxbury.[2]

Private donations, foundations, government grants, and residents have supported the RLT since 1970 when the non-profit organization was formed. More than half the people in Roxbury have donated land and dollars and the Connecticut Department of Environmental Protection has provided grants to help purchase and preserve open space, to launch a 1999 "Save Our Farms" initiative to preserve Roxbury's farming heritage, and to establish greenways around the town center.[3]

The land trust reaches out to the community through its educational programs. An example was a roving photo exhibit by Shepaug Valley High School senior Ashleigh Repko during the summer of 2006. Repko hiked deep inside the preserves and brought back stunning color photographs. Her photographs support the trust's efforts to preserve the history of Roxbury's land.

The permanently protected "necklace of green" has grown from that first gift of fifty-six acres of land in 1974 to 3, 318 acres as the Roxbury Land Trust approaches its fortieth anniversary in 2010.[4]

Allen S. Hurlbut Preserve. Former resident Sarah Houck donated the twenty-five-acre sanctuary in 2004 in memory of her father, Allen S. Hurlburt, first selectman from 1925 to 1955. The preserve includes wetlands, gently rolling hills, and a hiking trail.

Shepaug Valley High School student Kevin Parzuchowski cleared and blazed a trail in 2006, known as the Hurlburt Trail, that begins on Flag Swamp Road and meanders through some of Roxbury's most pristine woodlands.

Baldwin Connector. Land trust director Martha D. Baldwin created a valuable link in the landscape in 2004 with a three-acre gift that connects the Good Hill Farm, Styron, and

Widmark Preserves. This greenway protects the beauty of land between these preserves for all time. The Baldwin Preserve, named for her husband, Henry deForest Baldwin, is located near Lower County Road.

Baldwin Preserve. This preserve is in memory of Henry deForest Baldwin, a trusts and estates attorney whose knowledge was invaluable when he helped found the Roxbury Land Trust. *Growing Up with Harry: Stories of Character* is a book of recollections written by his son Sherman Baldwin. It is an inspiring memorial to the remarkable man, devoted husband, and loving father.[5]

In 2001, others remembered Baldwin with a land gift. Richard and Sheila Gross, the family and friends of Harry, and the Connecticut Department of Environmental Protection all contributed to this fifty-nine-acre preserve. Enter it from either Route 317 or Lower County Road.

Battle Swamp Brook Preserve. In 1987, Ethan Allen, a longtime resident and member of the RLT, donated a six-acre parcel on Judds Bridge Road in memory of his wife and son. A granite monument and bronze plaque stand in memory of Jean Brice Allen and John Brice Allen. In 1997, singer, songwriter, and resident James Taylor and neighbors donated additional land. The twenty-five-acre parcel is a habitat for birds and a wildlife corridor along the brook's western bank. Two large stone pillars mark the entrance to the preserve.

Beardsley Preserve. Naturalist and environmentalist Emily Griffith Beardsley lived on the property from 1901 to 1937. Caroline H. Beaumont, Elizabeth Boardman, and Hugh Hazelton Jr., in 1977, gifted this 121-acre parcel in memory of their great-aunt Emily Griffith Beardsley and their parents, Hugh and Caroline Norton Hazelton.[6]

The preserve shares parking and trails with the Humphrey Preserve. The trails are easy to walk, and this hiker paradise hides an old sawmill site, hemlock groves, and the Caroline Glen where water cascades through a rocky gorge.

Bray Preserve. In 1993, resident and realtor Malcolm Bray donated one and one-half acres blanketed with beech trees and mountain laurel. Trails lead to the Van Deusen Preserve, a beaver lodge, and a picnic site.

Brian E. Tierney Preserve. Brian Edward Tierney (1948-1968) was a Roxbury son who gave his life for his country in Vietnam. Drs. Ruth and Robert Sherman donated the fifty-six-acre parcel in 1974 in his memory.[7] It was the first gift of land donated to the Roxbury Land Trust.

Specialist 4 Tierney had served less than six months in Company D, First Battalion, and Twelfth Cavalry in the United States Army when he lost his life on May 21, 1968 during an enemy attack near Quang Tri City, South Vietnam. Tierney exhibited extraordinary courage when he lunged towards a grenade to shield himself and his companions. He saved his companions from injury, but lost his life when the grenade exploded. The U. S. Army awarded Tierney the Distinguished Service Cross for his heroic actions. The Vietnam War Memorial and this preserve memorialize Brian in the hearts of his friends and family.[8]

Carter Preserve. Resident Arthur L. Carter, former publisher of *The Litchfield County Times,* and honorary director of the Roxbury Land Trust has donated hundreds of acres to land trusts in Roxbury and neighboring towns. The Carter Preserve is a 160-acre parcel that encompasses part of Mine Hill. It includes dense woods, wetlands, and a vernal pond.[9]

Erbacher Preserve. The name honors Joseph A. Erbacher (1871-1963) and his family who owned a farm on River Road. In

1984, Joan Erbacher McMahan and Edward Erbacher donated the 262-acre parcel that lies across the river from the River Road Preserve, just over Volunteers' Bridge. A wide trail leads along an old railroad bed through hilly terrain and follows the bends in the river. Enter the preserve from Minor Bridge Road near Roxbury Falls or from Volunteers' Bridge.

Fulkerson Preserve. Resident Charles Fulkerson donated this nine-acre property in 1995. The landlocked nature preserve has no parking area or trails.

Gavel Family Farm Preserve. Named for the Gavel family, this two-hundred-acre preserve was once part of Martin Gavel's farm, started in 1908. Locals today still recall Martin Gavel's sons, Frank and Henry, racing around on motorcycles to round up their cattle.[10]

This stretch of land where cattle once grazed was an apt location for a Roxbury Land Trust celebration. During their "Save Our Farms" campaign, the RLT sought farms to preserve in perpetuity. In 2001, after much discussion and negotiation, the Gavel family and the Trust achieved their shared goal—to keep this as farmland. Different people may lease it, but this parcel of earth will remain farmland until the end of time.

The Roxbury Land Trust chose the Gavel Preserve as the site to celebrate its thirty-fifth anniversary. On a crisp autumn day in September 2005, an enthusiastic crowd gathered to talk with neighbors, walk the fields, and enjoy lots of food. A special treat awaited them.

A chorus line of board members sang, "Oh give us land, lots of land under sunny skies above, save open space; Let us hike through the wide open country that we love, save open space..." to the tune of Cole Porter.

The crowd laughed, whooped, and tried to sing along, as RLT board members let down their hair and had a rip-roaring time singing at the tops of their voices. The crowd applauded in agreement that saving open space was a high priority in Roxbury and that they would continue to support the dedicated board members in their efforts to acquire farmland, fields, and other bits of earth to preserve forever.

Glaves Preserve. This five-acre parcel, donated in 1990 by residents Terry and Pat Glaves, is set back from Flag Swamp Road and has no parking or trails, but protects the open space that Roxbury people so dearly love.

Golden Harvest Preserve. The Golden Harvest Farms Limited Partnership donated one hundred acres in 1993 to extend River Road and Erbacher Preserves. Enter this preserve from the Volunteers' Bridge or from Botsford Hill Road through the Orzech Family Preserve.

Good Hill Farm Preserve. This preserve on the eastern edge of town extends into Woodbury and is visible from Good Hill. Over seventy-five years ago, Sebastian Pond's World War I Jenny fell out of the sky in a crash landing near Nate Beardsley's home. Pond swooped down over the open land, liked the looks of the flat plowed fields, and brought his plane down right there. Years later he returned and bought five hundred acres.[11]

Pond's family farmed the land until 1959 and later leased it to farmers and nurserymen. Larry Pond, a descendant of Sebastian and Marguerite Pond, arranged for the trust to purchase 467 acres with the understanding that it would remain a farm always. The arrangement, completed in March 2004, protects one of the largest remaining active farms in Roxbury.

This historic property spreads across a ridgeline with woods and meadows and long views toward the south, east, and west.[12] Locals know the private airport, with its homemade metal hangar on a fifteen-foot-wide airstrip in a hayfield, as the "Roxbury International Airport."[13]

Horrigan Family Preserve. In 2006, Robert, and William Horrigan donated six acres in memory of two young men who died in tragic accidents. The preserve is a lasting tribute to William Horrigan Jr. and Richard Tyler Horrigan, known to their friends and family as Billy and Tyler. The preserve protects a portion of Cross Brook; enter it from Painter Hill Road.[14]

Humphrey Preserve. John Hersey Humphrey, former librarian of the Hodge Memorial Library, gave this fifteen-acre parcel in 1978 in memory of his parents Walter Downes Humphrey and Helen Hunt Humphrey. Walter Humphrey was founder of Roxbury's first library and rector of Christ Church for thirty-nine years until his death in 1931. Helen Humphrey was a co-founder of the Roxbury League of Women Voters, served on the school board, was librarian and library trustee, and author of *Sketches of Roxbury, Conn.*[15] The Humphrey Preserve shares its trails and parking with the Beardsley Preserve.

Jagiri Loomba Preserve. This five-acre island, a 1997 gift from Dr. N. Paul Loomba and Mary Adams Loomba, pays tribute to Dr. Loomba's father who passed away at the young age of forty-seven. This wildlife habitat is near the Roxbury Station Bridge.

Leander Woods Preserve. Leander Blakeman (1807-1895) farmed this property in the Warners Mill District, but when Capt. Cyrus E. Prindle and a journalist passed by in May 1894, they did not stop. The Captain explained that Blakeman, an eighty-seven-year-old "well known citizen" was in mourning for his wife.[16]

Wallace Murkland bought the Blakeman property in 1924 to use as a summer residence. He loved the brook that ran through the property and hoped to name it Leander Brook, but somehow his dream went unrealized until after his death.[17] Murkland's daughter, Mrs. Walter H. Glass, donated the thirty-four-acre parcel in 1989 in her father's memory and named it Leander Woods. No trails cross the preserve, though if you peak through the hemlock woods off Flag Swamp Road you will see the remains of stone walls that Blakeman probably built when he cleared the land over a century and a half ago.

Lilly Preserve. A succession of gifts from Thomas Robert Lilly's family has expanded the Lilly Preserve to 140 acres. Natalie Todd Lilly and Dione Todd Lilly Bowers donated the major parcel of 126 acres in 1975 in memory of their husband and father, a widely acclaimed landscape architect and longtime Roxbury resident.[18]

A plaque set in stone near the entrance tells of later family donations, "This property is given to the Roxbury Land Trust in memory of a gracious lady Natalie Todd Lilly by her daughter, Dione, and grandsons Thomas and Stewart Bowers October 9, 1983."

Two entrances lead to trails ablaze with pink flowers of mountain laurel in the spring, one on Good Hill Road two miles east of the center green and another on Old Tophet Road. From the Old Tophet Road entrance, a path to the right leads to a narrow bridge that crosses Jacks Brook. Follow the trail up the hill to view masses of wild flowers, mosses, and ferns that spread across the landscape. Some trails are steep and pass through marshes; other trails are flatter and wind through fields and along old stone walls.

Matthau Preserve. In the summer of 1999 stage and screen-actor Walter Matthau and his wife, Carol, donated the thirty-two-acre parcel they had owned for twenty years. Today these open meadows, stone walls, and wetlands on Tophet Road will forever be a protected habitat for wildlife.[19]

McMahan Preserve. Joan Erbacher McMahan donated six acres in 1991. Over the years, she has given additional parcels so that today this forty-four-acre preserve encompasses the land to the north of High Bridge Road.

Miller Preserve. The name honors playwright Arthur Miller and his wife, the esteemed photographer, Inge Morath Miller. Arthur Miller moved to Roxbury in 1948 when land was five dollars an acre. As a writer, he wanted to enjoy the farmland, walk the open fields, and be alone to do his work. He also wanted to meet his neighbors. Miller's estate donated the fifty-five-acre parcel in November 2005 making their donation part of more than six hundred acres of preserved land that stretches from the Matthau Preserve to the Good Hill Farm Preserve.[20]

Mine Hill Preserve. From its beginnings, the Roxbury Land Trust set its sights on the hills along Roxbury's western border. Its goals—to study and survey the archaeological site known as Mine Hill, to preserve the artifacts from the mid-1800s iron mines, quarries, and railroads that represented the town's industrial past, and to protect the wildlife.

It all began in 1978 when the RLT, with funds from Roxbury residents, the Knapp Foundation, and others acquired land for a preserve from its owners William O. and Adelaide J. Mathews. A year later, the National Register of Historic Places added Mine Hill Preserve to its list, and in 1981, two Yale graduate students published *Time and the Land: the Story of Mine Hill.*[21] The preserve grew in 1988 when the Sun Pond Woods Association gave an additional fifty-five acres; in 1994, Mabel B. Smith donated land on Quarry Drive and in 1998, the trust purchased an additional twenty-eight acres.

The Connecticut State Historical Society recognized the need to restore remaining artifacts from the mining industry and provided funds in 1982 to stabilize the blast furnace and conduct an archaeological study. Blast furnace, roasting ovens, granite quarries, and abandoned mines were repaired as part of an extensive restoration project.[22]

These restorations and the remains of a Shepaug Railroad turntable make this 360-acre preserve different from any other

in the portfolio of preserves and further enhance its historical significance.

Go back in time with a visit to Mine Hill. Signs peppered with facts and legends tell about the mineworkers, illustrate how iron was mined, explain how the blast furnace worked, and describe how granite quarries have prospered here for nearly two centuries.

Follow the Main Loop blazed in blue and begin the uphill climb along the Donkey Trail where you'll pass two mine tunnels and a series of grated airshafts that are now entryways to bat hibernacula. Listen to the clicking wings. Not to worry; the grates will protect you from the little brown flying objects.

As you begin to walk downhill, you'll pass abandoned quarries and an old quarry bridge. The trail eventually joins Hodge Road and ends at the furnace complex.[23]

Moosehorn Access. Joseph T. Foster Jr., a journalist, moved from Ohio to Roxbury in the mid-1950s and wrote for the *New Milford Times* until his death in 1987.[24] This two-acre parcel, given in 1985, creates a passage from Moosehorn Road to the Humphrey and Beardsley Preserves.

Natalie White Preserve. Natalie White was the great-grand-daughter of Stanford White, the distinguished turn-of-the century architect, and daughter of the well-known sculptor Robert Win-throp White. When seventeen-year-old Natalie died in 1975 in a

tragic automobile accident, authors Rose and William Styron donated a nine-acre parcel in her memory. A year later, Joseph and Marion Adams donated additional land to complete the preserve that consists of two parcels totaling sixteen acres on both sides of Rucum Road.

Friendship between the Styrons and Claire and Robert White began in the early 1950s when they were together at the American Academy in Rome. The Whites were matron of honor and best man at the Styron's wedding in Rome, neighbors during the Styron's honeymoon in Ravello, and close friends when they all returned to America to raise their families. The Whites lived on Long Island and the Styrons lived in Connecticut. The families visited each other often, though, and the children from both families played together on the hill that is now part of the preserve. Visit the preserve, and admire the memorial sculpture that Robert White carved to honor his daughter—the airy granite sailboat is perched on the highest spot in the preserve, "to sail between grass and sky forever." [25]

Orzech Family Preserve. On September 11, 2002, the RLT purchased this 112-acre stretch of green from Ed Orzech under the "Save Our Farms" initiative. A bronze plaque nearby reminds us that this stretch of earth will be protected through eternity

The Orzech family farmed this land since 1927 and kept a herd of a hundred Holstein cows. When the Shepaug Railroad ran along the river, the Roxbury Creamery bottled milk from the Orzech dairy farm and shipped it to New York City by rail. The old railroad bed is now a favorite hiking trail that connects this land to the River Road, Erbacher, and Golden Harvest Preserves. [26]

In addition to tending a dairy farm, the Orzechs also produced corn, hay, potatoes, and other vegetables. When Ed Orzech took over the farm in the 1950s, he opened a feed and farm supply store. His long-standing gas pumps and bright blue barns dominate the landscape at the bottom of Botsford Hill and are reminders of the large farms that once supported this rural community. After selling much of his land to the land trust, Orzech retained thirty acres to grow corn and hay and continued to operate the feed store until his death in 2008.

Raven Rock Preserve. This preserve represents resident Rod Thorne's donation of twenty acres to connect to the Battle Swamp Brook Preserve.

River's Edge Preserve. This twenty-four-acre parcel stretches along the eastern bank of Lake Lillinonah at the mouth of the Shepaug River. It lies on a section of the lake created when the Connecticut Light and Power Company built the Shepaug Dam in 1953. The man-made lake on the Housatonic River is a fisherman's paradise full of pike, bass, and large pan fish.

To catch the big one, student Jamie Curren needed access to the water, but there was no trail. In 2006, for his Shepaug Valley High School senior project, he decided to solve the problem. He cleared and blazed a wide trail that makes a one-mile loop leading to the lake and connects with Sherman Park. Curren also published a guide to fishing in these waters.[27]

River Road Preserve. Frasier McCann, a local gentleman farmer and honorary director of the land trust, gifted fifty-two acres in 1982 along the Shepaug River where residents swim in the town pond, fish, hike, picnic, and enjoy the wildlife. Trails loop uphill through a hemlock knoll and along the river to Volunteers Bridge, a suspension bridge built by volunteers in 1991.

Erbacher, Golden Harvest, and River Road Preserves total 453 contiguous acres with extensive hemlock forests, natural floodplains, and wetlands along the riverbanks.[28]

Styron Preserve. Resident writers William and Rose Styron donated the twenty-two-acre property in 1997. Though the Styrons lived in another part of town, they wanted to protect the dense forests, open meadows, and old trees that grew along Old Tophet Road.

Van Deusen Preserve. In 1986 resident Maizda Van Deusen gifted twenty-one acres off Bacon Road. A wooden-plank path leads to a viewing deck where frogs, beavers, ducks, and other wildlife frolic in Jacks Brook. In winter, children gather at this favorite ice-skating rink on the beaver pond in this preserve.

Widmark Preserve. Film star Richard Widmark's wife, Jean, loved the old schoolhouse and scenic hill on Tophet Road, and in 1997, Widmark donated nearly five acres and Roxbury's last-remaining one-room schoolhouse in her memory. Later, Widmark and his daughter, Anne, expanded the preserve with their 2004 gift of another twenty-three acres in memory of Jean Widmark.

Students attended classes in the schoolhouse, built in the early 1800s, until the turn of the twentieth century. Ryan Walsh, a Shepaug Valley High School senior, refurbished the building. In a press interview, he expressed relief that he hadn't attended classes in the tiny building during hot New England summers and freezing winters.[29]

The preserve contains open meadows with large rock outcroppings and connects with the Matthau and Styron Preserves on Tophet Road. The Baldwin Connector, a gift from RLT director Martha D. Baldwin, connects the three and creates a continuous greenbelt to the Good Hill Farm Preserve.[30]

9 Roxbury Center

Roxbury designated its historic district in 1966, according to the carved white sign at the north end of Roxbury's town green. What is not stated is that in 1983, the National Register of Historic Places added the town center to its list of local historic areas.[1] The district includes the Seth Warner Monument and seventy-two buildings that represent a variety of architectural styles— Georgian, Federal, Queen Anne, Cape—dating from the eighteenth century. Roxbury's Historic District Commission has published a survey and a walking-tour guide that details the architectural features of the buildings and this chapter will not duplicate that information.[2]

The center includes private homes, businesses, and government buildings—some built in the twentieth century. Its commercial area includes the Roxbury Market, post office, bank, and other offices that appear to be all in one building. The Roxbury Garage, the only full-service gas station in town, is farther south. Opposite the commercial area, a garden planted in front of a long, low stone wall decorates an area of public buildings, including the town hall, town garage, and fire station.

On October 18, 1996, in a salute to the future, townspeople buried a Bicentennial Time Capsule. They placed artwork, stories, and memorabilia inside. Students from the Booth Free School entered a contest to guess the population of Roxbury in 2046. A granite marker identifies the place where people will gather on October 18, 2046 to open the capsule. On that day, a student will receive a prize of old and new $100 bills.[3]

Booth Free School. The name is from the original benefactor, Hervey Minor Booth, who, in 1890, donated $10,000 to open a school in the Congregational Church Chapel. To qualify for enrollment, a student had to be at least twelve years old and have a basic knowledge of elementary studies; forty students qualified. Subsequent donations from Mary Somers and George Lendeveg, in memory of his son, Frederick Flower Lendeveg, added to the original gift.[4]

Students moved from the chapel to the one-room schoolhouse on South Street. In time, that building was enlarged and later became a high school and now, an elementary school. Once it had a belfry, but no electricity, no running water, and no bathrooms.

Amenities remained sparse until Health Officer Dr. Mary C. McIntyre wrote that the school should have electricity because the lack of electricity was a severe handicap for students. Electricity would improve the instruction of chemistry and physics, she said, and stressed that it was detrimental to students to work in a laboratory without lights. In addition to electricity, the doctor pressed for running water and sanitary toilets. Officials accepted the doctor's recommendation and town reports for 1934 and 1935 noted that the school was finally equipped with wiring and modern plumbing.

Changes are still taking place at this school, as renovations are currently underway for the upcoming school year. Meanwhile, young scholars walk through the doors of Booth Free School and pass a large portrait of the dour-looking genius and benefactor who wanted to ensure that student life would be easier for them than it had been for him.

Hodge Memorial Library and Museum. The name is from Charles W. Hodge (1856-1936) who, in his will, donated $30,000 for a library in memory of his father, Albert L. Hodge. Charles Hodge directed his executors to spend $15,000 to build the library and use the interest from the remaining funds for books

and upkeep. He further specified that builders use stone from Mine Hill.[5]

Roxbury had little space for a library collection before the building, fondly known as the Hodge, was built. One of Roxbury's first libraries was a collection of five hundred books in Benjamin S. Preston's store. Members paid two dollars for the first year, then a dollar a year after that for the privilege of borrowing books. Rules about borrowing were strict. The first book was free, additional books were ten cents, and all had to be returned by 7:00 PM on the first Friday of each month. Fines were fifteen cents a book. Membership was no doubt worth the rules, though, because a committee selected books from the "most worthy publications of the day."[6]

After the Preston store closed, the old town hall housed the collection, but space was at a premium—books stacked everywhere. Finally, in 1937, the Hodge Library was built and the town had a place dedicated solely to library activities.

Roxbury is a town of readers and writers and as the Hodge collection grew, space shrank and a new library was built on South Street. The Hodge Library became a museum. Usually a quiet place, once a year, it's as if a storm comes through. Dealers, book collectors, and browsers from all over New England attend the annual book sale. Opening night is always a gala Friday affair with a reception, entertainment, and a rush for the best buys. The rest of the weekend, visitors focus on finding treasures among the thousands of books, videos, and records that volunteers have collected, priced, and carefully organized months in advance.

Minor Memorial Library. The name honors Rachel Minor. In 1988, her daughter and son-in-law, Mabel Bernhardt Smith

and Sanford Smith, donated three and a half acres of land near their home for this library.[7] Private individuals and federal and state governments contributed to building and maintaining it.

Town Historian Timothy Beard was librarian at the Hodge Memorial Library and became library director of the Minor Memorial Library when it opened in 1994. He held that position until his retirement.

Valerie G. Annis became library director, having served in various positions at the Brookfield Library for eleven years. The Minor Memorial Library houses about 39,000 books, videos, and audio books. In addition, it has a well-stocked children's room, a formal reading room, and computers available for patrons. Local writers generously give their time and talent by displaying their works and joining a "Meet the Author" program. Paintings, sculpture, and photography by local artists are on display and the Calder sculpture, *Mountain*, graces the lawn near the front entrance.

In warmer months, the library is often a gathering place for receptions and parties. Wide French doors facing west open onto a covered veranda overlooking the fields beyond. The Contemplation Garden offers additional quiet space.

Munson Meadow. The name is from the Munson family who owned the land and the neighboring Roxbury Market from 1963 to 1993. This five-acre landmark property on Route 67, a state-designated scenic route, sits at the gateway to the town center. The town purchased the meadow through its land acquisition program to preserve the open space.

First Selectman Barbara Henry then sought private and state funding for a stone wall preservation project which was completed in June 2007. The run-down farmer's stone wall, now cleared of brush, runs 700 feet north of Hurlbut Bridge to the center and enhances not only the entrance to the town center but also the vista along the state road.[8]

R. M. Bernhardt Meat Market. Rulley McKinstry Bernhardt (1878-1955) owned and operated this one-room, one-story white building at 15 South Street. Bernhardt butchered cattle from his slaughterhouse in Roxbury Hollow and sold it in the meat market. Most of his native beef were Holstein and Guernsey, though, in later years, he bought from large meat packinghouses.

Bernhardt's son-in-law, Sanford Smith, ran the market until it closed in the early 1960s. Locals today recall buying meat at the market and remember the sweet aroma of sawdust on the floor. While customers waited for their meat to be cut and ground, they sat on a row of white chairs and caught up on town news. In 2002, the town purchased the meat market and the surrounding 3.62 acres and agreed to keep the land as open space and never allow the market to be moved.[9]

Roxbury Firehouse. The Roxbury Volunteer Fire Department was incorporated in 1948, as a result of a Roxbury Grange community service project. In those days, one small firehouse on Church Street serviced the community. Today, this small town has two firehouses, the older one used by scouts to store collected cans and bottles, the newer one to store fire trucks, ambulances, and emergency equipment. One truck, known as Old Betsy, parked in front of the old firehouse and was the only fire engine in town until 1950.[10]

Emergency volunteers live all over town. In earlier days, it was difficult to alert them about a fire or medical emergency, but three women who lived in sight of the old firehouse met the challenge. Elinor Hurlbut, Ethel Hurlbut, and Doris Richardson each had a phone system in her house to notify volunteers about emergencies. They were Roxbury's first responders and were in  charge of testing the fire whistle and answering the fire phone that called everyone to action. Every day at noon, Elinor Hurlbut pressed a button to test the fire whistle to be sure it worked. She coordinated her button pressing with the "beep" on radio station WTIC in Hartford. No one needed a watch; the whistle told them what time it was.

Each woman had a fire phone and when it rang, she ran to answer it, wrote down the caller's information, and immediately sent a signal to the firehouse. That signal set off a siren. The siren was a call for volunteers to drop everything and get moving. Whoever answered the fire phone pressed the signal to keep the siren blaring. At the same time, eyes on the firehouse, she pressed the siren button until a firefighter arrived to shut it off.[11]

A picture of the new firehouse, built in 1977, decorated that year's town report. The fire whistles and fire phones were silent, and the women found other things to keep them busy. Today, a siren at the new firehouse sounds the time at noon.

Roxbury Historical Society Barn. In 1974, Robert Hodges, David Gillette, Russell Montgomery, Alden Hurlbut, and Bud Squire became the first officers of the Roxbury Historical Society, Inc. They wanted to collect and preserve antique tools and farm equipment.[12]

The men met in the little firehouse on Church Street and set their sights on an old barn to store the treasures. It was on the old Asahel Bacon property on South Street. The group sought funding to buy the barn and then moved it behind the senior center. They renovated it and filled it with artifacts of Roxbury's agricultural history.[13]

Longtime resident Andy Piskura is an expert on antique farm equipment, is a member of the Society, and knows the architecture of this barn. On a tour of the barn, this man of few words pointed to the ceiling and said—wide chestnut timbers, all hand-hewn, no nails. He explained that even though no nails were used to construct the barn, the timbers were set to provide brute-strength support. The solid red structure on South Street stands empty now. In 2009, the Society moved its contents to Toplands Farm where new barns were built to house the artifacts.

The new barn is chock-full of stuff—old carriages, a Bronson Plow, an antique corn husker, and an odd assortment of hand tools. A mailbox that looks like a dollhouse is a replica of the former Ognan house. A sorting box with pigeonholes for mail is a reminder of the days of Rural Free Delivery. An antique icebox, utensils, and spinning wheels are on display in an old-fashioned kitchen, all reminders of the days when life was slow and the past was perfect.[14]

Roxbury Museum. Formerly the Roxbury Hall of Records, it's brick, it's fireproof, and it's now a museum. It also exists because of a near tragedy.

In the 1930s, a fire raged in the old town hall. Schools closed, students scrambled to rescue records, and bucket brigades put out

the fire. Once volunteers doused the fire, people began to worry about the safety of official records. At the time, records were stored in a vault that was large, moveable, and flammable. The town needed something better.

A farmer and a selectman donated dollars and land. Herman Beardsley, a cattle farmer on Good Hill, gave $800 to build a fireproof building and Allen S. Hurlburt, first selectman, sold the town a parcel of land for one dollar. Soon the little red building appeared on the landscape.[15] The tiny building dates from 1932, but the date carved above the door is Roxbury's incorporation date. Today the museum houses a collection of historic photographs, artifacts, and memorabilia.

Roxbury Senior Center/ Roxbury Land Trust. This building, formerly the old town hall, was renovated to make a senior center, and in 2004, Roxbury built a new town hall. The old hall was the center of social life for people of all ages who came from miles around to attend plays, potluck dinners, and dances. One of the most popular events was the Shepaug Club annual Thanksgiving dance. Hundreds of couples came from neighboring towns to join the fun. Women made sandwiches, men brought wood for heat, and people lugged cans of water— the hall had no water. They danced until the old floors shook and at midnight, the dancing stopped and everyone went home on foot or by horse and buggy. In 2009, the Shepaug Club celebrates its 105th anniversary.

The club still meets in the old town hall, now the Senior Center. During its renovation, men jacked up the old town hall eight feet off the ground and built a new foundation to replace the one-hundred-year-old stone sill. A state grant, secured by the town, funded the preservation and renovation of this historic building. The result is a modern center for seniors and land trust offices.[16]

The center is light, spacious, and modern, but retains many of the architectural features of the original nineteenth century building. A computer center, health-screening room, and entertainment area have taken center stage. The first floor has offices, a meeting room, dining area, and kitchen, and the upstairs has a large meeting room, a stage, and offices. In warm weather, a patio overlooking fields and a community garden are welcome retreats.

Alice Griffin, senior center director, municipal agent, and longtime resident, wore many hats as she worked to identify senior needs and organize programs. With added staff and a band of volunteers, the center bounces with activities and festivities, each one announced in the monthly "7 South Street" newsletter and Roxbury's elderly, who met for nearly twenty-five years in the town hall, now have a place to call their own.

The Roxbury Land Trust staff migrated from place to place until a wing was added. The staff last worked in a corner of the Hodge Museum. The RLT staff finally has office space and a large conference room where they conduct the business of preserving valuable undeveloped land.

Roxbury Town Hall. Once upon a time, this village had two town halls—one old, one new. The old town hall, built in 1879, was cramped and dark. Candles and gas lamps lit the hall until the mid-1920s when Connecticut Light and Power sent its first bill for electric lights.[17] The building was so small that officials held town meetings on the front 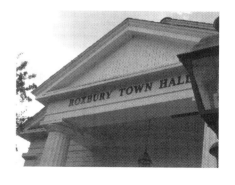 porch or in the basement of the Congregational Church.[18] There was scant space to store records and no rooms for town officers. The town clerk shared a small space with the probate judge, and the tax collector worked in a vault. The first public library was in a back room, books stacked everywhere, even in the bathroom. Horses, not cars, were in the parking lot. A theatre on the second floor, however, guaranteed that this little wooden building would be one of the liveliest places in town. Plays, ice cream socials, and other gatherings kept the crowds coming, but space was cramped for a long time.

It was 1989 before someone proposed building a larger town hall, eventually built on a 1.5 acre raised knoll on North Street. At a dedication ceremony in 1991, flags flew over the new hall. People toured the building and marveled at the four imposing, round white columns across the front. They admired the modern offices and spacious meeting rooms and praised the works of twenty local artists.[19] In 2006-2007, a photograph of this imposing Greek-Revival-style building adorned the cover of the *Roxbury Annual Report*, courtesy of Barbara Henry, first selectman.

10 Road Stories

*Y*ou may not get excited about the roads you travel every day, but they were a hot topic on a cold December 6, 1796 when Roxbury held its first town meeting and appointed nine highway surveyors to build, repair, and clear roads.

In those days, roads had no names or signs, because folks knew their way around. In fact, in 1865, when selectmen called for a vote to put eight road signs around town, town rebels yelled, "We don't need any!" [1] Hence, if a stranger came looking for Mallory's place, for example, he was told to walk down a rocky dirt path for a mile, turn left at the heap of stones under a hemlock tree, stop at the last fence post, climb the hill, and he would be at Mallory's place.

Then something happened. People began to travel from town to town and more strangers passed through, often peddlers selling their wares. For a while, word-of-mouth directions worked, but as the town grew, people needed names and signs to help them find their way. The path to Mallory's place officially became Mallory Road.

Roxbury's one hundred roads stretch across sixty miles and each has a name and each name has its own story. The names fall into categories: surnames, plant and tree names, animal and bird names, commercial, biblical, and quirky, foreign, or unusual.

Twenty-two names are topographical; that is, they describe the landscape or location relative to the compass or to another place, as in West Street, Lower Falls Road, and Southbury Road. Don't be fooled by the apparent simplicity of these names; each has a rich history.

Personal names make up the largest group with twenty-nine roads. Most are surnames; one is a Christian name; none is a woman's name. The town has attracted many well-known writers, artists, sculptors, and other famous people, but no celebrity name is on a road. Personal names on roads are mostly names from the eighteenth century, when 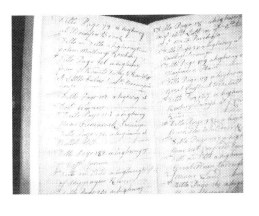 the tradition was to name roads for property owners and that tradition has carried over to modern times. For example, Crofut Lane, Welton Road, and Wakelee Road were early labels, whereas, Judge Road and Kressfield Farm Lane are of a more recent vintage.

With its roots in farming, Roxbury grew into a community of tree-huggers and animal lovers who selected road names to reflect those passions. For example, twenty-four roads have tree and plant-related names, such as Apple Lane, Cedar Ridge, and Pine Tree Hill. Wild animals roamed the hills in earlier days, and still do, yet only four roads have animal or bird names. Moosehorn Road and Bear Borough Road are among them.

Although mining was a prominent part of Roxbury history, commerce and industry provided only five road labels: Garnet Road, Mine Hill Road, and Quarry Drive.

Given the deep religious fervor among the first settlers, one wonders why they gave only one road a biblical name and that name refers to Hades. In the quirky, foreign, or unusual group, Brandywine Crossing, Chalybes Road, and Rucum Road are among my favorites.

You'll discover from these stories that roads move, discontinue, and change names. Here then, are this town's one-hundred road stories.

Acorn Hill. A developer named Acorn Hill after he built the first home there in 1983. It's true that thousands of acorns were strewn across the hill, but the namer may have selected the label out of compassion for the little brown nugget.[2]

Think about it; pretend you're an acorn. Your goal in life is to become a mighty oak, but your life cannot even begin without the cooperation of another oak tree.

Cooperation is hard to come by, though, since most oak trees are slow pokes. They prefer to hang around for twenty years before they make even one acorn.

Suppose you were the first-born acorn on a twenty-year-old oak tree—a tiny, green, thin-skinned nugget. You get older, turn brown, gain weight; you ripen. Finally, you're an acorn. Suddenly you hit the ground—ping, like a tiny ice cube. You barely feel the cold earth before a deer, a squirrel, a blue jay, a chipmunk, or a wild turkey scoops you into his mouth. You're a goner—you'll never become a tree.

Don't feel bad—only one in ten-thousand acorns becomes an oak tree. Had you known, you may have chosen a different goal in life.[3]

Apple Lane. If any road in town has an identity crisis, it's Apple Lane. The apple orchards that gave the lane its name are gone, but the street name has changed so many times it's a wonder the people who live here can find their way home.

For example, Elwell Road was its unofficial name in 1785 when the Norton-Elwell House was built along this road. The house still stands and nearly two-hundred years later a 1971 property deed still referred to Elwell Road. By the twentieth century, most folks were comfortable with the name Apple Lane and probably never heard of Norton-Elwell.[4]

South Street cuts the lane nearly in half even though local maps identify both ends as Apple Lane. Apple Lane East and Apple Lane West have also been favorite tags used to distinguish the two. For example, an advertisement in *Roxbury Cookery* promoted a business at Apple Lane W.

A local newspaper names West Apple Lane as the gathering place for the weekly Roxbury Road Race Series sponsored by the Roxbury Recreation Commission. To add to the confusion, a 1979 property map fashioned the name Apple Lane Way.[5] Never mind trying to find your way home, probably no one other than the mapmaker can locate Apple Lane Way.

Sanford and Mabel Bernhardt Smith grew apple orchards along this lane in earlier days, but someone dismantled their cider press more than thirty years ago. The plan had been to display it in the Roxbury Historical Society Barn, but that never happened and today, only the remains of its foundation lie at the bottom of a hill near South Street.[6]

A trip down this lane is more than a study of multiple names, lost apple orchards, and a dismantled cider press; it's a jaunt to the zoo, a peek at a botanical garden, and a romp in a public park. Scottish Highland cattle graze at the Rob-Low Farm, horses nibble grass in paddocks across the way, donkeys peer over a fence farther west, wild turkeys mingle with deer in a nearby yard, and an occasional stray cow crashes through fences near Crofut Lane.

Prize-winning, long-coated Scottish Highland cattle at the Rob-Low Farm stare over the fence to greet anyone who stops to visit. The owner, Robert Lowe, known as Bucky, raises the cattle for show and food. When I stopped by one day, he told me several name stories. One was about why his surname is Lowe and his farm's name is Low. He said that census takers changed the spelling when his grandfather came to this country. They dropped the "*e*" from the surname. To honor his grandfather, Bucky named the farm with his grandfather's surname, even though his own family added an "*e*" to Lowe.

Lowe had another story about seven-day old Fred, a Scottish Highland calf who stood on the other side of the fence while Bucky and I talked. Fred was still wobbly as he clung to his mother. Fred's father, Sir James, was at another farm. Bucky said that his grandchildren had outsmarted him when they named the newborn calf. Pointing to Fred, he said, "Once they have a name, you can't eat them."[7]

Bucky then turned my attention to the horses in the paddocks at Canterbury Farm across the road and said the field used to be an airfield. I flew a few times, he said, but it was hairy because when we took off, we barely cleared the treetops. He didn't describe what it felt like to fly over the windmill that towers above the manicured field.[8]

Farther along Apple Lane, brown and white patch-quilt-colored donkeys lean over a fence waiting for a handout. Flocks of wild turkeys feast under bird feeders at a neighbor's house and prance around the yard or march single-file atop a stone wall, plumes in full display. The turkeys occasionally wander over to celebrated composer and lyricist Stephen Sondheim's house or cross the road to visit Peter Wooster's fields, bypassing his distinctive show garden.

Once you've passed the sites on the eastern side of this lane, you'll encounter more as you cross South Street. One is the J and H Flower Farm run by Jack and Henny Reelick who came to Roxbury from Holland forty years ago. "Wild apple trees were all along here when we came," Jack said. He also said that he was surprised to learn that someone had grown potatoes in the fields, but added that the sandy loam and low water table were good for this particular crop. Jack should know because he was six when he started gardening. Reelick retired in 2000 and sold part of the land where he once raised 10,000 chrysanthemums.[9]

Follow the small round red and white signs marking the Shepaug Trail if you're hiking or jogging. Complete your trip with a stop at Hurlburt Park and enjoy a picnic in the pavilion, a trek around the track, or a swing on the jungle gyms. While you're there, consider the apple trees in the park that gave the lane its name or imagine enjoying a mug of cider from Sanford and Mabel Bernhardt Smith's apple orchard.

Apple Ridge. Apple orchards grew on this ridge, as they did on Apple Lane, but this ridge is best known among locals as the home of father and son Nathan and Percy Beardsley. Nathan Thompson Beardsley (1868- 1943), known as Nate, was a descendant of five generations of Connecticut Yankees.[10] His family lived in Roxbury from the days when his great-grandfather fought in the American Revolution to when his eldest son Percy Peck Beardsley (1891-1968) ran the family farm.[11]

Nate Beardsley was above average height with a mustache and a twinkle in his eye and had a pleasant personality. He was concerned about his son. Because Percy remained single for so long, his father worried that he would never meet the right woman.[12] Percy was tall and slender with dark brown eyes and hair. He was a taciturn man and a World War I hero. Percy's small, neat handwriting suggested a man deliberate in his ways.[13]

They were sociable men who entertained, spent long hours managing their vast farm, and achieved notoriety for their cider cellar and Devon cattle. They frequently invited locals and celebrities to tour the farm and enjoy the cider cellar. Two film stars, one from out of town, the other a neighbor, made a lasting impression on father and son. The visiting celebrity was Norma Talmadge, star of the silent screen. She stopped at the farm to make a film with the Beardsley's ruby-red Devon oxen, and like most guests, Talmadge joined the Beardsley men for a drink in the cider cellar. After the film star left, Nate found her gloves on one of the barrels, and he insisted that the gloves remain on that barrel as long as he was alive.[14]

If Nate was obsessed with gloves, Percy was obsessed with footprints. When their neighbors, playwright Arthur Miller and his wife, actress Marilyn Monroe, visited, it wasn't stardom and fame that impressed Percy. It was Marilyn Monroe's footprints or rather her high-heeled-shoe prints that made him swoon. He never let anyone walk on those heel prints; when an old friend scuffed the prints Percy never forgive him.[15]

Even Percy and Nate's friends were fixated with the barest trace left behind by visiting celebrities. Their friend Bud Squire was a carpenter who had a business selling wood. Actor Dustin Hoffman allowed Squire to cut wood from his property. Squire said it was one of his favorite places to collect wood. He called it Tootsie's Place.[16] When Squire finished cutting, he delivered the wood to customers around town. After a  long day, he stopped at Percy's house to say hello.

Inevitably, a hello turned into a chat and a chat led to an invitation to the cider cellar. Squire's favorite drink was cider brandy with a hard cider chaser. The men would wrangle about which was better cider—that from the Norma Talmadge barrel or that from the Marilyn Monroe barrel. A drink from either would have had the same effect, but Squire chuckled, he always selected from the MM barrel. He later admitted that, being a little tipsy, he had some difficulty making more than two deliveries after visiting Percy's basement.[17]

Nate and Percy were more than cider-makers and hosts though; they were serious farmers who raised oxen. One newspaper observed that Henry Ford, who could afford the best oxen around, bought his prize-winning Devon animals from the Beardsleys.[18] Senator Wayne Morse from Oregon also raised Devon cattle and went to see the Beardsley's herd. After viewing the cattle, the men headed for the cider cellar.

Percy liked to show off his basement even though it had a moist, damp smell and no floor. The senator gasped when he went down the stairs. "You would not believe it," Morse said, "but this smells just like the cellar back home did when I was a boy."[19]

When the Beardsleys were not entertaining in their cellar, they were driving a team of twenty oxen to the Danbury Fair to capture prizes. Bud Squire recalled that Nate had a bull lead and several pairs of oxen in yokes that pulled a two-wheel cart. People would line up to watch father and son parade their oxen, taking them to the ox draws contest at the fair.

Percy was famous for his Devon cattle, but he was also a decorated World War I hero who served with Sergeant Alvin C. York. Percy was in the squad that killed twenty-one German soldiers and captured 132 on October 8, 1918 in the Argonne Forest in France. He rarely spoke of the event but when he did, Percy gave all credit to Sergeant York for capturing the enemy.[20]

He was a shy man, but knew what he wanted. In 1949, photographers from the *Republican-American* snapped a photo of a tall, formal-looking man standing beside his bride, Gertrude E. Lingsch of Mount Vernon, New York. His father need not have worried; Percy finally met the right woman.[21]

Bacon Road. In 1916, Frederick Bacon (1869-1943) bought two and one-quarter acres of land and a small dwelling on this road. In those days, his closest neighbor was north and west of the intersection with Rucum Road. A Roxbury map dated 1934, showed F. Bacon as the only resident on a section of road known today as Transylvania Road.

People familiar with Roxbury history might have expected this road to be named for Asahel Bacon (1764-1838), one of Roxbury's wealthiest men. Neither Asahel Bacon nor any member of his family, however, owned property along this road as far as I have been able to determine. The name is from Frederick Bacon, a more modest man, a man born thirty years after Asahel Bacon died.

Both men were farmers, one a gentleman farmer, the other a farm laborer. Asahel owned an elegant home and vast properties including most of Mine Hill; Frederick owned less than three acres. If photographs of Frederick ever existed, they are lost to history. Asahel lived in an age before photography, but commissioned oil-on-canvas portraits of his family that today hang in a Williamsburg, Virginia gallery for the world to see.[22]

Asahel's children attended elite private schools; Frederick had no children; in fact, records are inconsistent about whether he married. History has recorded Asahel's life, but little about his death. Yet most of what we know about Frederick comes from a death certificate, an obituary, and his last will and testament.

Someone carefully inserted Frederick Bacon's death certificate into a neat black binder entitled *Death Certificates 1940-1959*. Words scribbled on the document stated that his parents were Lorenzo Bacon and Betsy Bowdy. He had been a laborer before he retired, but the space designated for married, widowed, etc. said, "Unknown." He died on March 7, 1943 and was buried in the Wooster Cemetery in Danbury three days later.

Curiously, Frederick's obituary painted a slightly different picture. It said that he was born in Roxbury, December 17, 1869 and lived his entire life in Roxbury, and that he died at home at 7:30 AM on Sunday morning. Family and friends paid their respects, the Rev. Robert B. Day, rector of Roxbury's Christ Church, officiated at the funeral services, and Frederick was buried in the family plot in Danbury. Two sisters, Mrs. James Stott and Mrs. Ethel Waterman, and several nieces and nephews survived him.

Frederick Bacon's last will and testament named three sisters and valued his two and one-quarter acres and barn in Roxbury at

$500. One Sadie M. Seltzer bought his property for $650.[23] Other public records revealed additional scraps of information. His name first appeared in the 1870 census when he was three months old. His parents were living in Maine at the time and both his father and grandfather were born in Maine. Later censuses reported that when Frederick was forty, he lived in Sheldon F. Seeley's household and worked as a farm laborer. At age fifty, according to the census, he was a widower.[24] In 1928, a brief entry in a town annual report noted that he was paid $72.63 for highway work.

Both men lived to the age of seventy-four. Asahel died a wealthy man who left his elegant home to his daughter. Frederick died a poor man who, in 1937, had applied for Old Age Assistance. After his death, the state of Connecticut filed a claim for $2,318.97 against his estate.[25]

Asahel's elegant eighteenth-century home still stands on South Street. Frederick's home, a lean-to, is either gone or hidden deeply in the woods. He left barely a trace of his life in the town where he was born. One of Frederick Bacon's neighbors remembered him as an unhappy man. Another, Bucky Lowe, remembered that when officials went through Bacon's belongings after he died, they found a railroad worker's watch. They assumed that Bacon had worked on the railroad, but it's more likely that the watch was a memento from his father who was a teamster and car man on the railroad in Danbury or another relative who was a railroad commissioner in Danbury.[26]

Baker Road. The Baker family originated in Boston, but when John Baker (1681-1750) settled in Woodbury, he could never have imagined that people would remember his family's surname two and a half centuries after his death. Nor could he have foreseen that both his son and grandson would die young—one in a tragic accident, the other in battle.

John Baker married Sarah Hurlbut, daughter of the man reputed to be Roxbury's first settler. Sarah's father gave the newlyweds land next to his property in an area known as Fort Shippauge.[27] It has been said that they were the first young couple to make their home in Roxbury. In 1733, they built the house where they would raise seven children. The house at 112 Sentry Hill Road remained in the family for sixty-three years.[28]

Their son Remember Baker (1712-1740) was a thirty-eight-year-old married man with two young children when he died in a tragic accident. As a hunter, he knew he could see his target better if he sat in a tree above his prey, but no sooner had Baker climbed a tree than another hunter, Abram Hurlbut, mistook him for a wild turkey. A shot rang out and Remember Baker was dead. He left a three-year-old son.[29]

Remember Baker Jr. (1737-1775) grew up in his grandfather's house and probably spent his boyhood playing games with the soldiers at Fort Shippauge. At eighteen, the tough, redheaded, freckle-faced young giant joined the militia, set his sights north, and followed his cousins Colonel Ethan Allen and Seth Warner. Before leaving Roxbury on April 3, 1760, Baker married Desire Hurlbut and soon moved to Vermont where his cousin Ethan Allen lived. Land in Vermont was available for the taking. The Colonel and his lesser-known brother, Ira Allen, were ready to take.

Baker became a land speculator and by 1763, in a partnership with Ira Allen, owned 5,000 acres. The following year, the town fathers of Arlington, Vermont offered fifty acres of land to the first man who would set up a gristmill in Vermont. Baker accepted the offer. He and Allen continued to buy, and by 1773, the Allen and Baker Land Company owned 45,000 acres of virgin Vermont land.[30]

Baker joined the Green Mountain Boys, led by Colonel Ethan Allen, and on May 10, 1775, the heroes captured Fort Ticonderoga, New York. In August, Baker left the fort to serve as a scout for General Philip Schuyler in Canada. It was there that Remember Baker Jr. lost his life.

English troops and Indians camped nearby, and while Baker was on a scouting expedition along the Richelieu River, Indians stole his boat, captured him, then shot and killed him. They cut off his head, raised it on a pole, and carried it in triumph to the British officers stationed at Saint-Jean-sur-Richelieu, thirty-one miles southeast of Montreal, Canada. The British were horrified at the Indians' barbarity, but they wanted Baker's body returned. They bought it from the Indians so they could bury the hero's body. Baker was thirty-five.[31]

Battle Swamp Road. In spite of the name, a battle may never have occurred on the one mile, half-paved, half-dirt road that curves through northwestern Roxbury. In earlier days, people sometimes turned to folklore to name a waterway and hearsay was enough for folks to name a brook for a real or imagined battle, skirmish, or feud among neighbors. Even though someone named the swamp and the road for a battle, not even a footnote has recorded a skirmish at Battle Swamp.[32]

Bayberry Hill. According to local architect Phil deVries, in 1967, developer John K. Smart (1910-1996) created a subdivision, built a house, and lived there for eighteen years. At that time, the road had no name and when Smart sold it to the Shulman family in 1978, the road was still nameless.[33]

A few years later, to meet Roxbury's new emergency system requirements, the town needed to name the road. Dana Schulman said one day she arrived and found a sign marked Bayberry Hill posted in her driveway, but did not know put it there.[34]

The sweet-sounding name, though, is a disappointment—the green aromatic leaves and winterberries are gone. Too bad, the shrub, also known as candleberry, could come in handy during a power failure. Like the early pioneers, we could boil the berries and use the wax coating to make candles.

Bear Burrow Road. This unpaved town road runs a scant 0.39 miles northeast from Goldmine Road, and land records first mentioned the name in 1801.[35] Its name probably came about something like this: Someone peeked into a hole, saw a bear sleeping, and said to himself, "look at that bear burrow." He told a friend; word spread. Some names landed on the landscape just that way. The bear was probably one of the many black bears that lumbered through town, toppled over garbage cans, ate scraps, grew fat, got sleepy, and hunkered down for the winter.

Black bears still amble through Roxbury and inevitably make headline news. When local farmer Ernest Gavel saw a black bear trudge through his fields, he poured plaster of Paris into one of the footprints to make a mold, let it harden, then took it home, and lost the cast.[36]

Another bear made the headlines when Roxbury resident and journalist Deborah Donnelly caught one making mischief.[37] It stopped by veterinarian Dr. Elwell's house. The bear weighed about three hundred pounds and was six-feet tall. "A black bear was standing on his tiptoes on the deck eating out of the bird feeder," said Dr. Elwell, "and yes, I had my glasses on. He or she was pretty proud of itself."

Dr. Elwell said that bears, deer, coyotes, mountain lions and bobcats belong in Connecticut with plenty of rocks and ledges that the animals like. He added that his visiting bear was not aggressive, just eating suet; but when it saw the doctor, the bear decided it was time to go.

Bernhardt Meadow Lane. The name honors Rulley McKinstry Bernhardt (1878-1955), Mabel Bernhardt Smith's (1905-2000) father who owned the R. M. Bernhardt Meat Market on South Street.

As a senior citizen herself, Mabel B. Smith understood that older people had special needs and she wanted to build a different kind of home for them. Her first dream was to build a senior center, but that was not to be. Then she had another dream—to build comfortable housing for lower income elderly. With her 1996 gift of ten acres and funding from the federal government, her dream became a reality.[38]

The eighteen housing units nestled in a circle in a meadow are the reality. Sadly, Mabel Bernhardt Smith died before she saw her dream fulfilled. She died in the early morning hours of January 1, 2000 at age ninety-four.

Berry Road. Ghosts did not stop James Berry from buying an 1812 house on this road. The thirty-two-year-old farmer needed a large house for his wife and four children, and either the realtor didn't warn Berry about the house, or the realtor did warn him, but he didn't listen.[39] The story told was that one snowy night while a former owner sat downstairs sipping cider, his mother burned to death in a fire upstairs and ever since, a ghost has roamed the house. Berry had bought a haunted house.[40] According to land records, Berry bought and sold several properties between 1903 and 1929, though we don't know whether any others were haunted.[41]

Farmer and carpenter Clayton Squire remembered a Jim Berry and his family lived in the woods near Bill Dickinson's place. Berry's son lived with the family, Squire said, but he didn't know the son's name or the names of other family members. The manager of Judds Bridge Farm from 1933 to 1947, George DeVoe, recalled that a Jim Berry cooked for the single men who worked on the farm, but DeVoe remembered nothing about him.[42]

A neatly written death certificate for James Bruce Berry (1877-1941) revealed that he emigrated from Canada when he was seven years old. He was married to Daisy Dickenson, lived at Judds Bridge Farm, had been a chef, and owned an "eating house." The 1920 census noted that he and his wife had four children. James Berry was buried in the Center Cemetery on August 1, 1941.[43]

Another Berry or Barry passed this way so long ago that folks barely remember when, though a few recall the sad story of Bridget Barry who lived near Paradise Valley.

Nobody knows where she came from, but the story has been told that she owned a boardinghouse and took in half-starved strangers, miners, and quarrymen. She fed and boarded the "hard rock men" and helped them find work at the quarry, the garnet mines, and the iron furnaces at Mine Hill. She never asked why a man was down on his luck; if he was hungry, cold, or discouraged, she took care of him.

She kept stables for sixty mules that hauled silica out of Paradise Valley and carried it to the grinders at Roxbury Falls. Bridget's real work began when she heard the rumbling Concord stagecoach screech to a stop at her door. She brought out food, drink, and relief horses for the stage and all its passengers. She welcomed everyone. Even outlaws never troubled her because she was a hulking brute of a woman said to have a hand like a ham and the heart of a Devon bull.

Bridget's place was clean and respectable. According to legend, the doorstep measured thirty-by-four feet and was made of Roxbury granite with just a trace of cobalt blue that glistened in the sunlight, and the hearthstone had blood-red garnets sprinkled through it like the raisins in her loaf cake.

One boarder, a poor man named Seth Buel, noticed how much Bridget loved garnets and he was determined to give her some. It took him a while, but he finally collected enough garnets to make a necklace. He sent them by boat from Derby to New York to have a strand made, then asked other boarders to help him give a party so he could present the necklace in style.

Seth Buel was a shy man, but when he presented the jewelry to Bridget, he announced, "Miss Barry, me'n the boys decided to make you a gift, so we had a mess o' garnets shined up and put on a string for you to wear." The strand had set him back two months wages, but he was overjoyed when he saw the little red sparklers around her neck.

In her own way, Bridget was also shy, so she waited until everyone left the party before she thanked him. "That was downright handsome of you, my boy! I allas wanted me a string of beads," she beamed, then gave him a big kiss and pinched his shoulders so hard his muscles ached.

Their flirtation, however, was brief. A few weeks after the party, Bridget's barn caught fire. She was trapped trying to free the horses, and though four men tried to rescue her, she was severely burned. Bridget lived only until morning. Seth was heartbroken that he had been too late to help her, but he made sure to bury the garnet necklace with her.

Soon after that, terrible things happened in Paradise. Bridget's house burned down, the silica mill caught fire, a coon hunter fell into a quarry and died, and an out-of-town company set up a mill near the waterfalls and blasted away the snow-white stone from the quarry. Silica powder was shipped to Boston, and before anyone knew what was happening, people were dying from a strange disease. One doctor inspected pantries and kitchens and found silica dust in the pancake flower. Silica fever was killing men who worked at the mill.

People blamed Seth Buel for the bad things that happened. They griped that he should have stayed with Bridget; he should have helped her run the boardinghouse; he should have helped her mind the stables; he should have married Bridget. It was, they complained, Seth's fault that Paradise was gone.[44]

Blueberry Lane. The name is from the blueberry patch at the entrance to this lane. Blueberries like wet acid soil and once grew wild in this area. Now locals plant the ten-foot-tall high-bush blueberries. In May and June, bell-shaped white or pink flowers drape the bushes, and from mid-July until September, berries hang from the bushes, ready for birds to come and devour them.

At one time, you could buy blueberries at a nearby farm stand, but the farm is now gone and the stand is in ruins. Good news is in sight, though; rumor has it that plans are under way to restore the blueberry patch and rebuild the stand.

Booth Road. Despite having a name that reaches back to the seventeenth century, according to former resident Larry Nourse, in 1977, this road was only five-hundred-feet long—a paper road, not passable. As new houses were built, the road became longer and longer.[45] The dirt road, now 0.72 miles long, climbs the hill between Upper County Road and Goldmine Road.

Once called the "highway to Booth's place," its name is from descendants of Englishman Richard Booth (b.1607) who settled in Stratford in 1640 and later moved to Woodbury.[46] Richard Booth's descendants were farmers, hatters, painters, and merchants, but one heir, Hervey Minor Booth (1813-1893), stands out. He was a wealthy farmer, a man obsessed with numbers, a man considered eccentric.

Mostly Booth used his love of numbers to make successful investment decisions that led to him becoming a rich man, but despite his wealth, some people thought he was a miser because he walked eighteen miles to Waterbury rather than hitch up a horse and ride. When he attended Yale College, he walked thirty-five miles every week from Roxbury to New Haven. The walk was apparently beneficial because he graduated in 1843 at the head of his class in mathematics.

After graduating from Yale, Booth tried to teach, but gave it up because, he said, he could not understand girls. In spite of that, he married Fannie M. Bunnell on February 6, 1854, and immediately realized his mistake.[47] The morning after the wedding, he gave his bride a large sum of money for a divorce. She took the money and ran.[48]

He read, studied, and solved mathematical problems in between doing chores on his farm. His sister took care of household chores. After their mother died, Booth and his sister lived a quiet, secluded life in their ancestral home.[49]

Hervey M. Booth was a brilliant mathematician who no doubt enjoyed exactness and might have been irritated to learn that census takers repeatedly listed his Christian name incorrectly as Hervey M., Henry, Harvey M., and just plain Harvey. One who listed his name incorrectly was Albert L. Hodge, the census taker for Roxbury in 1880. On Tuesday, June 1, when Hodge counted the population, he listed his house and family first. By Friday, June 4, when he reached Hervey Minor Booth's house, he jotted down the number fifty-five in columns one and two to designate that he was visiting the fifty-fifth house and the fifty-fifth family.

Booth may have been at his desk figuring out a numerical puzzle and the men may have chuckled over their exchange regarding the number fifty-five. Knowing Booth's love for numbers, Hodge probably told Booth about being number fifty-five in the population count, and Booth may have enjoyed pointing out to Hodge that the number fifty-five is the sum of the numbers one through ten.

Botsford Hill Road. Captain David Botsford (1753-1825) served in the Connecticut Line during the American Revolution and was one of the first of his family in Roxbury, though no historic house bears his name.[50]

Glover, Isaac, and George Botsford left two houses worthy of architectural interest. One house was built in 1790; the other was constructed in the mid-1800s. Both are reminders of the challenges farmers faced taming Roxbury's rocky land. The earlier Glover Botsford House at 119 Botsford Hill Road is well preserved and represents a more affluent farmhouse than its neighbor the Isaac and George Botsford House represents.[51]

On November 11, 1850, a census taker rode into Roxbury to count the population and his first stop was Glover Botsford's house. The enumerator marked the first two columns of the census form with the number one. The numbers signified that this was the first house and the first family he visited that cold morning. The census taker wrote in a neat hand, carefully filling in blank spaces on the form as Glover Botsford (1795-1859) answered questions. Glover had some experience answering the questions because he had lived in Roxbury for thirty years.

Glover Botsford said he was a fifty-five-year-old farmer who lived with his wife, two sons, and a daughter. His teenage sons were also farmers and all his children had attended school within the year. Everyone in the household was born in Connecticut and everyone could read and write. For some reason, the census taker put two check marks next to the sons' names in the column headed "Married within the year." The marks were probably a mistake, since both were teenagers and it's unlikely they were married. A sixty-five-year-old farmer lived with them, but the census form had no place to indicate whether he was a boarder or a relative.

Glover Botsford was affluent compared to his neighbors; he owned real estate valued at $4,000, but little is known about him. When he died two years after the 1850 census, his eldest son Charles inherited the property, turned it over to his mother, and left town. Charles and his family moved to Naugatuck where he worked in a fish market. Thirty years later, Charles Botsford (b. 1832) returned to Roxbury with his family and lived with his mother.[52]

The property passed through several hands until 1935, when Frasier W. McCann (1908-1987), a gentleman farmer, bought it. McCann was a different kind of farmer than the Botsfords. He raised prize Guernsey cattle and Dartmouth ponies, the elegant, even-tempered animal that once ran wild in the forests of Devon, England. McCann expanded the property, purchased other farms and formed the Golden Harvest Farm, LLP.

Others bought and farmed the land, like John and Mary Pokrywka, whose son, Albert J. Pokrywka, still lives and works in Roxbury. More owners followed, until 1985, when Golden Harvest Farm, LLP bought the property.[53] Historians know this as the Glover Botsford House, but to the McCann family, it's Thistledown Farm.

Brandywine Crossing. One could say that Andrew Wyeth was responsible for naming this road, but that would be an

exaggeration; former resident Larry Nourse named it. He owned and loved several Andrew Wyeth prints and decided to name the road for the group of artists Wyeth belonged to known as the Brandywine Artists.[54]

About 1977, Nourse bought property on Booth Road and named his horse farm the Brandywine Farm. Three years later, he subdivided the property and built Brandywine Crossing, a private unpaved road that runs between Booth Road and Upper County Road.

One story told was that Brandywine was the name of a tavern Nourse owned and that story was partially true. Nourse had owned a tavern that bore three colorful names during the fifteen years he owned it: Burgundy Lounge, Good Company, and Glass Menagerie.

Bronson Mountain Road. Bronson Mountain Road snakes up a serpentine drive to a seventy-five-acre subdivision that stretches across three town lines. Although the bridge entrance is in Woodbury, most of the road is in Roxbury. This twenty-first century road has a seventeenth-century name taken from Ebenezer Bronson who settled in Woodbury about 1690 and built a house near the mountain. When news spread that Indians were about to attack, neighbors chose Bronson's house as a place to hide, and his home became a fort.[55]

Daniel Gaylord Bronson (d. 1878), a descendant of Ebenezer Bronson, settled on Squire Road, far from the mountain. He was a farmer, carpenter, and creator of the Bronson plow. He was also a mechanical genius and an astute entrepreneur who passed his talents on to his two sons. Both were carpenters who carried on the business after his death.[56] Plow making was in its glory during the 1910s and 1920s when Gaylord Bronson seized the opportunity to expand his business. He bought Wakelee Plows of Southbury and began shipping all over New England. His company was named the Wakelee and Roxbury Plow, though most locals refer to the plows as Wakelee plows; others call them Bronson plows, as did Robert Hodges, former President of

Roxbury's Historical Society, when he described them as walking plows for one man; one or two horses drew it. Hodges said it was "about the best plow of its kind ever made."[57]

Gaylord Bronson's sons Henry Merwin and William Nathaniel were as energetic and industrious as their father was; they were men who could do almost anything and whatever the men did, they did well. One thing they did well was make plows, and like their father, they were shrewd businessmen. The Bronsons operated a sawmill and shingle mill and sold their plows and scrapers in Waterbury, Bridgeport, New London, and other large cities in Connecticut.[58] They managed the family business until their deaths—William in 1919 and Henry in 1932. The mill was sold and a few years later, the mill, along with much of the plow-making equipment, burned to the ground.[59]

Carriage Lane. Carriages took the rich and the poor, the honest and the dishonest, the drunk and the sober, the happy and the sad over bumpy, muddy roads in earlier days, but this name is from 1978, when the Carriage Lane Corporation named it.[60]

Roxbury histories did not mention carriages, but neighboring town reports did. East Windsor had a one-horse chair in 1756 and Bethlehem saw its first pleasure carriage in 1778. Goshen saw its first pleasure carriage a few years later and East Windsor counted fifty carriages by 1806. The carriage race was on and in 1812, Goshen reported thirty carriages, if you counted all the four-wheelers.[61]

Resident and local historian William James Walker (1916-1997) recalled when families came to church on horseback, buggy, or foot. They hitched their buggies and wagons in stalls in the barn behind Christ Church.[62] Today, automobiles cruise this smooth paved lane, but not for long—after 2,150 feet, it ends.

Cedar Ridge. Barely a passageway, it had no name until the 1980s when a town committee went to work to name all roads for the 911 emergency system. The committee tossed around several names like Dirt Road and Penny Lane until it selected the name suggested by residents Donald and Bonnie Westerberg. This private unpaved road runs 0.2 miles off Chalybes Road West.[63]

Chalybes Road. Chalybes was the name of a small village and a post office on the western edge of town at the bottom of Mine Hill. Both were later called Roxbury Station. Chalybes, pronounced *SHA le bees* or *KAE leb* by locals, is a Greek word for a Scythian tribe who lived in Asia Minor near the Black Sea.

According to James M. Swank, an officer in the American Iron and Steel Association for twenty years from 1872-1892, Chalybia was a small district in Armenia near the Black Sea. Its inhabitants, called Chalibees or Chalybians, were famous for the quality of their iron and steel. Swank also wrote that the Greek historian Herodotus who lived in the fifth century before Christ spoke of "the Chalybians, a people of ironworkers." An online source noted that the Chalybes, also called Khalib, were a tribe credited with the invention of the iron industry. It further mentioned that the tribe's name in Greek meant "tempered iron, steel," a term that passed into Latin as *chalybs*, 'steel.'[64]

Cothren wrote in 1872 that "a few years ago," the Rev. Dr. Horace Bushnell (1802-1876) named the village. Since the historian did not mention this fact in his 1854 two-volume history, we might assume that the Rev. Bushnell named the village sometime between 1854 and 1872.

The Rev. Bushnell was a Congregational clergyman, theologian, and prolific writer. He was born in Bantam, graduated from Yale College, and served as a clergyman in Hartford for twenty-three years until he retired in 1859. How he came to name a Roxbury village since he never lived here, never worked here, and had no association with mining remains a mystery.[65]

During the 1860s and 1870s, Chalybes was home to two-hundred miners and 140 stonecutters who worked in granite and silica quarries. It flour-

ished with its general store, school, lumberyard, coal yard, creamery, gristmill, hat factory, cigar factory, brass factory, hotel, boardinghouses, and bar.

The Chalybes post office opened in January 1867 and delivered its first mail on February 20, 1868.[66] Mail came on the Shepaug Valley Railroad that operated a spur to the little village. Unfortunately, by the time the railroad opened, the mines were closing. Miners left, the population declined, trains stopped running, and the village vanished. Over a century later, only three buildings remain in the former village: a private home, once the general store, an antique woodworking business that housed a cigar factory and a warehouse that was once the railroad station.

Aside from the alien name and peculiar pronunciation, Chalybes holds other curiosities that relate to the road's direction and official name. According to resident Alice Griffin, this road changed direction. It once crossed Hemlock Road, ran along a white fence and joined its western spur. The road crossed a triangular-shaped parcel that Everett B. Hurlburt donated to the town in 1961, but the road was moved and the corner triangle became a square. The paved road runs downhill for 0.4 miles from Hemlock Road to North Street. Signs at each end give the name as Chalybes Road. Never mind that in 1980, the official name became Chalybes Road East and that today's local maps still call it by that name.[67]

Chalybes Road West. A house on the corner of this road and Hemlock Road, built about 1770, was once home to the British seaman and writer William McFee. Its name origin is the same as the Chalybes Road story above.[68]

The road stretches from Baker Road to Hemlock Road, but has a strange street pattern. Each end of the road is less than 0.2 mile long and is wide enough for cars, but the middle is a narrow path through the woods. Forget trying to drive from one end to the other; it's not possible.

Added to the confusion of trying to drive on a road where you can't go from one end to the other, is the map versus sign puzzle. Signs will tell you that you're on Chalybes Road West; local maps will tell you that you're on Chalybes Road.[69]

Church Street. This Scenic Road is part of Route 317 and is one of only three "streets" in town. Before the churches moved in, it looked like an unpaved boulevard lined with stately homes and was called Main Street.[70] In the 1700s, prominent men like General Ephraim Hinman (b. 1753) and Judge Nathan Smith (1767-1835) built homes along this stretch of land.

General Hinman was from an important military family in Southbury. He and Judge Nathan Smith, a United States senator, both built elegant Georgian Colonial homes on Main Street. They prided themselves on the sophisticated architecture of homes that displayed their wealth.[71] Their homes upstaged the plain architecture of nearby churches. The Congregational Church was the first to move into the neighborhood. Then the

Episcopal Church moved nearby and the Roman Catholics followed, building across the street from the Congregational Church.

Religion was the center of life in those days, so when churches began to line the boulevard, people wanted to live nearby. New families moved in—merchants, hatters, and farmers built Cape, Federal and Greek-style houses. They all came to find their fortune, but also to grow and support the new town.

Clover Knolls. Despite its plural name, only one knoll exists. When Bob and Evelyn Williams bought their land in 1983, they chose the name Clover Knoll because much of the land had been pastures full of clover. Even though numerous maps and records have listed it as plural, Evelyn believes it will probably always be known as more than one knoll.

Initially, the Williams did not need a road because no houses stood on the land. After they started to build, however, they needed a driveway and turned an old cow path, once impassable in spring and overgrown with weeds in summer, into a driveway. Today, it is a private road.[72]

Crofut Lane. John F. Crofut (1825-1890) was born in Connecticut and was one of many men who worked in the local hat fabricator factories. In 1844, he married Mary C. Squire (1826-1915). John A. Squire, Crofut's father-in-law, was a farmer and hat maker who rented rooms to his employees and may have employed his son-in-law.

In 1850, Crofut bought twenty-four acres on Apple Lane, though he and his family continued to live next door to his father-in-law.[73] Crofut may have wanted to strike out on his own, or he may have realized that Roxbury's hat business was on the wane, because by 1870, he moved his family to Bridgeport where he worked in a hat factory.[74]

In 1884, when John was fifty, he deeded two-thirds of his extensive Roxbury property to his son George.[75] The son, George R. Crofut (1856-1932), returned to Roxbury with his wife and son and became a farmer. In 1910, George and his wife told the census taker that only three of their four children were still living.[76]

George must have been a man of means and one who believed in modern improvements. His thirty-by-forty-foot barn had a billiards room and he owned two "labor-saving" windmills.[77] Like many men, he worked on town roads, and in later years, he worked at Hillside Farm, a creamery or dairy. By 1930, he was a widower who lived on his farm with a housekeeper. When he died in the spring of 1932, his estate included a cider mill and seven acres of land. Stephen Sondheim, the lyricist of *Gypsy*, *Sunday in the Park with George*, and *A Little Night Music*, now owns the former Crofut property.[78]

Cross Brook Road. *Connecticut Place Names* gave two explanations for the name of the brook. One was that the usual drainage of brooks in the area was north and south; the other noted that the brook crossed a town line.[79]

Whatever the origin, the name Cross Brook appeared in Roxbury town records in 1798, a half-century before Edward Tracy (1808-1871) lived there.[80] Edward Tracy was one of the few Irish immigrant farmers to own property in Roxbury in the mid-1800s. His son, Edward Tracy Jr.(1848-1925), a gunsmith and blacksmith, inherited the property and it remained in the family for nearly a century. It passed through several hands until 1977 when film critic Rex Reed bought the house as a country retreat.[81]

Cross Brook Road must have been humming with activity in earlier days when Edward Tracy Jr. and others built a dam and operated a sawmill.[82] Frederick Ungeheuer, an author of *Roxbury Remembered* and his wife, Barbara Ungeheuer, past president of the Roxbury Land Trust, bought property on the road and said that a saddle-maker built their house shortly before the American Revolution.[83]

Davenport Road. On a crisp autumn day on September 17, 1828, Benjamin M. Davenport (1793-1880) and Sally Pope (1798-1871) were married.[84] Six years later, they became the first Davenports to buy property in Roxbury and their descendents stayed for over a century.

Two properties caught their attention. The parcels curved around the bend in the road where Davenport Road and Pickett Road met and even though a house was already on the property, Benjamin and Sally built a new one.[85]

When a census taker visited in 1850, Benjamin said he was a fifty-seven-year-old farmer who lived with his wife, son, and daughter-in-law. They were all born in Connecticut and could read and write. The census taker dutifully recorded the information, but left out Benjamin's middle initial, M., and failed to note Benjamin's nickname, Uncle Ben.[86]

During the next two decades, the Davenports lived a quiet life on the farm. Then Benjamin's son and wife died—his son in the summer of 1870 and his wife in the fall of 1871.[87] Saddened by the losses of his wife and son, he gathered his remaining family around him and his daughter-in-law and older grandson Walter G. moved in with him. His other grandson Noble B. Davenport (1852-1934) and his family bought property next door.

After Benjamin's death, at eighty-eight, Walter G. Davenport (1850-1933) inherited his grandfather's property and passed the one-hundred-acre estate to his heirs. For over a century, Davenport children, grandchildren, and great-grandchildren have lived in and remodeled the house that Uncle Ben and Sally built in 1834. It is the historic home known as the Benjamin Davenport House.[88]

Deer Ridge. A developer loved the little dears so much that he named the road for the whitetail *Odocoileus virginianus*. Enter this private unpaved road from Mallory Road and watch for white tails flashing in the woods. Today, the deer population is booming, yet they were once an endangered species. Colonial settlers used the skins to keep warm and were so desperate for deerskins that the general court passed a law making it illegal to take skins out of the colony.[89]

East Flag Swamp Road. The road is east of Flag Swamp Road and many locals believe the name refers to the invasive yellow irises that grow in nearby wetlands. This unpaved road runs 1.02 miles until it reaches Southbury. Read about its name origins in the Flag Swamp Road story.

East Woods Road. Named partly for its direction on the eastern edge of town and partly for the woods along the road, it runs 0.52 miles north to south. It is unpaved at the upper end toward Grassy Hill and paved at the lower end where it intersects with Rucum Road. The name is probably a more recent name and one given by a Roxburian. Had a Woodbury settler named this road, we would know it as West Woods Road.

Evergreen Drive. From New England's earliest days, people built log cabins from evergreens; later they built frame houses, churches, and other public buildings from the pine and hemlocks they found in the forest. A developer named this private road for the evergreens bordering the drive or as a salute to the long history of evergreens in this part of the country.[90] The unpaved drive runs east to west off Baker Road.

Evergreen Lane. This private unpaved path runs north and south off Evergreen Drive. Many New England towns named their roads for conspicuous trees in the landscape and this town was no exception. Evergreens easily grew in the damp acid soil of

New England; they have become one of the most common types of trees to blanket the northeast and their enduring green is a welcome sight in the dead of winter.

Falls Road. The name is from the waterfalls in the Shepaug River, but historian Helen Humphrey referred them as rapids. Unfortunately, the beauty of the roaring, rushing waters was marred when Shepaug Railroad builders blasted rocks and cut down trees along the riverbanks.[91]

The railroad has long since closed, but locals still enjoy the falls. Bud Squire said his five children all learned to swim at the falls. Kids would jump off a rope tied under the bridge and go swimming in the falls, and every year on the first day of trout fishing, someone brought a trailer with hot dogs and sodas.

Falls Road curves for a half-mile from South Street to Minor Bridge Road, winding through hemlock woods that soar like cathedral arches on both sides of the road, keeping it in deep shade year-round. Only an occasional fishing lure hitting the waters and the sound of gushing white water break the silence of the hemlock woods.

Farm Road. It first appeared as a fine line on maps from the 1990s, but the name was a misnomer. By the time the road had a name, the farms were gone. At one time, though, Golden Harvest Farm, LLP, covered this land.[92] The unpaved private road runs off Judge Road.

Flag Swamp Road. The name is from a flower, though some people believe the name was from a family called Flag or Flagg. Town Historian Timothy Beard said many people named Flagg lived in Connecticut, but not around here. They lived in the northern and eastern sections of the state.[93]

European settlers brought flowers to this state and one they brought was the *Iris pseudacorus,* also known as yellow flag iris, yellow iris, water flag, pale yellow iris, and European yellow iris. Its long narrow leaves looked like flags waving in the breeze. By the early nineteenth century, settlers had cultivated a dozen or more hybrids in various colors, leading some to call the iris "the rainbow flower."[94]

For more detail on the name origin, see the Flag Swamp story. Even though all parts of the iris are poisonous, growers all over the world have planted it as a showy garden and pond plant. Unfortunately, it often escapes its intended planting place, forms dense clumps, takes over wetlands, displaces native species, and upsets wildlife habitats. The plant is so invasive that many states, including Connecticut, do not allow it to be sold.[95]

Garden writer and resident Tovah Martin wrote in the *New York Times* that, "All these aliens have become naturalized or occur without being planted. In other words, they've broken loose from gardens; they are wild. They spread rapidly by many reproductive methods under all sorts of growing conditions. And, here's the rub: they bull out native plants."[96]

Even though the flood of 1955 washed out Flag Swamp Road, it reopened in 2000 and the flags still wave.

Forest Farms Drive. Developers named the road for a subdivision of the same name that was created about 1987, but the origin of the name is unknown. Forest may refer to the surrounding woodlands or it may be a personal name. Some confusion in recording the name of this paved private drive is evident. Town records indicated Farms as plural, but the road sign reads Farm as singular.

Garnet Road. Connecticut once had one of the finest sources of almandine garnets in the world, and a catch phrase for Roxbury was The Garnet Capital of the Northeast. In 1977, Connecticut named the blood-red almandine stone its state mineral, and in

April 2001, Roxbury designated Garnet Road a Scenic Road. Not to be confused with the bright red birthstones found in jewelry, Roxbury's garnets look like small, red-hot coals. The industrial strength stones were used to make grinding wheels, saws, garnet paper, and sandpaper.[97]

Extracting garnets from rocks that contained chunks of pale-reddish-brown garnets was an arduous process. Workers blasted the stone, hauled it from a pit, and then smashed it to bits with a 1600-pound ball. Horses then carried the crushed stone to a mill where it was ground into finer pieces, spread on a moving belt, and covered with water. The water made the garnets shine so it was easier for workers to pick them out. Later, men packed the garnets onto horses or mules, sent the stones to other mills, re-ground the gems, and used them to produce abrasive sand paper.[98]

In the 1880s and 1890s, Roxbury had three garnet mines and a 1934 Roxbury League of Women Voters map marked "X" for each of the mines—one at the end of South Street, one near Garnet Road, one on Rocky Mountain.

Charles Thomas Squire (1839-1935) owned the 180-acre garnet mine at the end of South Street and the Armour Company managed it, but the operation closed after three years because the stone was too hard and too expensive to mine. When the mine closed, its buildings were moved to Nova Scotia where the stone was softer and less expensive to cut and extract.[99]

The Union Sand Paper and Emery Wheel Company of Boston owned and operated the mine on Garnet Hill south of Mallory Road. Twenty-five to thirty mostly Polish-speaking workers mined the garnets and some believed that the men found black garnets. By 1894, the company had spent $18,000 on buildings and other improvements and had planned to buy four crushers, a blower, and other machinery to separate the garnets from the stone.[100] In spite of the investment, the venture failed; the company closed its doors and left garnet rubble all over the place.

Lyman E. Green (1887-1963), a farmer in Southbury, had no use for the rubble left on his property from the Garnet Hill mine. In 1935, Roxbury paid Green $600 for the "entire pile of garnet wastestone" to spread on its dirt roads.[101]

The Sanford family operated the Rocky Mountain garnet mine.[102] In winter, many of their Norwegian workers traveled to the mine on cross-country skis. The venture was short-lived, though, because the miners couldn't find enough water. They drilled down ninety feet—not deep enough. They stuck dynamite down a hole. That loosened the bedrock and cracked the stone so much the miners ended up with no water at all.[103]

Look closely and you will see the blood-red stones in stone walls and on roads. Garnets are supposed to be the best fill for a dirt road. One man had a place behind his house that was always a mud hole. He tried everything, but the mud kept coming back. He claimed that since he filled the hole with garnet waste, the mud has disappeared.[104]

Golden Harvest Road. The name is a reminder of the golden fields that once dominated the countryside. The fields are gone now, sold to developers, and subdivided. In the 1930s, Woolworth heir Frasier McCann bought five contiguous farms, some that stretched into Bridgewater, to create one of the last dairy farms in town.

In 1985, the Golden Harvest Partnership bought the 857-acre Golden Harvest Farm for $2.7 million and within a year began to sell off parcels. Soon roads, houses, and driveways dotted the landscape where, in the past, only feet and tractors had traveled.[105]

Goldmine Road. Enoch Woodruff (1800-1890) lived on the south side of the road. He was a farmer who lived here from at least 1850 until 1880. It has been said that he came in search of gold. Local historians have not written about Enoch Woodruff's gold mine, but census records provided a few details about his family.[106]

When the 1850 census counted Enoch Woodruff, he was a fifty-year-old farmer who lived with his wife and eight children that ranged in age between twenty-seven-years old and nine-months old. Everyone in the family had been born in Connecticut. Twenty years later his three youngest children still lived at home.

The youngest son, John A. Woodruff (b. 1842), was a Union soldier in the Civil War. He had enlisted as a Private on November 19, 1861 and served in Company E, Eleventh Regiment Connecticut. He received a disability discharge on February 28, 1863 and returned home, perhaps because of injuries, perhaps to help on his father's farm.[107]

By 1880, Enoch's youngest daughter had married and moved away, but his sons still worked on the family farm and his wife kept house. Enoch was eighty-years old and blind, but continued to farm until his death at age ninety.

Despite Enoch Woodruff's optimism about gold in the hills, Norman Hurlbut was told there was so little it wouldn't pay to mine it.[108] Jacqueline "Jackie" Dooley, whose family lived nearby for decades, said that Woodruff's search for gold was a failure. No matter what Hurlbut and Dooley said—where's there's gold, there are gold diggers. To find Enoch Woodruff's gold mine, search the

1.44 miles of Goldmine Road between Tophet and Painter Ridge Roads in the northeast corner of Roxbury.

Good Hill Lane. Some place-names seem to bump into each other and this is one of them. The narrow private passageway is one of three Good Hill roads in Roxbury and the name is from the original story, told in chapter one, of settlers arriving on this hill. The unpaved lane juts off Good Hill Road in a straight line east of Good Hill Terrace.

Good Hill Road. Kids never minded the cold winter in the early 1900s when they could run over to the Holmes Ranch at the top of the hill in search of excitement. They went to watch the parade of big bay draft horses from the Barnum & Bailey Circus trudge up from the old Southbury train station, along Main Street in Woodbury, to Good Hill Road. The horses boarded for the winter in two huge barns on the ranch.[109]

In 1672, the first settlers were not thinking about circuses and draft horses when their journey ended on this hill. After all, they had come to settle a town and had traveled a long way from Stratford. The tired, weary travelers fell on their knees and gave thanks to the Heavens. They whispered the words Good Hill and those words became the first English place-name in the Pomperaug Plantation.

One historian applauded the name, saying it was a place of good hope, good views, and good lands.[110] The hill, surrounded by plains, rivers, and valleys held promise for a good life. The land was fertile because Indians had planted it with corn, beans, and tobacco and had burned the land to clear brush, leaving open space to hunt.[111] The land is still fertile, corn still grows, and the views from the hilltop are still good. At least one thing has changed, though; Good Hill is protected land and no longer a place to hunt.

Good Hill Terrace. A terrace suggests a place with houses along the side or top of rising ground above the level of the roadway. Officials must have fallen in love with the name Good Hill and decided to plant it in triplicate, in this case on a private unpaved passageway that runs off the road of the same name.

Grassy Hill Road. Grassy Hill, also known as the Pasture Division, was among this area's first place-names.[112] The road gained the additional designation Scenic Road in August 1999 when Roxbury officials granted that label for its original stone walls, streams, and scenic views.

According to resident Jan Napier, this Scenic Road was once a cow path.[113] Youngsters walked to the one-room schoolhouse at the intersection of Bacon and Grassy Hill Roads. Today, instead of schoolchildren, small goats wander the grounds at a private residence. Resident Betty Blyn said that in the decades between the schoolchildren and the goats, the schoolhouse property was put to serious use. During the American Revolution, it was a winter hospital for injured Yankee soldiers. Considering the sparse conditions, Blyn wondered how many of the wounded survived.

Blyn recalled another story a neighbor told her when she first moved to Roxbury. Ernie Finch Sr., a nearby farmer, told her about a barn that had long since disappeared. The barn was so far away from the center of town, he told her, that most farmers called it the African barn. When they went for hay, these farmers felt like they were traveling to Africa.[114]

Hemlock Road. The name is from the hemlock tree that is native to the northeast. It is such a sturdy tree that, in 1895, one became the town's first flagpole. The town paid Frank Pierce two dollars for a hemlock tree trunk from his forest and it stood on the town green until someone decided metal was sturdier than hemlock.[115]

The majestic hemlock grows up to ninety-feet tall, but it's under threat of extinction from the woolly adelgid, a sap-sucking insect from Asia, that is rapidly killing the trees. The large stands of hemlocks that line this mile-long road offer hope that the trees will survive for future generations to enjoy.

Hickory Lane. A naming committee met on November 14, 1974 at a special town meeting and convinced officials to name this lane for the Shagbark Hickory, a tree common in the area.[116] The name seems like a misnomer because this lane winds through a subdivision of nineteen lots and ends in a cul-de-sac after meandering through a long row of white pine trees. Perhaps the hickory trees are hiding behind the evergreens. This unpaved town lane runs 0.3 miles off Rucum Road.

Hickory Lane West. This name is an echo of the one above and has the virtue of assuring you that you're west of Hickory Lane. The private unpaved road offers 0.1 mile of breathtaking views of the valley and hills to the south and west.

High Bridge Road. The fifty-foot-high bridge was gone by 1894, replaced by a stone bridge.[117] Both bridges are gone now. Maybe they fell down or maybe someone took them down because of the boy who was lost on the bridge. He didn't know he was lost. He was from the Bates family with so many children his mother couldn't keep track of them all. One day, though, she did notice that one of her sons had been gone a long time, and she started a frantic search to find him. Everyone thought the boy was dead until someone spotted him stretched out on the broad ledge. He was sound asleep.

If you had asked the Bates boy, he would have told you the high bridge was a good place to take a nap. He didn't know that one roll in the wrong direction and he would have plunged into the one-hundred-foot ravine into Jacks Brook.[118]

Beware, if you decide to take the high road where the old bridge used to cross. This unpaved road runs 0.72 miles with a posted speed limit of 10 miles per hour. Even that speed may be too fast for this rough and rutted road.

High Meadow Lane. The name evokes images of lofty heights and fits the high elevation of the meadows that stretch across the top of Bronson Mountain. Hilltop Builders developed the site and probably coined the name.[119] The private paved road runs straight up the mountain to views of the surrounding hills.

High Meadow Way. Try to find it. No one lives here, current maps don't show it, and no road sign marks it, but it is home to the High Meadow Riding Club, LLC.

While doing research in the Assessor's office about this road, I met a neighbor who lived nearby and mentioned to him that I might put High Meadow Way in the forgotten names section of this book. He was aghast. It still exists, he said; it's a private road; it's not forgotten. Keep it with the other roads. I was secretly glad. Roxbury seems so much neater with one-hundred roads than ninety-nine. On reflection, a round number is definitely preferable.

Hodge Road. Philo Hodge's (1756-1842) descendents have lived in Roxbury for over two hundred years. In 1782, he built a home where he and his first wife, Keturah Armstrong, raised four daughters.[120] She died in 1787 or 1788 and Philo married Lucy Newtown on New Year's Day 1789 in Roxbury's Congregational Church. Philo and Lucy raised eleven children on their farm and enjoyed over half a century of marriage. After he died, Lucy lived with her oldest child Chauncey Hodge (1790-1853) and survived another ten years.[121]

Chauncey married in 1815 and built a home near his father. He farmed, raised a family, and served as a representative in the state legislature. Chauncey died at sixty-three of lung fever and was buried in the family plot in the Center Cemetery.[122] He had two sons; one was a schoolteacher and a West Point Cadet who died at age twenty. The other, Albert Lafayette Hodge (1822-1920), like his father and grandfather, was a farmer and public servant.

Albert L. Hodge served two years in the state legislature and thirteen years as selectman. He was a Victorian-Age gentleman, financially successful, and well respected. He owned a lumberyard, sawmill, and hardware store. He also operated a gristmill and grain elevator, both of which burned in a spectacular fire in January 1918. Even though a hundred men fought the fire, it caused $50,000 in damage. The loss was more than just financial; it was the loss of a historic mill. The 150-year-old gristmill had been in the Hodge family for forty years.[123]

Hodge was an entrepreneur and a man of vision. In addition to his mills and stores, he owned part of Mine Hill and was one of the few men to make money from both mining and granite quarries. He fought to get a railroad through Roxbury and opened a post office at Roxbury Station. He loved adventure and kept himself in excellent physical condition and at age eighty-four, Hodge traveled to the farthest west he had ever been and climbed the Rocky Mountains.[124]

His daughter, Elizabeth Josephine Hodge (1853-1927), known as Libbie, married Dr. Louis Jacques Pons in 1886. Before medical school and before he married, Dr. Pons worked for Hervey M. Booth who funded the Booth Free School. Two years after his marriage, Pons built a home on South Street.[125]

The year 1910 must have been a busy one for Elizabeth. That summer, a local newspaper made frequent mention of Sunshine Club and Civic Club meetings at her home "to talk of flowers and trees." As president of the Sunshine Club, Libbie sent flowers every week to New Haven and she sent over one-hundred bunches of flowers that July to hospitals and the Lowell Settlement.[126]

Meanwhile, Dr. Pons took steps to make life easier for his wife. In June 1910, the doctor received a package from the Aermotor Company in Chicago; it was a pump for a windmill. He wanted a windmill in the back yard to generate power for a water system for a new bath and running water in the kitchen. For all the doctor's intentions for home improvements, the summer and fall must have been a nightmare.

Dr. Pons hired Robert N. White & Co., Sanitary Plumbing of Bethel, to install pipes. In letters between R. N. White and

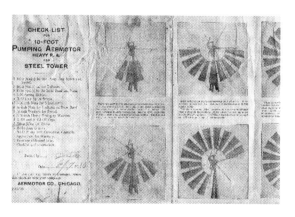

the doctor, it's clear that the work did not go smoothly and by September, the doctor was fuming. In a note to White, the doctor complained that the cellar was flooded, and a coupling on the hot water tank leaked enough to fill a bucket. Moreover, even though he had thrown "the wheel into the wind," the windmill would not start. This was supposed to be a satisfactory job the doctor grumbled and in a pique, he wrote, "Your boy left his overalls and you left your tape measure."[127]

Life must have calmed down by November. Dr. Pons had purchased a new motor car. In prior winters, Libbie was at the reins of a sleigh, drawn by their beloved horse, Daisy, taking the doctor on his rounds through town to see patients. Change came to their household in 1913, when Dr. Pons and his wife moved to Milford where he continued to practice medicine.

Though Albert L. Hodge's daughter left town, his son, Charles Watson Hodge, (1856-1963) lived in Roxbury his entire life and inherited his father's talent for business. He was this town's key benefactor, largest property owner, and a well-loved personality known as the Father of Roxbury.[128] Like his father and grandfather, Charles represented Roxbury in the state legislature. He also served on the board of directors of the fledgling Booth Free School, and as president of the First National Bank in New Milford, he held 51% of the stock. He continued to own and operate the A. L. Hodge & Son lumberyard and granite quarry and endowed the Hodge Memorial Library in honor of his father. At his death, Charles W. Hodge was buried in the Center Cemetery. He had willed his bank, lumberyard, granite quarry, and Mine Hill to his niece Adelaide Jane Pons Mathews.[129]

Though two hundred years have passed, descendants of Philo Hodge's family continue to contribute to the town. Burton Hodge and his son Philo managed the Hodge General Store during the 1920s and 30s and Burton was the postmaster in the days of rural free delivery.[130]

Philo Burton Hodge, known to friends as Bud, joined the Roxbury Volunteer Fire Department in 1968, served on the town Zoning Commission for seventeen years, and recently received the Municipal Award for thirty years of volunteer service.[131] His son Aaron J. Hodge, still in his teens, rode the fire engines with his father and joined the ambulance corps. In the 1990s, Eagle Scout Aaron renumbered town addresses for an emergency 911 system.[132]

Holmes Road. This unpaved road is less than a half-mile long. It lies off the beaten path in an area once known as the West

Mountain District. According to a survey of Roxbury homes, the name is from a New York City family named Holmes who bought properties at numbers 11 and 28 Holmes Road in 1937.[133]

Jonathan Drive. Little did baby Jonathan Scott know when he was born that he would make history. Instead of following the tradition of using a surname for this drive, a proud father was inspired to name this drive with his son's Christian name. Jonathan was the first-born son of developer James M. Scott, owner of Scott Swimming Pools, Inc.[134] At a ten-minute town meeting in September 1974, the vote was unanimous to accept the 1,700-foot drive in the Scotland Rise subdivision.[135]

Judds Bridge Road. Thomas Deacon Judd emigrated from England to Massachusetts in the 1600s.[136] One Daniel Judd (1782-1870) was among his descendants who settled in Roxbury and censuses first listed him here in 1830. He must have been a hard-working man be- cause, as a sixty-eight-year-old farmer in 1860, he reported $3,400 in real estate holdings,  comfortable compared to his neighbors. Ten years later, Daniel Judd listed his occupation as Gentleman. He was a widower and Polly Higgins, a housekeeper, lived in his household. By the time Daniel Judd was eighty-seven, he was living with Hubbell White- head's family. Whitehead was probably his son-in-law.[137]

Lewis Judd (b. 1823) was Daniel Judd's next-door neighbor, though we don't know whether he was related to Daniel. Lewis listed himself in the 1860 census as a thirty-seven-year-old farmer whose household included his wife, daughter, and two Higgins boys. With real estate valued at $2,000 and personal assets of $200, Lewis Judd was a prosperous man.[138]

He was also a decorated soldier. In the summer of 1851, when Litchfield County celebrated its one-hundredth anniversary with a two-day celebration, Capt. Lewis Judd's Warner Light Guards represented Roxbury. His troops, in elegant new uniforms, demonstrated their excellent maneuvers, military discipline, and gallantry as they escorted their fellow citizens and stood guard over the parade. One commentator noted that they looked like a veteran company with years of training.[139]

When the Civil War broke out in the spring of 1861, President Lincoln called for militia to serve for three months and Lewis Judd answered that call. A common practice during the Civil War was for local men to raise a company and then offer it to the Army. The war was not a popular one, but Capt. Lewis Judd and his troops joined the Union side.

Judd enlisted on August 17, 1861 as a Captain and the next day, he offered the Warner Light Guards, his company of sixty-four men, including twelve from Roxbury. They became part of the Connecticut Volunteers known as Company D., Tenth Infantry Regiment.[140] He mustered out on January 2, 1862.[141] After the war, he and his family headed west. By 1870, they had settled in Virginia and by 1880, they had settled in Burnsville, Minnesota.[142]

Judge Road. John S. Judge had a habit of going to the Roxbury Market to chat with friends while he waited for his morning newspaper. One morning in the 1960s, while he waited for his paper, he and First Selectman Harold Birchall talked. Birchall told Judge that the road he lived on needed a name. The men tossed around several ideas until they decided on Judge Road.[143]

The surname remained after John Judge passed his property to his son and daughter-in-law, Jerry and Margot Judge. Even though the house was a weekend retreat, Jerry remembered many cold winter nights when the family escaped the big city and headed to even colder rural Roxbury. As soon as they arrived, they built a fire and baked potatoes in the large fireplace. Margot recalled that, in winter, Birchall used to call them in New York City to ask if they were coming to Roxbury. If not, the town would not bother to plow the road.

The unpaved dead-end road is a curiosity; it was a road, then a driveway, then a road again. According to Margot Judge, the road was on the route of a post road that ran from Albany to New Haven and crossed a ford in the Shepaug River.[144]

Kressfield Farm Lane. The lane runs off Botsford Hill Road and its name is from the George Kress family who purchased land here in 1984.

The ingenuity of a realtor or a seller was on full display, according to Margot Judge, when a house near the lane was for sale. The house stood empty for so long, she said, that someone put a mannequin in a window to make it look lived in.[145]

Laurel Lane. The name is an old one, dating from the eighteenth century when Swedish botanist Carl Linnaeus gave the Latin name, *Kalmia latifolia,* to the mountain laurel in honor of his student and friend Pehr Kalm.

When Chuck and Doris Farrell bought property here in 1980, an old deer trail ran through it. Like early settlers, the Farrells used existing trails when they laid out their property and transformed the deer trail into a driveway. When the town asked the Farrells to name the lane so emergency services could find them, Doris Farrell's mother, Louise Hoddinott, offered an idea. She was especially enchanted with the delicate scent of the pink and white blossoms that bordered their driveway and suggested the name Laurel as a reminder of the plant's splendor.[146]

Don't make honey from its blossoms or chew on its leaves, though, because the Kalmias are among our most poisonous plants. Their foliage is more deadly than strychnine. The Indians knew this and were said to make death-dealing drinks from Kalmia leaves. Though aware of its poisonous nature, in 1907, Connecticut officials, charmed by its beauty, named it the state flower.

Loomba Lane. Dr. Narenda Paul Loomba and his wife, Mary Adams Loomba, purchased property here in 1970. They named this private lane in honor of Dr. Loomba's father, Jagiri Lal Loomba, who passed away at a young age. While Mary Adams Loomba's roots were in Roxbury, Dr. Loomba's roots were in India. Mary grew up in Roxbury where her stepfather, John K. Smart, lived for almost fifty years and her aunt, Louise Adams Metcalf, owned Judds Bridge Farm that, at one time, comprised 5,000 acres.

It was the water nearby that enticed the Loombas to build their home on this private lane. His homeland was Punjab, India and the name Punjab means Land of Five Rivers. Rivers and riverfronts have always been attractions for Dr. Loomba, he said, and the Shepaug River was no exception. It reminded him of the river that ran next to his village.[147]

One bit of confusion exists about the name. Town records and local maps name it Loomba Lane, but a road sign names it Loomba Drive.

Lower County Road. No remnants of this road's history are apparent today. Modern homes line the road, a telecommunications tower juts out above the skyline, and the town Transfer Station, opened in January 1991, ensures traffic on the dirt road three days a week.[148]

At one time, the road ran through the lower part of Litchfield County, and in the 1700s, it crossed into New Haven County.

Roxbury's first churches once stood at the southern end of this road, but when worshippers built new churches further north in a new town center, they abandoned the lower end of this road. In the 1940s, farmers planted cornfields where the old center had been.[149] Now the cornfields have disappeared, and the southern end of the road is a dirt path leading to private property.

This dirt path is quiet now, but may have been part of a dispute over Litchfield County's name. According to one report, the Connecticut General Assembly allowed Woodbury settlers to choose which county they wanted to join. At first, at least until May 1748, they chose to be part of Fairfield County. Then the settlers changed their minds, and a decades-long controversy resumed between the settlers and authorities. The settlers were adamant; they wanted their own county, and they wanted it named Woodbury County.

When the general assembly refused, the settlers were enraged, but suggested a compromise. They offered to pay to build and maintain all the county buildings, if only the name were Woodbury County. The assembly ignored them, and in October 1751, created Litchfield County. Townsmen were so furious they called an emergency meeting to try to reverse the decision—they lost. They petitioned again two decades later—they lost. They petitioned again ten years later—again, they lost. Litchfield County is now four centuries old and Woodbury is still part of it.[150]

Lower Falls Road. The name says it all; the road is downstream from the Shepaug River waterfalls. It ends at a boat launch, and at 250 feet, is the lowest elevation in Roxbury.

Lower River Road. Entered from South Street, it is at the lower end of the Shepaug River and runs less than a half mile before the pavement ends at the Southbury boat launch. In 1902, J. Coleman Smith of New York City bought the Jay Tyrrell House on this road and that same year leased it to the Roxbury Club. Twenty years later, the Connecticut Light and Power Company became an owner of this property.[151]

Mallory Road. Malary, Mallary, Mallery and Mallory families lived in the area, and according to a family genealogy, the Mallory stock was of a "marvelous productive vitality." Thomas Mallory (1682-1783) certainly fit that description. He settled in Woodbury where he and his wife raised six children. Mallory lived to be 101 years old.[152]

Adna Mallory and John Mallory were among nine Mallory heads-of-household listed in the Woodbury 1790 census, but records did not indicate how they were related. Both accepted official positions at Roxbury's first town meeting. The following year, John G. Mallory purchased a house on nearby Garnet Road that remained in the Mallory family for over a century.[153]

Adna Mallory was a religious man. He understood the strict rules of the church and demonstrated his willingness to enforce those rules when he became one of five men appointed to the office of tythingman. As a tythingman, he would see to it that people obeyed the rules of the church regarding the Sabbath.[154] One of his jobs was to keep the congregation awake. Ministers did not take kindly to sleepy children and adults snoozing during sermons, and some clergymen went so far as to shout a nodder's name to the whole congregation.

If that did not work, Mallory became a pest; some would say a brute. He carried a long stick with a heavy knob at one end and a dangling foxtail or rabbit's foot at the other. With one end, he popped unruly boys on the noggin and clobbered dozing men. With the other end, he tweaked nodding girls' noses and tickled sleepy women's chins. If he wasn't careful, as some tythingmen were not, he might use the masculine end to bop a drowsy maiden. Church elders would make him pay a fine for such a mistake.

If he wanted to, Mallory could wield his power outside the meetinghouse. He could arrest anyone who walked or rode too fast to services and he could arrest anyone who walked unnecessarily on the Sabbath. Mallory's job didn't end with the Sabbath. He could give a tongue-lashing to tavern keepers serving tipplers who drank too much. In addition, he kept an eye on newcomers, lest they be of a sort that would become paupers and a drain on the town budget.[155]

John Malary also had a job nailing people who broke the rules, but his job was more mundane—he was a leather sealer. He monitored the sale of leather to ensure it met government standards of quality. John Malary placed his seal or stamp of approval on items he inspected, tested, and certified.[156]

Capt. Cyrene Mallery must have been a popular figure. Both the 1800 and 1820 censuses listed him as a married man with a family, but his popularity came about because he owned an inn that had a store, a ballroom, a bar. It was a place to conduct business as well as a place to party.

When the press announced that anyone with claims against a certain estate should meet at Capt. Cyrene Mallery's Inn, men came to conduct business.[157] On other occasions, crowds came to celebrate. For example, at noon on a hot July 4, 1817, a procession of citizens and clergy, escorted by companies of artillery and infantry, met at the inn. From there, they moved to the Episcopal Church to hear speeches. Speeches ended, the crowd headed back to the inn to dine and drink. They held their glasses high for a round of toasts—each toast followed by artillery fire. The mob toasted the military, the President of the United States, the Governor, and the state of Connecticut.

They toasted the clergy of every denomination and the freemen of the state of Connecticut. Finally, they toasted to the fair sex, "Our only sovereigns!"[158]

Mine Hill Road. The road takes its name from the silica and granite mines on the hill on Roxbury's western border. Earlier names were Hurlbut Mountain and Spruce Hill. The first name referred to the mound of minerals found in 1751 by Moses Hurlbut and Abel Hawley, though some people believe others were there earlier. The second name is, presumably, from spruce trees that grew on the hill.[159]

Though mining began in the 1700s, the search for ore started in earnest around 1865 when the Civil War was raging. Workers constructed mines, trails, roasting ovens, furnaces, a rolling mill, and other buildings.[160]

A small town called Chalybes grew up around the mines, and in 1871, a railroad opened. Unfortunately, mining operations were already in trouble. Furnaces broke down, production techniques were out-of-date and inefficient, and competition from iron ore reserves in the west caused the mines to fail. Then the quarries closed, and by World War II, the village was a ghost town.[161]

When the mines and quarries were active, miners, stonecutters, and masons lived in tenement houses and boardinghouses. The town historian Timothy Beard said he had read of at least three bordellos to entertain the men. William Seward, known as Big Bill, a corpulent man said to weigh three hundred pounds, operated a three-story hotel near the boardinghouse. The Seward Hotel had a barroom, a drinking lounge, and bedrooms. At night, it became a rowdy place; some people said that "career ladies" occupied some of the bedrooms.

Today, only three buildings remain at the foot of the hill—a private home that was a general store, an antique woodworking business that housed a cigar factory, and a warehouse that was a railroad station. The remains of the mine are farther up the hill.

Three main tunnels—former passageways for miners and quarrymen—still exist. Now, bats hibernate and breed in the tunnels that stay cool all year round. Four rare species of bats in Connecticut have been known to winter in the tunnels— the pippistrel, the little brown bat, the big brown bat, and the Keen's bat.[162]

Drive or walk along Mine Hill Road and imagine the noises of the blast furnace and the smell of ore roasters spewing smoke. It's quiet now, but walk around the furnace and roasters and envision the vibrant industrial center on the edge of Roxbury. Marked trails cross the hill and signs tell the history of the mines.

Minor Bridge Road. The family name was Miner or Minor, but might have been Bullman had it not been for King Edward III (1312-1377). Henry Bullman, a miner by trade, supplied the king with one-hundred men armed with battle-axes and other weapons to fight the French in the Hundred Years War. The king was so impressed with Bullman's service and bravery that he knighted him with the surname Minor and awarded him a coat of arms. By naming him Sir Henry Minor, the king honored all the miners of the world by making their profession a surname.[163]

The first descendant of Sir Henry Minor to reach America's shores was Thomas Minor (1608-1690). This road name honors the Minor family. John Minor (1635-1719), Thomas' first son, was a captain in the militia, a man fluent in Indian languages, and a man who settled a Connecticut town.

Capt. John Minor and his wife, Elizabeth Booth (1641-1732), lived in Stratford until 1673, when the Connecticut General Court appointed him to lead a group of fifteen people out of that town.[164] The Court ordered the Captain to lead the group north through miles of deep forests until he reached the place where they would settle Pomperaug Plantation.[165]

Indians owned and occupied the land that the Captain and his group were to settle, and because he knew the Indian languages, he was the perfect man to negotiate to purchase their land. Capt. Minor signed many contracts with the Indians, but the one he signed in 1706 to create the Pomperaug Plantation was the most important because it confirmed all earlier grants and purchases. It was also the only one signed by women.

Women did not often serve in an official capacity, but here they were, witnesses and signatories to contracts that would settle a new town.

Four English and twelve Pootatucks signed the agreement, and Elizabeth and Rebeckah Minor were among the signatories. Two Pootatuck women, Mu-nmenepoosqua and Mut-tanumace also signed the document. They signed in the customary form of signature used by the Indians with a picture or icon representing a fish, a stone, or some other figure important to her.

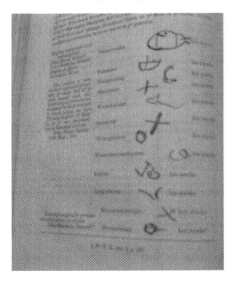

Capt. John Minor signed all of the Pomperaug Plantation deeds and was also one of the seventeen original signers of the 1673 Fundamental Articles that governed the settlement. The Captain lived to the age of eighty-five, having served as town clerk in Stratford for ten years and as town clerk in Woodbury for thirty years. His log house on Good Hill passed to one of his sons, then through several generations, until 1841, when one Albert Minor sold it.[166]

Moosehorn Road. Even though someone occasionally claims to see the noble moose in Roxbury, it has gone the way of the buffalo of the western plains. Moosehorn, sometimes spelled as two words, is the name of a hollow, a plain, a hill, a brook, and a road. In earlier days, moose shed their antlers here, thereby giving the area its name.

To some, this mile-long unpaved stretch was so beautiful that, in July 2004, they persuaded authorities to designate it a Scenic Road. To others, though, it was spooky. For example, the press wrote that stones left in the road scared Cyrus Prindle's horse.[167] A century later, when former resident Elizabeth Nourse tried to take the road as a shortcut to visit friends, her horses also shied. She was certain the horses saw ghosts.[168]

Murkland Road. S. W. Murkland's family owned property on this road from 1924-1997. A descendent Edward R. Murkland (1918-1972) lived here with his wife and three sons. He served on Roxbury's Board of Education and Zoning Board. He was an accomplished man who served in the U. S. Army Signal Corps, was a Lieutenant in World War II, and won awards for his educational and industrial films at the Cannes Film Festival.[169] His widow, Jean Murkland Luberg, said that in the 1950s, a realtor wanted to publish a map of Roxbury, and named this road for Edward Murkland.

North Street. The name describes the street's location north of the town green, but was called Bradley Street in the 1800s. Today, the paved stretch bears two state highway numbers— Route 67 and Route 199.

Three historic homes attributed to the Bradleys still stand on this street, although only two carry the Bradley surname. The first, the Alson Bradley House, built in 1790, remained in the family through most of the nineteenth century. One of Alson Bradley's four sons, Edson Bradley (1806-1889), built the second in 1835—a Greek Revival-style farmhouse at 76 North Street. Eli Bradley (1857-1911) owned the third property, but sold it in 1870 to the Rev. Austin Isham. It was the Reverend's second home in Roxbury and bears his name.[170]

During the late summer and fall of 1893, the press reported a bit of excitement in the minister's neighborhood. A chicken thief had the neighbors in a quandary when he stole ten chickens from the Rev. Isham and a dozen from George W. Smith, his next-door neighbor. Six months later the chicken thief was still at work and at large. Then the thief got careless and left his footprints in the snow as he carried off sixteen chickens. Authorities did not divulge his name, but were hot on his trail. They said that they knew the size of his foot.[171]

Old Boston Post Drive. Local veterinarian Dr. Paul A. Elwell named the drive because it ran parallel to, and incorporated part of the original Boston Post Road, a system of roads that ran from New York to Boston.[172]

The post roads were main roads built to deliver mail and carry news between towns. Created in 1673, the roads were just wide enough for a lone horse and rider, known as a post rider, who took four weeks to deliver mail between New York City and Boston. By 1772, stagecoaches completed the route in a week, and during the American Revolution, troops and equipment moved along the Boston Post Road.

In the early 1800s, post rider David Mallory rode his horse on the isolated post road to take news and deliver mail to his fellow neighbors. One of his stops was the Roswell Ransom Tavern. In those days, customers paid the post rider to carry the mail, but

Mallory's customers were slow to pay, so he placed a notice in a newspaper and demanded his customers to pay up and be quick about it.[173] When the automobile became popular in the early twentieth century, paving, paint, and a numbering system turned the Boston Post Road into a national highway system.

Old Lane. The name expressed the emotions people felt about an older, lower path lined with aging stone walls that was a favorite hiking path before a new one was built in 1980. The lane is a 0.3 mile-long slope off Baker Road near the intersection with Botsford Hill Road. In earlier days, students used the older path as a shortcut to the Botsford Hill schoolhouse.[174]

Resident Steve Zaleta said that, in the past, this lane might have connected to the nearby Old Town Highway. A Bridgewater resident who owns Old Lane received approval for subdivisions about twenty-five years ago and property owners have deeded easements to this lane with rights to travel over "the possible Old Town Highway."[175]

Old Roxbury Road. The label seems to be a misnomer— why isn't it labeled Old Roxbury Center Road? In the eighteenth century, it led to the town center, the heart of Roxbury where people attended church. For a period, at least until the mid-1950s, this road was also known as Route 67A.[176]

Before Roxbury had a center, folks walked or rode horseback six miles over rocky roads to worship in Woodbury. In the 1740s, the general court allowed Roxbury inhabitants to build their own churches. Suddenly, a town center popped up and what a center it was— two churches, a noon-house, a cemetery. As the population grew, churches bulged at the seams, and folks needed larger churches. They built their new churches two-and-a-half miles north, and a new town center was born—and this road was left with an apparent misnomer.

Old Turnpike Road. Now a wide paved stretch, this was once a dirt road and part of the New Milford-Roxbury Turnpike. It runs less than one-tenth of a mile through Roxbury.

After the Revolution, towns had no money to build connecting roads to other towns, so the government encouraged private businesses to build roads and collect tolls. The era of turnpike roads started. When the Old Turnpike Road opened, if you wanted to travel on it, you had to pay a toll.

Here's how it worked. Imagine you're walking, riding horseback, or lounging in a carriage on your way across town. Suddenly, you're faced with a long stick hung across the road. You can't go any farther. A man hollers, "Pay up." You do; he raises the barrier, and you're on your way. The long stick was a turnpike, and the man who hollered was a toll collector. If you had refused to pay up, he would have refused to raise the turnpike.

Painter Hill Road. In 1743, Woodbury land records listed a highway that was laid out on Panther Hill, and an 1821 Roxbury deed listed property on Panther Hill. Whether this hill was a favorite hangout for the big cats or whether someone made a spelling error in public records, two hundred years later the name remains. For example, on a Connecticut Department of Environmental Protection map dated June 16, 1998, the words Panther Dam appeared next to a small blue circle designating a pond. Another name for this area was Planter Hill, possibly a misspelling in public records, but locals prefer to believe the name was from panthers.[177]

More likely, the name was from the Painter families. In 1789, Lt. Lamberton Painter successfully petitioned the court to incorporate Roxbury, and in the 1800s, he and his relatives bought and sold hundreds of parcels of land in this area.[178] A relative and representative to the Connecticut General Court,

Capt. Deliverance L. Painter (1764-1841), operated one of Roxbury's earliest stores on the south side of Castle Street.[179]

The Captain served with the Connecticut Continental Army in the Revolutionary War and collected an annual pension of $50 for his military service. As of June 30, 1840, he was living with Henry Painter, probably his son.[180] Capt. Painter died at age seventy-seven and was buried in the family plot in the Squire Road Cemetery.

Painter Hill has a number of attractions that draw visitors from around the state. One is the five-hundred-acre Toplands Farm. For years, a sign at the entrance read Toplands Farm, Home of the Tops. A farm hand was certain that one of the owners invented tops—the spinning kind that kids play with. Owner Dudley Diebold liked the story, but said the sign was there in 1942 when his family bought the farm. In 2008, the Diebolds added The Diebold Foundation, Inc. and DD Living History Farm, Inc. to the sign.

Diebold admitted he had never seen panthers prowling the hills, but quickly added that they were not very big, more like bobcats with long tails. Even though panthers may not roam, coyotes do, therefore, every evening Diebold's friend Bucky Lowe, who keeps a herd at Toplands Farm, drives three miles north from his farm to count his longhaired Scottish Highland cattle. Lowe has raised these cattle for years, but on July 4, 2005, he got a surprise. Twins were born—among the first in Lowe's herd. When I saw them at two-weeks old, the calves were about the size of a Labrador retriever. The twins were not identical though, at least not in terms of habits. One twin persisted in crawling under the rail fence and dashing into the fields. The other twin was a couch potato; he stayed in the barn and slept.

A favorite attraction is a pair of donkeys. They are not always the same donkeys, but always a pair—sometimes they are black, sometimes multicolored, and sometimes white. People come from all around to see them, like the couple from Oxford who come by motorcycle every Sunday to pet and feed the donkeys. They've also given the animals names like Michael, Sam, and Samantha.

A schoolhouse and an artist's home are also popular sites on Painter Hill Road. The one-room schoolhouse, built in 1889, was a school until 1939, when it became a private home. Its original dome ceiling remains, but the blackboard hides behind a plaster wall, and a large stone fireplace in the living room has replaced the wood stove that heated the school.

An outhouse with separate entrances for boys and girls remains. It used to face the road, but a teacher was horror-struck at the thought that passers-by would see children using it. She notified officials, selectmen called a town meeting, and residents voted to turn the outhouse so the doors faced the school, not the road. When the former owner tried to sell the outhouse to make room for a garden, locals persuaded her to keep it intact as a bit of local history.[181]

The artist's home is a 1750 house associated with Alexander Calder (1898-1976), the renowned sculptor and creator of mobiles. From the 1930s until his death, he and his family divided their time between France and Roxbury. After a fire in the 1950s, Calder became enamored with the color charcoal-black and painted the entire house that color.[182] Calder's sculpture, *Mountain* stands at the entrance to the Minor Memorial Library.

Painter Ridge Road. Tucked away in the quiet northeast corner of town, this ridge may also have been a panther haunt, and its name origin is the same as Painter Hill Road. This road runs less than a mile in Roxbury, passing two historic homes built in the 1800s, before it crosses the town line into Washington.

Phaeton Drive. The phaeton, a light four-wheeled carriage, drawn by two horses, was popular in the nineteenth century. Residents who lived here in the 1980s and owned a horse farm nearby gave this drive its magical name. Resident Tracey Andrews, who lives in the house formerly owned by her grandmother, recalled that before this drive had a name, there was only one house here. Its address was on Lower County Road.[183]

Pickett Road. Several Picketts emigrated from Ireland in the 1850s, moved to Roxbury, bought property, raised their families, and became successful dairy farmers. Two of the most prominent were Michael and William Pickett. It is likely the road was named for William Pickett's family, since early maps show his name on this road.

Michael Pickett (1839-1904) was one of the first of his family to move to Roxbury. At sixteen, he and eighteen-year-old Mary Pickett, boarded the passenger ship *Lucy Thompson* in Liverpool, England and immigrated to the United States. On May 26, 1857, they arrived in New York harbor. The passenger manifest listed them as British, but later censuses listed them as Irish. They both found work, but in different Roxbury homes. Mary became a servant in Herman Frisbie's home and Michael became a farmhand on Edwin Seeley's farm on Painter Hill Road.[184]

At some point, though the date is unclear, Michael rented a house east of Sheldon B. Smith's property on Church Street and worked in Smith's cheese shop. Michael's ties, though, were with Edwin Seeley, a dairyman, cattle breeder, and importer of purebred Dutch Holsteins. In 1872, Seeley conveyed part of a farm with a house that he owned elsewhere on Painter Hill Road to Michael Pickett.

Michael must have been an industrious farmer and saved his hard-earned money because by 1870 he was married to Margaret who had emigrated from Ireland three years after he did. During the course of their forty-year marriage, they raised five children. Their son Michael J. (1866-1934), a dairyman, inherited the family farm and passed it down to his son.[185]

William Pickett (1843-1909) was the second Pickett to arrive in the United States and buy property here. He was fourteen-years old when he arrived in New York harbor on November 23, 1858 on the *Aurora*. He was listed as Irish.[186]

William's future wife, Bridget Costigan (1845-1884), was a twenty-year old servant who traveled alone from Ireland on the *Star of the West*, arriving in New York harbor on March 8, 1865. Five years later, William's household included his wife, Bridget, and three children. Bridget died in 1884, leaving William with six children.

William married his second wife, Margaret Costigan (1855-1937), in 1891 and they had two children. Margaret had emigrated in 1867 from Ireland, but I found no record that indicated whether she and Bridget, William's first wife, were related.

Little information is available about William, though, in addition to farming, he performed other jobs. For example, in

August 1888, he worked on town roads. The following year, the town paid him $18.00 for keeping Michael Costigan, a poor relative of Margaret Pickett.[187] William worked in School District No. 2 during the 1890-91 fall and winter terms, but reports did not record what kind of work he did.

After William died, Margaret continued to farm with the help of their two teenage children and a farm hand. Margaret passed the family farm to her son, Leo William (1893-1955), who became a successful farmer and milk producer, as well as selectman. His descendants, who still live in Washington and Roxbury, sold part of the extensive Pickett property that straddled the Roxbury-Washington town line. Today, Regional School District No. 12 owns most of the property along this road that runs only 0.20 miles in Roxbury.

Pine Tree Hill. Town records and a road sign call this unpaved lane Pine Tree Hill; local maps call it Pine Tree Lane—long names for a private path that's less than one-tenth of a mile long. The namer may have thought all evergreens were pine trees or maybe a ribbon of pines covered the hill when someone dubbed it Pine Tree Hill. Today, rhododendrons, hemlock, spruce, and other evergreens line the lane.

The widest pine tree in town is a portly white pine with a waistline dubbed by the Conservation Commission as a winner in their 2003 Tree Contest. It's around the corner on Hemlock Road.[188]

Quarry Drive. Quarrying lasted almost forty years in Roxbury, though much of the history of its eight quarries has been lost. Skilled workers and unskilled day laborers worked the quarries from 1880 to 1900, creating a population boom and a housing shortage. Roxbury's population rose to 1,087 in 1900, the highest it had been in fifty years. Nearly every household in or near the quarries took in boarders.

Quarry bosses were American or Irish; stonecutters, quarrymen, and derrick tenders were from Ireland, Russia Poland, and Italy. In 1900, fourteen quarrymen, all of them English or American, lived at William (Bill) Seward's hotel. His staff of four included three African Americans who worked as cook, waitress, and waiter.[189]

The first quarries were at the top of Mine Hill. Oxcarts carried the quarried rocks to Roxbury and New Milford, but probably not much farther, since transporting the stone was extremely difficult. When the Shepaug Valley Railroad opened in 1872, it became easier to ship the stone, but in 1890, when quarries opened at the bottom of Mine Hill, the upper quarries closed temporarily. The railroad shipped large granite slabs to Bridgeport, and barges carried the stone to New York City to build part of Grand Central Station.

When the Rockside Quarry near Judds Bridge was open, stoneworkers who lived on the town side walked across a suspension bridge that spanned the Shepaug River, but when work slowed down, the Rockside Quarry closed.[190]

By the spring of 1899, Mine Hill Quarry Company had opened with a small workforce. In the fall, a press notice mentioned that the newly built company houses gave the little hamlet a brighter appearance and cheer that had been lacking. That same year, the Company hired men to handle a large order from the Consolidated Railroad of Bridgeport. To meet the demand for the contract, the Mine Hill Quarry Company installed a switch and boiler at the abandoned Rockside Quarry, and employed one hundred and fifty men for three years to fulfill the contract.[191]

The Mowers Brothers Company leased quarry rights from Albert Hodge, and William Mowers, who lived at Roxbury Station, opened two granite quarries.[192]

During the early 1950s and 1960s, men came again to cut and sell stone. One was a stonemason from Southbury who salvaged stone from the quarries and sold it for hearths and doorsteps in houses near Roxbury and New Milford, much as the quarrymen on Mine Hill had done over a century ago.[193] The Hodge Library and stone chimney at the Minor Memorial Library were built from Roxbury granite. Quarrying continues today at Mine Hill.[194]

Ranney Hill Road. Variations in spelling—Ranney, Ranny, Reany, and Reny— presented challenges to finding the surname in public records. For example, Woodbury records from 1753 to 1786 listed deeds for Jeremiah, Nathan, and Stephen Ranney. In 1881, records listed John Reany. Roxbury listed no Ranney or variation of the name in land records for any of those years. According to historian William Cothren, one Joseph Reny from Roxbury served in the French and Indian Wars and was a soldier in Capt. Ebenezer Downs' Company at the Fort William Henry Alarm near Fort George, New York in August 1757.[195]

Nathaniel Ranney was a head of household in Roxbury in 1800 when the census was counted, but he was not required to answer questions about the names or relationships of people who lived in his household. The people in Ranney's household were free white people, including one male and one female between twenty-six and forty-five years old, meaning they were born sometime between 1756 and 1774. One boy and three girls under ten years old, and one boy and one girl between ten and sixteen years old also lived in the household.[196]

Though we know little of the Ranney family, we know that Ranney Hill Road is the only Roxbury road documented to have had "thank-you-marms," though certainly other hilly roads had them. "Thank-you-marms," also called "water bars" and "thank-you-mums," were bumps in the road where the wheels of a cart or wagon could rest while horses caught their breaths going uphill. They were like speed bumps, but served a different purpose. Besides being resting places, they funneled water off the road into a ditch that followed the road all the way down.[197]

"Thank-you-marms" by day became "kiss-me-quicks" at night, so a hilly road did have its high spots and Ranney Hill was one of them. Elinor Hurlbut wrote that when she came to Roxbury in the 1940s, it was a narrow dirt road with grass growing between the wheel tracks. Open fields and large apple and peach orchards grew on the hill. There were many "thank-you-mums" to carry water off the road so it wouldn't wash away.

Elinor recalled pushing her first-born in a baby carriage up this road. "I would push the carriage up the hill to the first thank-you-mum, push over it, and anchor the wheels so it could not roll down. Then I'd pick a soft spot of grass in the middle of the road, sit down, and begin mending some socks I'd brought along." She remembered it as peaceful and quiet; no cars came along. She cherished the earlier times, writing, "I'm glad I enjoyed it way back when." Paved now, cars go whizzing by one house after another with no thank-you-mums to slow them down.[198]

Raven Rock. Ravens may have nested in the rocky cliffs, though there is no record of ravens in Roxbury. Ravens, the largest members of the crow family are smart, solitary, high-flying stunt pilots and scavengers with a raucous, deep "kaw" sound. They can imitate an amazing number of sounds and thirty distinct vocalizations.[199]

Something more ominous than ravens and crows, however, lurked in the hills of Raven Rock. They were smart scavengers, famous for their stunts; they tended to be solitary, hiding out in dusky dens and caves. They were counterfeiters, and Gamaliel's Den at Raven Rock was their favorite hideout.

Gamaliel Hurlbut, born December 20, 1714, was the first son of Cornelius and Sarah Hurlbut, and one of nine children. Some people believe he was a counterfeiter.[200] Records about him, however, are confusing. A footnote on an online Hurlbut family tree stated that Gamaliel Hurlbut lived in Woodbury in 1740 and later moved to New Milford.[201] Admitting the "absence of any evidence," the footnote also stated that Gamaliel Hurlbut had a son, Gamaliel Jr., who was married to Jerusha Drinkwater and was the father of three children. Further, it claimed that it was Gamaliel Jr., not his father, who was the counterfeiter.[202]

Other records confirmed that Gamaliel Hurlbut married Jerusha Drinkwater on Feb. 19, 1758/59 and had three children.[203] In 1790, Gamaliel Hurlbut lived in New Milford and told the census taker that he was single. By that time, Gamaliel may have been widowed or divorced and his children may have been living elsewhere.

William Stuart, Connecticut's first counterfeiter and a known horse thief printed money in Canada and hid it in local caves in Bridgewater and Roxbury.[204] Yet another counterfeiter, Steve Rance, led a band called the Gamaliel Gang. Their underground rendezvous was near Pootatuck Indian caves at Raven Rock. Rance's mob named their gang and their hiding place for Gamaliel Hurlbut.[205]

River Road. The two-mile stretch that follows the Shepaug River along Roxbury's western border was designated a Scenic Road in February 2004. In the petition for scenic designation, resident actor Jack Gilpin wrote, "Just next to the entrance to the River Road Preserve, in fact, lies the ruined foundation of what local lore holds to be Colonel Ethan Allen's birthplace."[206] Gary Steinman, another resident, confirmed the story.[207]

Roxbury is so rich in legends and luminaries that it's easy to confuse its history and heroes. For example, local historian Elmer Worthington said that Ethan Allen lived on Sentry Hill Road, and Seth Warner lived on River Road.[208] Other local histories also gave River Road as Seth Warner's home.[209] According to *Roxbury's Early Days*, Seth Warner was born on River Road on May 17, 1743 to Dr. Benjamin Warner and Silence Hurd. Dr. Ebenezer Warner, Seth Warner's grandfather, built the Warner home in 1715 on property given to him by the town in exchange for his medical services. In 1900, the house was still standing, though now only a foundation remains on the west side of River Road, a mile below the Wellers Bridge.

One local historian described five historic houses on River Road. One was the eighteenth century house at 191 River Road owned by the Warner family that operated Warners Mill. Later industries on the same property included a hat factory, a file factory, and a soap factory.[210] Aldophus M. Baglin (b. 1837), sometimes spelled Baglan and Baglan, owned the file factory and sold the files all over New England.[211]

Another historic house, at 183 River Road, was once a stagecoach stop, known as the Old Erbacher Place, even though decades have passed since Joseph A. Erbacher (1871-1963) owned the property. The Erbacher home replaced a pre-Revolutionary house that burned to the ground in 1820. When the stagecoach ran from Stamford to Hartford, it stopped at this house so passengers could rest and have refreshments. The stage came through Brookfield, crossed the new bridge over the Housatonic River, traveled over the hills, and down to the Shepaug River where it crossed behind the house. Since the stop was about midway, the house took on the name Halfway House.[212]

Rocky Mountain Road. The seven-hundred-foot mound of stones, boulders, and garnets rises above open fields to create one of the most breathtaking panoramic views in Roxbury.[213] In summer, the land is an uninterrupted carpet of green as far as the eye can see. In autumn, an unknown painter has splashed it all over with oranges, yellows, and reds. In winter, snow covers the mountain like a white fleece blanket.

This road follows the hill less than a mile south from Wellers Bridge Road until it becomes a steep dirt footpath where, as the Shepaug Trail, it pushes through deep woods.

Rucum Road. In earlier days, folks pointed to Rocum Hill, Reukum Hill, Rucum Hill, Rucum Plain, and Rucum Mountain,

all names in land records. No one bothered about the *o* and the *u* until a finicky speller came along. The fuss was over the letter *u* and how many to use. It took a ruling by the U. S. government to settle the matter.

On September 26, 2002, Woodbury selectmen sent a request to the U. S. Board of Geographic Names, stating that *rucuum* was the correct spelling. It was in common use, the selectmen pointed out. As proof, they presented a map showing Rucuum Hill. Three years passed before the U. S. Board of Geographic Names decided what to do. After all, the neighboring town, Roxbury spelled the name Rucum. The feds were in a quandary, but finally voted at their July 2005 meeting—Rucum was the correct and official spelling.[214]

Some feuds never end, though, no matter what the feds say. So today, if you're in Roxbury, you're on Rucum Road; if you're in Woodbury, you're on Rucuum Road. No matter—when you ask locals about the label, they scratch their heads and wonder where the name came from.

I spoke with a number of locals about the word "rucum." Some thought it might be a family name, but Town Historian Timothy Beard said no public records listed Rucum as a surname.

He added that the word was a variation of one that described the rocky landscape.[215]

Some people thought rucum might be American Indian. I contacted Ruth G. Torres, a Schaghticoke, whose relatives were among the Pootatucks and Weantinocks who settled near Kent. Torres knows the Indian languages of western Connecticut and is familiar  with words used by her ancestors during Colonial times. Torres explained that it was not an American Indian word. The primary language spoken in western Connecticut was a dialect of Algonquian, a derivative of the Mahican language, and it was rare for words to begin with the letter *r* in that dialect.[216]

Nora Dougherty Costello, reference librarian at the Mashantucket Pequot Research Library, confirmed that few Mahican words began with the letter *r*. She searched numerous sources of Native American names in New England, north of Mexico, and Long Island and found no reference to the word *rucum* and its various spellings.[217]

Resident writer Stewart Kellerman searched the *Oxford English Dictionary*. He found no variations of rucum, but said parts of the word could be relevant. He noted that *ruc* was an obsolete word for rock or rook. As part of his work with the Conservation Commission, Kellerman collected information on Roxbury's scenic ridgelines and pointed out that *ruck* was an obscure word for "ridge." Alternatively, there could have been a ruckus or rucas in the area, though no local historians have recorded it.[218]

After all the speculation about this strange word, we are left with an unknown. A simple explanation may have to do—in the 1600s, a tired and hurried clerk jotted a squiggle in a town record—rucum or rocum—his version of rocky.

School House Road. The brown, sturdy-looking building that looks like a large dollhouse is Roxbury's only remaining one-room schoolhouse. The schoolhouse is on Tophet Road near the corner of School House Road. In the days of district schools, it was in Good Hill District No. 4. In 1997, resident actor Richard Widmark donated the building and five acres to the Roxbury Land Trust.

The rustic wooden schoolhouse stood abandoned for years, until 2005, when Shepaug Valley High School student Ryan Walsh refurbished the building. He cleaned it inside and out, added period furniture, old school books, and wall maps. He also wrote a brief history of school life in the 1800s.

In those days, students walked to a school in their district, that is, the one nearest their home. The names and numbers of school districts changed over the years, but an 1874 map included Baptist, Painter Hill, Warner Mill, Weller, Center, Good Hill, and West Mountain Half District. Half District. District No. 3 was at the corner of Grassy Hill Road and Bacon Road.[219]

As student population dwindled, schools closed, districts disappeared, and the educational system changed to a regional structure. In 1930, only five schools remained with eighty-eight students.[220] By 1940, the town had consolidated them all into one school.

As each school closed, it took on other functions. For example, the Weller District school became the Roxbury Grange, and later, a private home. The Center District schoolhouse became the Christ Church Parish House and the one on Grassy Hill Road became a private home. Built in 1899, the Painter Hill School closed in 1939 and today is a private home.[221]

Sentry Hill Road. Recent topographical maps give the elevation of the hill as 450 feet, but the contour of the hill might have changed over the centuries. In any case, by order of the court, settlers used this hill as a lookout point to spot potential danger.

The Connecticut General Court put the entire colony under martial law in October 1675. Although Indians in this area were generally friendly, they were involved in skirmishes with tribes from other parts of Connecticut, and war raged between Indians and white men in the eastern part of the state. Members of the court were concerned about the dangers to inland frontier towns like Woodbury and ordered every plantation to station guards at high points on hills, in meetinghouse belfries, and in sentry boxes. It was from the brave sentries that stood watch over the safety of the inhabitants that we have the name Sentry Hill. Guards protected the scattered settlers when Indian troubles threatened again in 1726 and the court ordered another garrison of men to stand watch in the fort on Sentry Hill.[222]

South Street. The name reflects its location south of the town center, and in 1894, it was called the longest street in Roxbury Center and the main road to Shepaug Falls.[223] In earlier days, when Roswell Ransom's Tavern was jumping, and the Episcopal Church faced east, this road threaded north between the church and the tavern. But when the Episcopalians turned their church to face south, the town rerouted this street to its present location.[224] Today, it lies between Wellers Bridge Road and the town line with Southbury.

This street had undergone many changes in its history, but historians have written little about them. For example, Christian Street was its former name, but I found nothing about the origin of that name or when it was given that name.[225]

In the 1930's, the state renumbered highways in the area, took over this road, and named it Route 199. In 1963, the state gave it back to the town, and the town named it South Street.[226] Today, it has the distinction of being one of only three "streets" in town and part of it lies within Roxbury's historic district. Though only a small section of this street lies in the historic district, it is dotted with eighteenth and nineteenth century houses. The elegant Georgian Colonial home, built in 1784 by Asahel Bacon, one of the town's wealthiest merchants, stands at the corner of South Street and Wellers Bridge Road.

Roxbury was a farming community in the nineteenth century, and both large and small farms were part of this street's landscape. South Street, however, was also the center of trade and commerce. Its cobbler's shop, meat market, blacksmith shop, and foundry and casting shop are now museums and private homes. By the twentieth century, farming was on the decline, the small tradesmen were gone, and Roxbury became a retreat for people looking for an escape from large cities.

New Yorkers discovered life in the country and moved to rural Roxbury. One was actress Sylvia Sydney who bought the Asahel Barnes House that had been in the Barnes' family for over a century. She lived in that house for thirty years. Mystery writer Manfred B. Lee (1905-1971), a. k. a. Ellery Queen and his family moved into foundry-man Josiah Bronson's house. Hamlin's shoe-maker shop remained on this street, but was moved, attached to a barn, and converted to a private residence, enjoyed by well-known garden writer Tovah Martin.

The diminutive building that was the R. M. Bernhardt Meat Market, open until the

1960s, is now a museum. In three centuries, Asahel Bacon's grand house has passed to only three other families.

Southbury Road. The name is not seductive, but it tells you where you're going. In addition to being Southbury Road, it's also Route 67, a state highway that sweeps through several towns between New Milford and Woodbridge. In the nineteenth century, part of Route 67 followed the Oxford Turnpike and the New Milford-Roxbury Turnpike.[227]

The turnpike era started after the Revolution when budgets were tight, and towns had no funds to repair roads. The state was also short of funds to build roads, therefore, in 1792, the Connecticut General Assembly issued its first charters to entrepreneurs to create turnpike companies. Roxbury's Phineas Smith joined the turnpike movement and founded the Oxford Turnpike Company. Roads were in wretched condition, so his company and others took over the roads and put them in good order. Laws allowed companies to capitalize their expenses to build the turnpikes and divide the profits until they got back their original investment and an annual 12 percent interest.

Building a road was no easy matter. Men and animals had to remove boulders, stumps and trees, level a path, and dig drainage ditches. In this rocky land, the first step was obvious. Nevertheless,

Smith may have turned to a 1799 article in the *Philadelphia Magazine and Review* entitled "Directions for Making Roads," in which an anonymous road builder gave detailed advice on how to remove and break up stones.[228]

Tolls were posted, but many people were exempt from paying. For example, a man passing through on farm business was exempt. People traveling to worship, going to and from a gristmill, and soldiers attending to military duties were all exempt. Frequent travelers could pay an annual lump sum to turnpike company proprietors, rather than pay for each trip, like an early EZ-Pass.

Most toll roads in Connecticut were laid out between 1825 and 1830, and at one time, the Oxford Turnpike was one of 120 turnpikes in the state. In 1854, the state allowed turnpike companies to give the roads back to the towns. The assembly that had issued the charter for Phineas Smith's Oxford Turnpike Company annulled that charter in 1885. By then, Connecticut had only six turnpike companies still operating.[229]

Spargo Road. James, William, and Thomas Spargo emigrated from Cornwall, England in 1887 and settled in Roxbury. William and Thomas were brothers, but it is unclear what James' relationship was to them.

James Spargo (b.1844) was the oldest of the three men who came to Roxbury. What kind of work he did in England is unknown, but in Roxbury, he worked as a stonecutter in the quarries. In 1900, when the census taker stopped by his rented house he told the enumerator that he was in his mid-fifties, had been married for thirty-five years, and that his son and daughter were born in Connecticut.[230]

William Spargo (b. 1864) came alone to the United States and was the youngest of the three men. Two years later, his wife and older son joined him. By 1900, William had been in the United

States for thirteen years, rented a farm, and worked as a stonecutter. He was thirty-six years old, and his family included his wife, two sons, and two daughters ranging in age from five to eleven.[231]

For some reason, the census did not count Thomas Spargo (1854-1933) until 1910. His family included his wife, a son, three nephews, a niece, and a fifty-eight-year-old boarder. The niece and nephews were William's children. By 1930, Thomas owned property valued at $8,000. He had lived in Roxbury for fifty years and had retired from work on the state roads.[232]

Another Spargo lived in Roxbury his entire life. He was Thomas Henry Spargo (1892-1959), one of William's sons. Thomas Henry was twenty-four, married, a father, and required to register for the World War I draft. His registration card described him: medium height, blue eyes, light brown hair, not bald. Nathan T. Beardsley witnessed and signed the card on January 5, 1917. When World War II started, even though he was fifty, Thomas Henry was required to register with the military again. This time, he said that he worked on the state roads at the Maintenance Terminal in Hartford. He lived in Roxbury, but had a New Milford telephone number.[233]

Thomas Henry's life must have been a struggle; he and his family never owned their own home and never reported any assets. He died at the age of sixty-six.[234]

When census takers made the rounds in 1930, they asked a question never before asked during a population count. The government's interest in technology and communication, combined with new attention to consumer purchasing power led census takers to ask people if they owned a radio. Thomas Henry, the younger man who reported no assets answered "yes"; his uncle who owned his own home and had substantial assets answered "no."

Squire Road. This road stretches between Southbury Road and South Street. Formerly named Castle Street, it was renamed for Charles Thomas Squire (1839-1935), although I found no record of why or when the road's name changed. The surname is also spelled Squier and Squires. Today, no Castles live in Roxbury, and no Squires live on Squire Road.

Horace Squire's (1807-1898?) house, built circa 1860, stands on this road as a well-preserved nineteenth-century farmhouse and its present owners call the property Squire Meadows. Squire was a cattle dealer and drover who became affluent and built this house when the railroad came to town. He owned another property on South Street where he, his wife, and five children lived before he built the Squire Road house.

Horace Squire's South Street house passed through several generations and today, his great-grandson, Charles M. "Bud" Squire and his family live in the house. Bud Squire, an amiable, jolly man followed his father's example and became a carpenter. Like his father and great-grandfather, he and his wife raised five children. Bud has lived in Roxbury his entire life and his many stories are scattered throughout this book, but some of his favorites are about his father and grandfather.[235]

Bud's father, Clayton Barber Squire (1881-1978), operated a general farm with cows, chickens, and pigs; he also sold milk, worked as a carpenter, and built several houses in Roxbury, until 1953, when he retired from the building business. Clayton lived to be ninety-seven years old and was the oldest living Roxbury resident at that time. Clayton learned a great deal about carpentry when, as a young man, he worked and studied with the Bronson Brothers who were skilled carpenters and plowmakers. He put his skills to good use when someone built a warehouse at Roxbury Falls, but forgot to put in windows. The reason, according to

Bud, was because "that's what the blueprint said." To Clayton's good fortune, he was contracted to add windows and doors to the already built warehouse and was paid a considerable amount of money for his efforts.

In interviews with Bud, it was clear he was equally proud of his grandfather, Charles Thomas Squire, who served with the Union Army during the Civil War and was assigned to Company I, 2nd Regiment, Connecticut Heavy Artillery. He enlisted as a Private and within two years was promoted to Full Corporal. Squire was wounded in the battle at Winchester, Virginia on September 19, 1864. He was transferred to another regiment and later received a disability discharge. Family photos, family trees, and other memorabilia cover the walls and cupboards in Bud's house. Among his most treasured items is a copy of his grandfather's mustering-out papers. Bud says these framed military papers have been on that wall forever and will stay there always.[236]

Tamarack Lane. A developer named this private lane for the only native conifer that sheds all of its leaves in the fall. The tree grew in the surrounding wetlands of Tamarack Swamp.

Early settlers used tamarack wood to make snowshoe frames, ladders, and fence posts and used the gum to sooth cuts and bruises. Tamarack trees, also known as American larch, fortified the shafts at Mine Hill and seven Tamarack trees at 13 Mine Hill Road are similar to those used in the mines.[237]

Tophet Road. Its name means hell. But we will probably never know how or why someone assigned it to a hollow, ravine, valley, and road. In the 1800s, a writer described Tophet Hollow as a deep long ravine that was a dark, damp, heavily wooded, dismal place, yet in 2001, the road was designated a Scenic Road.[238]

Perhaps dark ravines in the valley conjured up images of Hades; perhaps people burned refuse in the hollow; perhaps folks believed tales about Indians beating drums to drown the cries of children being sacrificed; or perhaps the hex of a witch caused people to name it for a place where Satan lived.

One person told me of a former neighbor who believed it was a dumping ground for bodies, especially people who were ill, possibly lepers. The *Oxford English Dictionary* noted that a later usage of the word Tophet was for a place to deposit refuse and became symbolic of the torments of hell. It made no mention of lepers.[239] One dictionary gave the pronunciation *tō-fat*. Locals differ, however, about how to pronounce it: *'tō'fet* or *tŏ'fet*. According to Marion Hawley, no matter how locals pronounce it, they have long used the expression "hotter than Tophet."[240]

The Bible identified Tophet as a place in the valley of Hinnom, near Jerusalem, where children were sacrificed to the god Moloch. In Jeremiah, the Lord called for an end to the name Tophet and said that, in the future, it would be known as the valley of slaughter.[241] The 1897 *Easton's Bible Dictionary* listed *toph* as a Hebrew word meaning a drum referring to one used to drown out the cries of children. The reference also said that the origin could have been from *taph* or *toph* meaning "to burn."

As far as some locals today are concerned, none of the above matters. They believe what their parents told them and still shudder in the telling. For example, when Lois Hodges was a child, her parents told her to stay away from that place—a witch lived there and the witch would cast a spell on her. Hodges was talking about Moll Cramer. In 1753, Adam Cramer, a poor blacksmith, lived on the western edges of Woodbury. Adam was a Christian man, but Satan possessed his wife. Since Adam depended on the public for support, when Moll became eccentric and outrageous, the community forced him to throw his wife and son out of the house.

Moll and her son moved to Good Hill and built a pole cabin to shelter them from the "storms of heaven." They slept on straw, lived in filth, and eked out a living by begging. Moll's young son was under her spell and followed her everywhere she went. No one dared refuse them when they came begging, because if Moll begged a man for a piece of pork and he denied her, she put a hex on his pig. The curse was so strong that the pig would never get fat again.[242]

Town Line Road. The name of this mile-long paved road describes its purpose as a boundary between Roxbury and Bridgewater. Its scenery is like a postcard—green fields, rolling hills, and the sky at your fingertips. Face east, plant your feet in the wide sweeping fields at the Jane Pratt Farm Preserve, and drink in the scene across the Shepaug River and through the valley to the hills.

The bucolic setting is enhanced by Greyledge Farm, Town Line Farm Preserve, and the Stuart Family Farm with its red barns and silos, a sign featuring All Natural Beef, and a modest white house surrounded by open fields. Restored barns and houses pepper the fields at the Meadow Sweet and Botsford Hill Farms. Enjoy the vista, but be careful of the sharp curve in the road as it dips steeply down past Keeler Road to become Botsford Hill Road.

Transylvania Road. No, the name is not from Dracula. That tome, published in 1897, was too late to have influenced the road name. Transylvania, sometimes spelled Transilvania, is from the Latin meaning "beyond the forest," and the road name comes from a nearby brook, named in a 1705 agreement between settlers and the Pootatuck Indians.[243]

A special feature of Transylvania Road is a black oak dubbed "Miss Personality" because she has the best personality of all the trees in town. It is said that wildlife flock to her tangled web of grape vines, poison ivy, and fringed fungi.[244]

Tunnel Road. This road leads to a tunnel that runs through a mammoth boulder, a reminder of the days when the Shepaug Railroad chugged its way north through the rocky hills to Washington. The train sped through the thirty-rod long tunnel north of Judds Bridge Farm.

Ralph Mumford, a railroad worker, recalled the tunnel and the train that ran through it. The tunnel is longer than most people realize, he said, and it's got a bend in it. The train raced right through the fields and barns and screamed through the long tunnel, he said, and you'd really hear the engine bellow. The roar was deafening. Then the train hurried on to Washington Depot, and quiet returned to Judds Bridge Farm.[245]

Two Rod Highway. Most of this road is in Washington and is barely a driveway in Roxbury. Before either town was settled, the general court addressed the issue of roads and in 1679, with a growing colony, the court urged plantations to clear roads at least a rod wide for the convenience of inhabitants. Perhaps, by the time Washington was settled, townsmen wanted to avoid the attention of the court, so they cleared a road twice the width recommended and centuries later named it Two Rod Highway.[246]

Upper County Road. This road once connected with others that linked Litchfield and New Haven counties. It had an official name in those days, but it may have been part of a raging controversy over county names.

When the Connecticut General Assembly assigned Woodbury to Litchfield County in October 1751, residents were furious; they wanted their own county, they wanted to be the center of it, and they wanted it to be named Woodbury County. Residents seethed and then sent five representatives to petition the assembly again. It's a wonder they bothered—one-hundred years had passed. Residents had calmed down, and though they wanted their representatives to succeed, they didn't allow them to spend any money to plead their case. Naturally, the men failed. The general assembly not only named the town of Litchfield as the county seat, but made Woodbury part of Litchfield County.[247]

Upper Grassy Hill Road. This woodland lane runs off Good Hill Road as a 0.8- mile paved town road. Its name pegs it as being at the higher, more elevated end of Grassy Hill Road where the hill rises to 964 feet near the town line with Woodbury.

Wakelee Road. Roxburians often associate the Wakelee name with the Wakelee Plow sold all over New England, but that Wakelee was from Southbury. Daniel Bronson of Roxbury bought the plow-making company in Southbury and named his company Wakelee and Roxbury Plow. His sons, William and Henry Bronson carried on their father's business after his death. You will find their story in the Bronson Mountain Road story above.

The Roxbury Wakelees that gave their name to this road are descendants of Henry Wakley (1620-1689), who emigrated from Gloucester, England in the 1600s and settled in Stratford. Abner Wakelee (1723-1769), Henry's grandson and first descendant, was born in Roxbury. Family members and public records spelled the surname: Wakelee, Wakeley, Wakley, Wakely, Weaklee, and Weaklin.[248]

One of Abner's grandsons was Abel Wakeley (1760-1850) who, according to local histories, was sixteen when he joined the military, served in numerous campaigns during the American Revolution, claimed to have been an eyewitness to General Benedict Arnold's escape at West Point, and received an Honorable discharge from General George Washington. Abel Wakeley died at the age of ninety, and in his later years, regaled friends with stories of the traitor's escape.[249]

Abel's brother Henry Wakeley also served in the American Revolution, and in October 1780, when British forces viciously attacked Fort George, they took Henry Wakeley prisoner. One source said he was part of Col. Seth Warner's Regiment; another reported that he served in Col. Wait Hinman's Regiment in Capt. Thadeus Lacey's Company.[250]

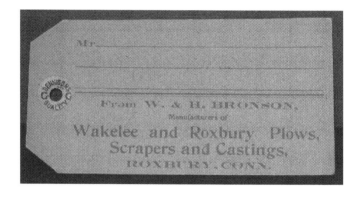

Daniel Wakely, another descendant, accepted two positions— highway surveyor and fence viewer at Roxbury's first town meeting. Often, men who lived on the edge of town were appointed surveyors. In winter, they could clear roads starting from the outskirts of town and work their way to the town center. Beginning at sunrise, a surveyor hitched his yoke of oxen to a plow, broke through snowdrifts to his neighbor's house where his neighbor added his yoke of oxen. Then, they went from neighbor to neighbor until they had collected fifteen or twenty yokes of oxen to hitch to the plow. As the oxen got tired, they would be unhitched, and left to cool down at a farmer's house until the job was finished.

Being a surveyor was backbreaking work, but had its rewards, especially in winter. After a snowfall, highway surveyors were in a hurry to finish clearing the roads. They raced to break out roads leading to the town center and then popped into the nearest tavern. The surveyors caught up on a bit of gossip, downed a few grogs, and pointed their team of oxen toward a school or church as they worked their way back home.[251]

To accept a post as fence viewer was asking for trouble—with people and animals. Cattle and swine liked to crash through fences, destroy crops, and devour gardens. Daniel's job was to make sure that didn't happen. Farmers had a choice—they could keep their cattle in nearby common areas or keep them fenced on their own property. Either way, each man had to work a certain amount of time each year to repair the fences.

Farmers built fences on their own private property. But if a farmer's fence was broken and his cattle crashed through it and devoured his neighbor's cornfield, the farmer had to pay for damages to his neighbor's crops. On the other hand, if a neighbor's cattle crashed through a farmer's sturdy fence, Daniel Wakely fined the neighbor for having unruly and destructive animals.[252]

James Wakeley (b. 1802) was another of Englishman Henry Wakley's descendants to live in Roxbury. In 1850, forty-eight-year-old James lived here with his family. He was a farmer and his eighteen-year-old son worked as a hatter. His farm was valued at $3,000, a substantial amount for the time. By 1870, his real estate and personal wealth totaled $8,000, and that year, he told the census taker to spell his surname Wakelee. James Wakeley's name appeared on an 1874 map; he lived on present-day Wakelee Road.[253] No census after 1870, however, counted a Wakeley family in Roxbury, under any variation of the surname.

The women may have married and changed surnames, and the men may have left in search of jobs after the Civil War.

Walker Brook Road. This rocky, bumpy road stretches less than half-a-mile in Roxbury as it twists along Walker Brook for miles on the western border of Washington. The name is probably from Walker families who lived in that town and were descendants of the Rev. Zechariah Walker (1637-1700) from Stratford.[254]

Washington Woodbury Road. This road connects two towns, and its double town name identifies its location between Washington and Woodbury. It is part of Route 47 that cuts across the northeast corner of Roxbury.

Wellers Bridge Road. Call it the road with many names—Main Street, West Street, and Sanfords Hill. In 1864, it was Main Street when a student wrote about the monument at the corner of Main Street and Bradley Street. That same year, a journalist referred to it as "the principal street of Roxbury."[255]

West Street was one name that stuck for a while. An undated photo in the *Bicentennial Calendar* was captioned West Street. Even in the twentieth century, Mabel B. Smith continued to use the directional name when she told a story to First Selectman Barbara Henry. Smith said she bought a horse with the first money she earned and named him Jack. She harnessed Jack to a sleigh and rode from A. R. Gurney's house on West Street down to the monument green. Another moniker was Sanfords Hill from the Sanford families who owned properties on this road for more than a century.[256]

Its present-day name is from the Weller family, even though none ever lived on this road. In 1712, property was laid out to Englishman Thomas Weller (1680-1751) on Baker Road. He did not build there, but his sons and grandsons did. Little has been written about Thomas who was buried with his wife and eight children in the Weller Cemetery. About 1770, Thomas' eldest son Daniel Weller (d. 1810) built a Cape-style house for his wife and nine children; it remained in the family for four generations. Daniel left the house to his son David Weller who gave it to others and built his own home nearby.

David Weller (1775-1845) was twenty-one when neighbors appointed him one of Roxbury's first surveyors of highways.[257] Even though he inherited the family homestead, he built a Federal-style home next door. An accomplished craftsman, David made the nails and other ironwork by hand in his blacksmith shop. David's son Andrew converted his father's blacksmith shop to a hat factory and worked in the hat making business until 1870. When the hat business was on the wane, Andrew Weller did what many others did and turned to farming.[258]

Other Weller descendants worked in the hat-making business, became farmers, served in the military, and held public office. In spite of all their good works, tragedy struck the Weller family. On May 30, 1814, the public woke up to the *Connecticut Journal* headline, "Horrid Murder." Lieutenant Thomas Weller (1789-1814), an officer in the United States Army, stationed at New Milford, was murdered. It seems Weller allowed the newly enlisted Archibald Warner Knapp to stay at home and work on his farm until his marching orders were delivered, but when the orders arrived and recruits reported for duty, Knapp was missing.

Lt. Weller and others went looking for Knapp and found him at home. When Weller called to Knapp to come out, Knapp said he was ready, but waved a pistol and pointed it at the officer. Weller was not intimidated, but when he stepped forward to take the firearm, Knapp shot him in the groin. The Lieutenant only survived a few hours; he was twenty-five years and nine-months old. He was buried in the Center Cemetery.

The shooting took place on Tuesday, May 14, but after Knapp killed Lt. Weller, he holed up in his house with three pistols and a hunting rifle. Knapp said he intended to kill anyone who tried to take him and would keep shooting until his ammunition ran out. Officers and recruits surrounded his house. Three days after the murder, Knapp was still holding them at bay when the *Connecticut Journal's* informant, a stagecoach driver, left the scene. A later account claimed that Knapp fled to New York and lived there until 1854, when authorities arrested him for killing Lt. Weller. He was not in custody long; a group of his friends from an independent militia company helped him escape.[259]

This road, a long, windy length of black pavement leading from the center to the bridge, has become a danger zone. It's often used as a racetrack for commuters speeding between Southbury and New Milford. A sign with flashing neon lights warns drivers of their excessive speed, but they often remain indifferent to potential tragedy and oblivious to the beautiful landscape around them.

Welton Road. The Eleazor Welton House, built circa 1830, stands at 72 Welton Road, but just how many Eleazor Weltons were associated with the property is a question. Records are confusing because of the variations in surname spellings—Welton and Walton, as well as variations in Christian name spellings— Eleazor, Eleazar, and Eleazer. According to public records, one Eleazer Welton was married to Nancy W.; another was married to Maria B.; yet another was married to Delia. But were they all the same man with several wives or were they different men?[260]

Homes of Old Woodbury stated that the house belonged to Eleazer Welton and that his widow, Nancy W. Welton, left the twenty-four-acre property to their son, William. Then, in 1873, William deeded it to a later Eleazer Welton. Nancy W. was the daughter of Syrenus Ward.[261] Connecticut marriage records listed Eleazer Welton and Adelia Beers as having been married in Woodbury on February 16, 1849 and living in Roxbury.[262]

The surname Welton first appeared in Roxbury census records in 1850 when Eleazar Welton told the census taker that he was born about 1806 in Connecticut, was a forty-four-year-old farmer, and owned property valued at $2,000. His household included Maria B., twenty-six, and children Harriett, Ellen, and Maria. The census did not indicate whether they were a wife and three daughters, four daughters, or four unrelated people. That same year, the census taker recorded four-year-old William W. Welton as living in Roxbury with Syrenus Ward's family.

The following census, taken in 1860, listed Eleazer Walton as a fifty-one-year-old farmer, born about 1809, with real estate valued at $1,500 and personal assets valued at $400. His household included thirty-three-year-old Delia and children: Helen K., Delia M., George W., and Jennie who ranged in age from four to sixteen. William W. was thirteen years old and living in another family.

In 1870, Eleazer Welton, now sixty-one, listed himself as a farmer, stonemason, and property owner. He was living with Delia, forty-four, and Jennie, twelve, who was in school. His total assets had increased to $5,250.

The 1880 census did not list Eleazer Welton, but it did name William W. Welton and J. E. Welton. William, a farmer, thirty-three, was married and living in Roxbury. Twenty-four-year-old Jennie Welton, listed as J. E. Welton, was divorced and doing housework in a neighbor's home.

There may have been only one Eleazor after all. His son William may not have sold the house in 1873 to another Eleazor Welton, but rather the conveyance may simply have been a quitclaim of his rights. Moreover, the most reasonable explanation for the confusion about Eleazor Welton is that after his wife, Nancy W., died, Welton left his son William in the care of his grandfather Syrenus Ward. Eleazor later remarried Adelia "Delia" Beers.[263]

West Flag Swamp Road. The Flag Swamp Road story above tells the name origin of this road that was marked as a thin squiggly line on an 1874 map. Today, it is a narrow path, less than a mile long, barely wide enough for a single car. It winds through forests, brooks, and pristine wetlands.

West Mountain Lane. The mountain was named for its location west of Woodbury and was first named in Woodbury land records in the 1600s. In the late 1900s, developers laid the road to access newly built houses on the hill. In 1975, a mapmaker named the hill Woodbury Ski Hill.[264] The private unpaved lane runs north and south off Painter Hill Road.

Willow Brook Drive. This name, given by Willow Brook Associates, gives the impression that a brook named Willow is nearby, but the bridge at the entrance crosses a branch of Jacks Brook. The private unpaved road climbs 0.2 miles off Bacon Road.

Notes

Introduction

1. Cothren, *History of Ancient Woodbury,* 1854. 1:276; Hurlbut, *Roxbury's Early Days,* 3.

2. *Colonial Connecticut Records, 1636-1776.* 8: 337, 537-538 and 9:16, 61.

3. The General Court was later named the General Assembly. For the sake of clarity, I will retain the earlier name when referring to this body.

4. Stewart, *Names on the Land,* 44.

5. *Colonial Connecticut Records, 1636-1776.* 8:537-538.

6. Stewart, *Names on the Land,* 49.

7. Sellers, *Connecticut Town Origins,* 70.

8. For a detailed discussion of place-name classifications, see Stewart, *Names on the Globe.*

Chapter 1. A Glimpse of the Past

1. Cothren, *History of Ancient Woodbury,* 1854. 1: 24-29.

2. Ibid., 39.

3. *Colonial Connecticut Records, 1636-1776.* 7: 362; 8:537-538.

4. *The Shepaug Railroad, 1872-1948,* 4-5.

5. "Roxbury," *Woodbury Reporter,* Jan. 2, Feb. 22, July 2, Aug. 2, 1879.

6. *Roxbury Past & Present,* 5.

Chapter 2. Gone But Not Forgotten

1   Hughes and Allen, *Connecticut Place Names*, 489; Barber, *Connecticut Historical Collections,* 485; *Colonial Connecticut Records, 1636-1776.* 9:200.

2   Early American Newspapers, *Danbury Gazette*, Oct. 26, 1813, 3; New York Genealogy & Biographical Society. http://www.newyorkfamilyhistory.org/

3   Cunningham, *Architectural Resource Survey,* 90; Hughes and Allen, *Connecticut Place Names*, 489.

4   Ungeheuer, *Roxbury Remembered*, 3; *U. S. Federal Census*, 1860.

5   *Brien E. Tierney Preserve* pamphlet (n. p.: Roxbury Land Trust, n. d.).

6   "Roxbury Trees Have Personality, Too," *Voices*, Nov. 12, 2003.

7   Humphrey, *Sketches,* 26; Hughes and Allen, *Connecticut Place Names*, 489.

8   Cunningham, *Architectural Resource Survey,* 171; *Roxbury Cookery*, 299.

9   *Litchfield Monitor,* Sept. 29, 1788, 3.

10   *U. S. Federal Censuses*, 1790-1880.

11   Hurlbut, *Roxbury's Early Days,* 40-41; "Roll of Representatives," *Connecticut Mirror*, Apr. 10, 1830, 3; *U. S. Federal Census* 1830, 1840.

12   "Rambles in Roxbury," *New Milford Gazette*, May 18, 1894; Deborah B. Donnelly, "Castle Street Lost in Pages of History," *Country Life,* June 6, 2002.

13   Cunningham, *Architectural Resource Survey*, 142-144.

14   Ungeheuer, *Roxbury Remembered*, 115.

15   Hughes and Allen, *Connecticut Place Names*, 489.

16   Cothren, *History of Ancient Woodbury*, 1872. 2: 852.

17   Ungeheuer, *Roxbury Remembered*, 3.

18   Humphrey, *Sketches,* 39; "Roxbury Station," *New Milford Gazette,* Apr. 7, 1899.

19   Cothren, *History of Ancient Woodbury,* 1854. 1: 29-30.

20   Humphrey, *Sketches,* 39.

21   *Woodbury Reporter,* Mar. 14, 1878; Ella Pierce diary, entry dated April 2, 1877.

22   Crescent Lodge No. 243 handbooks; *Quarterly return Nov. 1, 1886-Jan. 31, 1887.*

23   Orcutt, *History of the Towns of New Milford and Bridgewater,* 1882, 482-486; "Roxbury," *New Milford Gazette and Housatonic Ray,* Sept. 3 and 10, 1886.

24   *Roxbury Land Records,* 1828. 7:45 and 1828. 7:281.

25   Deborah B. Donnelly, "Castle Street Lost in Pages of History," *Country Life,* June 6, 2002.

26   *Roxbury Land Records,* 1829. 6: 291; Hughes and Allen, *Connecticut Place Names,* 489.

27   Marian Skedgell, conversation, summer 2005.

28   *Homes of Old Woodbury,* 252.

29   "Was It Murder?" *New Milford Gazette,* April 7, 1893; "The Mannering Trial," *New Milford Gazette,* Dec. 1, 1893.

30   "Glenacres School Roxbury, Connecticut," brochure; "Headmaster Closes School to Study for Ministry...," *Sunday Republican Magazine* (Waterbury, Conn.), June 1939.

31   *Roxbury Land Records,* 1808, 3:399 and 1828, 7:122.

32   Hughes and Allen, *Connecticut Place Names,* 489.

33   *Homes of Old Woodbury,* 234.

34   *Roxbury Land Records,* 1799. 1:484.

35   Sloane, *Diary of an Early American Boy,* 30-31.

36 U. S. Board on Geographic Names. http://geonames.usgs.gov/ domestic/monthly minutes.htm. See Minutes from July 14, 2005 meeting; Arthur Miller, letter to Barbara Henry, First Selectman. Stamped "Received Nov. 01 1998."

37 Cothren, *History of Ancient Woodbury*, 1854. 1: 363-364; 1872. 2: 852; Humphrey, *Sketches*, 6.

38 "Haunting Documentary Preserves Legend of Mysterious Leatherman," *The Hour (Norwalk)*, July 5, 1984; "Roxbury," *New Milford Gazette and Housatonic Ray*, June 18, 1886.

39 Jack Conway, "The Unhappy Wanderer," *Sunday Republican Magazine* (Waterbury, Conn.), Feb. 26, 1967.

40 *Roxbury Land Records*, 1798. 1:455.

41 *Homes of Old Woodbury*, 234.

42 Hurlbut, *Roxbury's Early Days,* 3; Cothren, *History of Ancient Woodbury,* 1854. 1: 274.

43 Ungeheuer, *Roxbury Remembered*, 3.

44 George Greenfield, "Rod and Gun," *New York Times*, Dec. 4, 1934, 26; Cunningham, *Architectural Resource Survey*, 102-103.

45 Hughes and Allen, *Connecticut Place Names,* 490.

46 New Hampshire Fish & Game Dept. http://www.wildlife.state. nh.us/Wildlife/ Wildlife_profiles/profile_moose.htm

47 *Roxbury Land Records*, May 5, 1802, 1: 367; Hughes and Allen, *Connecticut Place Names,* 490.

48 Hurlbut, *Roxbury's Early Days,* 3.

49 Cothren, *History of Ancient Woodbury,* 1854. 1: 25.

50 Marie White, "Roxbury Museum Opens Saturday for two-day run," *Republican-American* (Waterbury, Conn.), July 21, 1978; Debra Myers, "Old Roxbury Days Returns," *Voices*, July 22, 1998.

51 Hughes and Allen, *Connecticut Place Names*, 490.

52 Ibid., *Register and Manual of the State of Connecticut*, 1901, 371.

53 *Homes of Old Woodbury*, 224.

54 Cothren, *History of Ancient Woodbury*, 1854. 1:20; Hughes and Allen, *Connecticut Place Names*, 490.

55 Ungeheuer, *Roxbury Remembered*, 118.

56 Humphrey, *Sketches,* 7; Lenney, *Sightseeking,* 64-65.

57 *Roxbury Town Meeting Minutes*, Mar. 10, 1910, Book 20: 146.

58 Deborah B. Donnelly, "A Look at Roxbury's Rock of Ages," *Republican-American* (Waterbury, Conn.), Jan. 10, 2002.

59 Hurlbut, *Roxbury's Early Days,* 56; Humphrey, *Sketches*, 8. John Eliot lived nearly sixty years in Roxbury, Massachusetts and I found no record that he ever visited Roxbury, Connecticut.

60 "Roxbury Flower Show, Aug. 20," *New Milford Times*, Aug. 13, 1942, 1.

61 Humphrey. *Sketches,* 39.

62 "Litchfield, Nov. 5," *Connecticut Journal*, Nov. 5, 1787; Cothren, *History of Ancient Woodbury*, 1854. 1: 282.

63 *Norwich Packet*, Jan. 17, 1793, 3.

64 *Weekly Monitor*, Dec. 21 and 28, 1793, 3.

65 Scott Oglesby's Web site. http://www.kurumi.com/roads/ct/.

66 Ibid.

67 "Roxbury," *New Milford Gazette*, June 17 and Nov. 25, 1910.

68 "Rambles in Roxbury," *New Milford Gazette*, May 4, 1894.

69 *Roxbury Land Records*, Apr. 14, 1798. 1: 455.

70 Humphrey, *Sketches,* 31; Cunningham, *Architectural Resource Survey,* 201-202.

71 *Roxbury Cookery*, 299.

72 Cothren, *History of Ancient Woodbury*, 1854. 1: 25-26; Hughes and Allen, *Connecticut Place Names*, 491.

73 Hull, *Bewitched Mine Hill*, 28.

74   Cunningham, *Architectural Resource Survey,* 24, 58.

75   Hurlbut, *Roxbury's Early Days,* 3.

76   Deborah B. Donnelly, "Jack's Brook once powered Roxbury industry," *Country Life,* May 12, 2005; Hurlbut, *Roxbury's Early Days,* 43.

77   Cothren, *History of Ancient Woodbury,* 1854. 1: 274-276.

78   Ungeheuer, *Roxbury Remembered,* 3; Hurlbut, *Roxbury's Early Days,* 41.

79   Cothren, *History of Ancient Woodbury,* 1872. 2: 852; *Roxbury Land Records,* 1800. 2: 227; 1805. 2: 323.

Chapter 3. Water, Water Everywhere

1   Cothren, *History of Ancient Woodbury,* 1854. 1:74; 1872. 2: 851; Humphrey, *Sketches,* 7.

2   Cothren, *History of Ancient Woodbury,* 1854. 1:153; 1872. 2: 852; Humphrey, *Sketches,* 6.

3   *Roxbury Land Records,* 1796. 1: 286; Roxbury Land Trust Web site. http://www.roxburylandtrust.org/study.html.

4   *Roxbury Cookery,* 291.

5   Sterry and Garrigus, *They Found a Way,* 169; Humphrey, *Sketches,* 6; *Roxbury Cookery,* 11-12.

6   Cunningham, *Architectural Resource Survey,* 111, 169.

7   Hughes and Allen, *Connecticut Place Names,* 707.

8   Cothren, *History of Ancient Woodbury,* 1879. 3: 646; "A Confederate Soldier from Connecticut," *Sunday Republican Magazine,* Mar. 11, 1984.

9   Hughes and Allen, *Connecticut Place Names,* 489.

10   Timothy Beard, telephone conversation with author, Jan. 15, 2005.

11   Cothren, *History of Ancient Woodbury,* 1872. 2: 852.

12 *Woodbury Town Records*, 1693. 1: 42; 1:355.

13 Cothren, *History of Ancient Woodbury*, 1872. 2: 852; *Centennial Celebration at Roxbury, Connecticut July Fourth A. D. 1876,* 14.

14 Roxbury Assessor, *1992 Grand List of Real Estate and Personal Property*, 58.

15 Charles "Bud" Squire, conversation with author, Mar. 14, 2005.

16 Hughes and Allen, *Connecticut Place Names,* 489 and 490; Humphrey*, Sketches*, 7.

17 *U. S. Federal Census*, 1850 and 1860, Fairfield, CT.

18 *U.S. Civil War Soldier Records and Profiles; New York Passenger Lists, 1820-1957.* http:// www.ancestry.com.

19 *Roxbury Land Records*, 1890-1906; *Roxbury Annual Report*, years ending Sept. 28, 1890, 1 and Sept. 26, 1891, 2.

20 Bell and Mayerfeld, *Time and the Land*, 15.

21 Cothren, *History of Ancient Woodbury*, 1854. 1:87; Hurlbut, *Roxbury's Early Days,* 44.

22 Humphrey*, Sketches*, 6.

23 "Rambles in Roxbury," *New Milford Gazette*, May 25, 1894.

24 *Roxbury Land Records*, 1799. 1:149.

25 "Roxbury." *New Milford Gazette*, May 25, 1894.

26 *Roxbury Town Meeting Minutes*, Apr. 8, 1983. 5:86; *Roxbury Annual Report*, July 1, 2002-June 30, 2003, 40.

27 *Roxbury Annual Report*, fiscal ending June 30, 1976.

28 U. S. Geological Survey Map, Roxbury, Conn., 1955; Peter Hurlbut conversation with author, July 13, 2009.

29 Cothren, *History of Ancient Woodbury*, 1872. 2:798.

30 Ibid., 1854. 2: 847.

31 Jackie Dooley, conversation with author, Mar. 18, 2005; Mary Weaver, conversation with author, Jan. 28, 2005.

32 Sellers, *Connecticut Town Origins*, 70; Cothren, *History of Ancient Woodbury*, 1872. 2: 846.

33 Shepaug Organization. http://www.shepaug org/.

34 Romania Tourist Office Web site. http://www.romaniatourism.com/did-you-know.html.

35 Cothren, *History of Ancient Woodbury*, 1854. 1: 41; 2: 721.

36 *U. S. Federal Census*, 1850-1910; Beers, *County Atlas of Litchfield Connecticut*, 67.

37 Boyd and Boyd, *Roxbury Inscriptions*, Oct. 16, 1910, 11; Cunningham, *Architectural Resource Survey*, 110.

38 Cunningham, *Architectural Resource Survey*, 37.

39 *U. S. Federal Census*, 1850, New Milford, CT.; Cunningham, *Architectural Resource Survey*, 141.

40 "Rambles in Roxbury," *New Milford Gazette*, May 25, 1894; Boyd and Boyd, *Roxbury Inscriptions*, Oct. 16, 1910, 11.

41 "Pollution Persists in Second Test of Spring Water," *The Star*, July 4, 1992.

Chapter 4. Bridges Over Rushing Waters

1 *Roxbury Annual Report*, July 1, 2003-July 1, 2004, 9.

2 John Addyman, "Roxbury Bridge to Honor Founding Family," *Voices*, July 16, 2003.

3 Ungeheuer, *Roxbury Remembered*, 21.

4 John Addyman, "Roxbury Bridge to Honor Founding Family," *Voices*, July 16, 2003.

5 *Roxbury Annual Report*, year ending June 30, 1979; July 1, 2003-July 1, 2004, 10.

6 Ibid.; Cunningham, *Architectural Resource Survey*, 102.

7 *Roxbury Annual Report*, July 1, 2001-June 30, 2002,11.

8   Hurlbut, *Roxbury's Early Days,* 38.

9   Ibid., 40-41.

10   "Roxbury," *Housatonic Ray,* Oct. 8, 1881; "Drought of 1881,"
     New York Times, Oct. 21, 1881.

11   *New Milford Gazette and Housatonic Ray,* July 2, 1886.

12   *Roxbury Annual Report,* year ending Sept. 16, 1915 to Sept. 16,
     1916, 8.

13   *Roxbury Annual Report,* year ending Aug. 31, 1956, 4; year ending
     Aug. 31, 1958, 4.

Chapter 5. Cemeteries, Memorials, Quiet Places

1   Worthington, *Roxbury Cemeteries 1745-1934,* I; "Rambles in
     Roxbury," *New Milford Gazette,* May 4, 1894.

2   Cothren, *History of Ancient Woodbury,* 1854. 1: 65; Worthington,
     Roxbury Cemeteries 1745-1934, viii.

3   Ungeheuer, *Roxbury Remembered,* 186.

4   Gleason lived in Terryville and Bristol, Connecticut in the
     1930s and worked for the Emergency Relief Agency, part of the
     Works Progress Administration (WPA). He may have copied the
     inscriptions as part that project. *U. S. Federal Census,* 1931-1935.

5   Boyd and Boyd, *Roxbury Inscriptions,* Oct. 30, 1910, 19.

6   Leavenworth, Elias Warner. *A Genealogy of the Leavenworth Family
     in the United States.* Syracuse: S. G. Hitchcock, 1873, 81-82.

7   Cothren, *History of Ancient Woodbury,* 1854. 1: 204 and 208.

8   Barbara Mathews, e-mail to author, Oct. 24, 2004. Mathews'
     gave her source as the Charles R. Hale *Collection of Connecticut
     Headstone Inscriptions,* Town of Roxbury, Hartford, Dec. 1937, p.
     54. She noted that the Hale source indicated Morse Leavenworth
     was buried in Center Cemetery. (Hale, p. 19).

9   Jim Green, conversation with author, Summer, 2004; James Martin, conversation with author, Summer, 2007.

10 Charles M. "Bud" Squire, telephone conversation with author, Jan. 10, 2007.

11 Mary Jonker, conversation with author, June 22, 2006.

12 Marie Swanson, conversation with author, Mar. 20, 2007.

13 Worthington, *Roxbury Cemeteries 1745-1934*, ix.

14 Cothren, *History of Ancient Woodbury*, 1879. 3: 641.

15 Pepin, "Cemetery Inscriptions."

16 Hurlbut, *Roxbury's Early Days*, 35 called him "Seneca Durling"; In Civil War Pension Records, his name was "Seneca Durlin;" *U. S. Federal Census*, 1880, "Chas. S. Derling;" *U. S. Federal Census*, 1900, "Charles Derling." His wife, Maria's surname was "Derling" in the *U. S. Federal Census*, 1900 and Maria P. "Dearling" in the *U. S. Federal Census*, 1910.

17 Roxbury Town Clerk's office. *Marriage Certificates*, 1869-1940; *Roxbury Land Records*, 1886. 17: 92.

18 *American Civil War Soldiers; Civil War Pension Index: General Index to Pension Files, 1861-1934.* http:// www.ancestry.com.

19 "Parish Profile: Christ Church, Roxbury, CT." unpaged brochure; copies of Christ Church correspondence and papers provided to the author by Carolyn Goodrich on July 10, 2009.

20 Denise Dowling, "Stalwart oak rooted in town's past," *New Milford Times,* Aug. 18, 1994.

21 Peter Hurlbut, conversation with author, Jan. 25, 2007.

22 Worthington, *Roxbury Cemeteries 1745-1934,* vii.

23 "Rambles in Roxbury," *New Milford Gazette*, May 18, 1894.

24 Tracey Andrews, telephone conversation with author, Jan. 16, 2005.

25 Worthington, *Roxbury Cemeteries 1745-1934,* xiii.

26 Gen. Walter Harriman, "Seth Warner," *The New England Historical & Genealogical Register*, Boston: New England Historic, Genealogical Society 1880. 34: 363-370; "Rambles in Roxbury," *New Milford Gazette*, May 4, 1894.

27 *Centennial Celebration at Roxbury, Connecticut July Fourth A. D. 1876,* 11; Worthington, *Roxbury Cemeteries 1745-1934,* vi-vii.

28 Worthington, *Roxbury Cemeteries 1745-1934,* xiii.

29 Keith Eddings, "Forgotten hero of Revolution gets belated honors," *News Times*, Feb. 24, 1995.

30 Worthington, *Roxbury Cemeteries 1745-1934,* ii.

31 "Rambles in Roxbury," *New Milford Gazette*, May 25, 1894.

32 "Cemetery Fence Gets Needed Attention," *The Star*, Sept. 12, 1992.

33 Cathy Shufro, "Roxbury's Cemeteries Yield Glimpses of Past," *News Times,* Feb. 14, 1977.

34 Worthington, *Roxbury Cemeteries 1745-1934,* v.

35 Kevin Falconer's report and photographs of all headstones in the Weller Cemetery are in the Roxbury Town Clerk's office.

36 Deborah B. Donnelly, "Eagle Scout Project Includes Raising the Dead," *Republican-American* (Waterbury, Conn.), Nov. 9, 2006.

Chapter 6. Parks and Gardens

1 *Roxbury Land Records*, Oct. 2, 1965. 27: 406; Roxbury Planning Commission. *Roxbury, 1999 Plan of Conservation & Development*, 41.

2 Ungeheuer, *Roxbury Remembered*, 142.

3 John Addyman, "Hodge Park Neighbors Bring Concerns to Board," *Voices Weekender*, Sept. 11, 2005.

4 *Roxbury Town Meeting Minutes*, Sept. 30, 1963, 121.

5 *Roxbury Annual Report,* year ending Aug. 31, 1958, 4.

Chapter 7. Places to Worship and Rest

1   "Roxbury," *Housatonic Ray*, Oct. 8, 1881.

2   "Village and Vicinity – Notes and Gleanings," *New Milford Gazette*, Apr. 27, 1894.

3   *Centennial Celebration at Roxbury, Connecticut July Fourth, A. D. 1876*, 8.

4   Cunningham, *Architectural Resource Survey*, 22, 120; Beers, *County Atlas of Litchfield Connecticut*, 67.

5   *Centennial Celebration at Roxbury, Connecticut July Fourth, A. D. 1876*, 8; Cothren, *History of Ancient Woodbury*, 1854. 1: 298.

6   Cothren, *History of Ancient Woodbury*, 1854. 1: 292.

7   *Ancient Woodbury Tercentenary*, 51.

8   Hurlbut, *Roxbury's Early Days*, 50.

9   *Ancient Woodbury Tercentenary*, 51.

10   "Church History ," unpublished notes by Margot Judge; "Roxbury," *New Milford Gazette and Housatonic Ray*, June 5, 1885; Mar. 12, 1886.

11   "Christ Church Marks 200 Years in Roxbury," *New York Times*, June 17, 1940.

12   Cothren, *History of Ancient Woodbury*, 1854. 1: 282.

13   Ven. Lewis N. Tillson, "Alter Marks Old Church Site," *The Sunday Waterbury Republican*, Sept. 5, 1965, 7.

14   "Christ Church, Roxbury," unpublished notes by the Rev. Lewis N. Tillson and Timothy Field Beard.

15   "Miss Beigneux of Roxbury, A Pulitzer Prize Winner," *New Milford Times* May 8, 1941; "Christ Church, Roxbury," unpublished notes by the Rev. Lewis N. Tillson and Timothy Field Beard; Web site of Connecticut Society of Portrait Artists. http://www.csopa.camp8.org/.

16   *Roxbury Past & Present*, 64-65.

17   "Church History," unpublished notes by Margot Judge; "Christ Church, Roxbury," unpublished notes by the Rev. Lewis N. Tillson and Timothy Field Beard.

18   Fay, *Historical Sketch Roxbury Congregational Church, 1744-1944*, 24.

19   Worthington, *History of the Roxbury Congregational Church,1673-1974*, unpublished notes.

20   "Chapel May Have New Role," *Voices,* Sept. 16, 1981; "Roxbury on the Move: The History of Roxbury's Many Traveling Buildings,"1999.

21   "Rambles in Roxbury," *New Milford Gazette*, May 4, 1894; June 1, 1894.

22   Fay, *Historical Sketch Roxbury Congregational Church, 1744-1944*, 21.

23   "Rambles in Roxbury," *New Milford Gazette*, May 18, 1894.

24   Fay, *Historical Sketch Roxbury Congregational Church, 1744-1944*, 23.

25   "Rambles in Roxbury," *New Milford Gazette*, May 18, 1894.

26   Fay, *Historical Sketch Roxbury Congregational Church, 1744-1944*, 26-27.

27   Ibid., 24.

28   Worthington, *History of the Roxbury Congregational Church...1673-1974*, unpublished notes.

29   *Roxbury Past & Present*, 40-41; 46-47.

30   "Rambles in Roxbury," *New Milford Gazette*, May 11, 1894.

31   Deborah B. Donnelly. "Bears appear to find Roxbury pickings 'just right,"*Country Life*, Apr. 28, 2005, 5.

32   Cunningham, *Architectural Resource Survey*, 151.

33   *Centennial Celebration at Roxbury, Connecticut July Fourth, A. D. 1876,* 8-9; Humphrey, *Sketches*, 12.

34   Deborah B. Donnelly. "A modern view, Roxbury streetscape has changed," *Country Life*, Oct. 4, 2001.

35   Ungeheuer, *Roxbury Remembered*, 3, 8.

36   "Rambles in Roxbury," *New Milford Gazette*, May 11, 1894.

37   *New Milford Times,* Feb. 2, 1914.

38   *Ancient Woodbury Tercentenary,* 52.

39   Earle, *The Sabbath in Puritan New England*, 102-106.

40   Fay, *Historical Sketch Roxbury Congregational Church, 1744-1944*, 22.

41   Cothren, *History of Ancient Woodbury*, 1872. 2: 1416; *Ancient Woodbury Tercentenary*, 51; Cunningham, *Architectural Resource Survey*, 80, 15.

42   "Roxbury," *New Milford Gazette and Housatonic Ray,* July 9, 1886; Amy Biancolli, "Roxbury Church Celebrates 100th Among Friends," *Litchfield County Times*, Aug. 23, 1985.

43   Claire La Fleur, "Church to celebrate centennial," *Waterbury Republican,* Aug. 25, 1985; *Roxbury Past and Present*, 30-31.

44   "Church wants to use school facility…," *Republican-American* (Waterbury, Conn.), Nov. 9, 2004.

45   Harry Ong, interview with author, May 19, 2009.

Chapter 8. Roxbury's Land Trust – Preserving a Necklace of Green

1   John Addyman, "Land Trust Building Necklace of Green," *Voices*, June 23, 2004.

2   "Roxbury Land Trust Receives Gift," *Voices*, Mar. 15, 2006, 34; "Roxbury Land Trust,"(Summer, 2005), 3.

3   "Roxbury Land Trust Properties Total 1,356 Acres," *Focus on Roxbury Land Trust* (Spring, 1992), 2; *Roxbury Land Trust Since 1970* (Summer, 2005).

4   For a history of the Roxbury Land Trust, maps and descriptions of preserves, see their Web site at www.roxburylandtrust.org and Roxbury Land Trust Preserves Map, 2nd edition, (Roxbury, CT: RLT, 2005).

5   Baldwin, Sherman. *Growing Up with Harry, Stories of Character*. New York: iUniverse, 2008.

6   "Roxbury Land Trust," (Roxbury, CT, 1979).

7   *Roxbury Land Trust since 1970*, (Summer, 2005), 2-3.

8   National Archives and Records Administration Web site. http://www.archives.gov/research/vietnam-war/casualty-lists/ct-alpha.html; Tierney's platoon leader's Web site. http://peninsulapen.blogspot.com/2008/05/1968.html.

9   "Land Trust Receives Gift," *Voices*, Jan. 21, 1998.

10   John Addyman, "Land Trust Building Necklace of Green," *Voices*, June 23, 2004.

11   Ibid.

12   "Land Trust Picnic This Weekend," *Voices Weekender*, Sept. 19, 2004, 10.

13   Barbara Loecher, "Happy landings at Good Hill…," *News Times*, Dec. 30, 1991.

14   "Roxbury Land Trust Receives Gift," *Voices*, Mar. 15, 2006, 34.

15   "Roxbury Land Trust," (Roxbury, CT, 1979).

16   "Rambles in Roxbury," *New Milford Gazette*, May 25, 1894.

17   Julie Steers, e-mail to author, Nov. 20, 2006.

18   "The Lilly Preserve," *Roxbury Land Trust*, (RLT, n. d.).

19   Deborah B. Donnelly, "Walter Matthau's Wish Benefits Roxbury," *The Sunday Republican* (Waterbury, Conn.), Aug. 29, 1999, 1b-2b.

20   "Miller Land Given to Roxbury Land Trust," *New Milford Spectrum*, Nov. 18, 2005; "Miller Estate Thinks of Roxbury…" *Republican-American* (Waterbury, Conn.), Nov. 15, 2005.

21   Roxbury Land Trust Web site. *Time and the Land* and other detailed information about Mine Hill can be found at http://www.roxburylandtrust.org/.

22   "Mine Hill Time Line," *Roxbury Land Trust Since 1970*, (Summer, 2005), 3; "Mine Hill Preserve," *Roxbury Land Trust*, (1983), 1-4.

23   "Land Trust Will Unveil Signs at Roxbury's Mine Hill Preserve," *Voices*, June 6, 2007, 13; *Mine Hill Preserve Trail Map*, printed spring 2008.

24   "Beardsley and Humphrey Preserves and Moosehorn Access," *Focus on Roxbury Land Trust* (Spring, 1994), 3.

25   "The Natalie White Preserve," *Focus on Roxbury Land Trust* (Spring, 1992), 1.

26   Jessica Dyson, "Agreement Would Save Roxbury Farmland," *New Milford Times*, Mar. 15, 2002.

27   Jamie Curren, *A Guide to Fishing at River's Edge Preserve on Lake Lillinonah*" (n. p., 2006); "Project Gets Shepaug Teen Closer to the Fish," *Republican-American* (Waterbury, Conn.), May 23, 2006.

28   "The River Road Preserve," *Roxbury Land Trust*, (RLT, n. d.), 1-4.

29   Rebecca Ransom, "Shepaug Student Works to Restore a Schoolhouse in Roxbury," *Litchfield County Times*, Apr. 21, 2006.

30   "Land Trust Receives Gift," *Voices Weekender*, Dec. 19, 2004, 3.

Chapter 9. Roxbury Center

1   National Register of Historic Places Web site. www.nationalregisterofhistoricplaces.com/ct/Litchfield/districts.html.

2   Cunningham, *Architectural Resource Survey; Roxbury Past and Present*.

3   *Roxbury Annual Report*, year ending June 30, 1997, 10.

4   Humphrey, *Sketches*, 21.

5   "Roxbury's Ranking Citizen, Liberal Donor to Town Needs," *Republican-American* (Waterbury, Conn.), May 17, 1936.

6   "Roxbury," *New Milford Gazette and Housatonic Ray,* Feb. 19, 1886.

7   "Smiths Donate Land for Roxbury Library," *Voices*, Dec. 1988.

8   *Roxbury Annual Report*, July 1, 2007-June 30, 2008, inside cover.

9   *Roxbury Annual Report*, July 1, 2001-June 30, 2002, 11.

10   Joan LoBiondo, "Old Betsy, Roxbury firemen begin moving to new home," *News Times*, June 4, 1976.

11   John Addyman, "Roxbury Bridge to Honor Founding Family," *Voices*, July 16, 2003; *Roxbury Historical Society News*, Spring, 2003.

12   Marie White, "Cultivating an Interest in the Past," *Sunday Republican Magazine* (Waterbury, Conn.), Nov. 7, 1976.

13   Barbara Loecher, "Roxbury Gives Old Barn New Lease on Life," *News Times*, Dec. 14, 1990; Elizabeth Berner, "Roxbury Group Plans a Museum to Exhibit Antique Tools of Toil," *Litchfield County Times*, Dec. 18, 1990.

14   Deborah B. Donnelly, "Roxbury Native's Craftsmanship Opens Door to History," *Country Life*, Aug. 3, 2006.

15   Lewis Hurlbut, "A Couple of Points of History," *The Star*, June 22, 1991.

16   White, Marie, "History of Roxbury Shepaug Club," Oct. 12, 1996; *Roxbury Annual Report*, July 1, 2002-June 30, 2003.

17   The first mention of lights in the Town Hall was a payment to Connecticut Light and Power. *Roxbury Annual Report*, Sept. 15, 1925-Sept. 15, 1926.

18   Cunningham, *Architectural Resource Survey,* 149.

19   Robert Piasecki, "Larger town hall on town's horizon," *News Times*, Oct. 8, 1989; "New Town Hall Dedicated," *Voices*, Oct. 1991.

Chapter 10. Road Stories

1 Hurlbut, *Roxbury's Early Days*, 42.

2 Donna Nash, e-mail to author, Dec. 23, 2004.

3 Archytech.org. Web site. http://www.arcytech.org/java/population/facts_oaks.html.

4 *Roxbury Land Records*, Apr. 8, 1971. 33:332.

5 *Roxbury Property Maps*. vol. 11, map 9-47; map 16-77.

6 Peter Wooster, e-mail to author, Oct. 16, 2004.

7 Robert Lowe, conversation with author, May 20, 2005.

8 Ibid.

9 Jack Reelick, telephone conversation with author, Feb. 20, 2005.

10 "N. Beardsley of Roxbury Passes Away," *New Milford Times*, Sept. 23, 1943.

11 James Martin, conversation with author, Apr. 6, 2005.

12 del Po, *It Was a Way of Life*, unpaged.

13 See copies of Percy Peck Beardsley's draft registration cards. On June 5, 1917, he requested an exemption because he was superintendent of the family farm. Twenty-five years later, his World War II registration card noted that he was self-employed and named Nathan Beardsley as the person "who will always know your address." Percy signed only his first and last name. *U. S. World War I Draft Registration Cards, 1917-1918* and *U. S. World War II Draft Registration Cards, 1942*. http://www.ancestry.com.

14 Ungeheuer, *Roxbury Remembered*, 35.

15 James Martin, conversation with author, Apr. 6, 2005; Ungeheuer, *Roxbury Remembered,* 35.

16 Charles "Bud" Squire, telephone conversation with author, Mar. 18, 2005.

17 Ibid.

18 Joseph B. Stephens, "Roxbury Cider King," *Sunday Republican Weekly*, Apr. 21, 1963, 5.

19 "Morse on Beardsley: An Amazing Man," *Waterbury Republican*, July 1, 1954.

20 Charles "Bud" Squire, conversation with author, Mar. 14, 2005.

21 Photograph is in a collection of "Maroon Books" at the Roxbury Minor Memorial Library. The article was undated, but appears to be from the wedding reception held at Curtis House in Woodbury, Connecticut.

22 Rumford, *American Folk Portraits.*

23 "Frederick Bacon," *New Milford Times*, Mar. 11, 1943; Roxbury Probate Court. Probate file.

24 *U. S. Federal Census*, 1860-1870 and 1910-1920.

25 *Roxbury Land Records*, Dec. 31, 1943. 26: 374.

26 *U. S. Federal Census*, 1870 for Danbury under name Lorenzo Bacon; *U S. City Directories, Danbury, Connecticut, Webb's Danbury Directory, 1885-6*, 38. http:// www.ancestry.com.

27 Cothren, *History of Ancient Woodbury*, 1854. 2: 502-504. Genealogy of the Baker family.

28 Ungeheuer, *Roxbury Remembered*, 85; Cunningham, *Architectural Resource Survey,* 147.

29 Cothren, *History of Ancient Woodbury,* 1854. 1:157; 2:503.

30 Arlington,Vt. http://www.thisisvermont.com/story/arlistory.html; Hurlbut, *Roxbury's Early Days,* 23.

31 *American Revolution Bicentennial, 1776-1976;* Cothren, *History of Ancient Woodbury,* 1854. 1: 427.

32 Stewart, *American Place Names*, 37.

33 Phil de Vries, telephone conversation with author, May 12, 2005.

34 Dana Shulman, telephone conversation with author, Jan. 26, 2005.

35 *Roxbury Land Records*, 1801. 2:142.

36 Ed Lang, "Bear reported touring Roxbury," *Waterbury Republican*, Friday, June 4, 1976.

37 Deborah B. Donnelly, "Bears appear to find Roxbury pickings 'just right," *Country Life*, Apr. 28, 2005, 5.

38 *Roxbury Annual Report,* July 1, 1996 to June 30, 1997, 6.

39 *U. S. Federal Census*, 1910.

40 *Roxbury Cookery*, 295-296; Cunningham, *Architectural Resource Survey,* 67.

41 *Roxbury Land Records*, 1903. 20:54; 1911. 17:449; 1929. 20:488.

42 Ungeheuer, *Roxbury Remembered*, 175.

43 Roxbury Town Clerk. *Death Certificates*, 1940-1959. Death certificate for James Bruce Berry, born Sept. 24, 1877, died July 29, 1941.

44 Sterry and Garrigus, *They Found a Way,* 173-177.

45 Larry Nourse, telephone conversation with author, Feb. 24, 2005.

46 Cunningham, *Architectural Resource Survey,* 90.

47 Pepin, *Genealogy Information for the Town of Roxbury, CT*, 11, 16; Cothren, *History of Ancient Woodbury*, 1879. 3:614.

48 Ungeheuer, *Roxbury Remembered*, 36-37; *U. S. Federal Census*, 1870. The census records H. Booth as divorced.

49 "Rambles in Roxbury," *New Milford Gazette*, May 25, 1894.

50 *The Bicentennial Celebration Calendar 1996-1997*. June 8, 1997.

51 Cunningham, *Architectural Resource Survey,* 69-70.

52 Ibid., 70; *U. S. Federal Census*, 1850, 1870, 1880.

53 Cunningham, *Architectural Resource Survey,* 69-70.

54 Larry Nourse, telephone conversation with author, Feb. 24, 2005.

55 Cothren, *History of Ancient Woodbury*, 1854. 1: 79; 2: 504.

56 Ungeheuer, *Roxbury Remembered*, 120-121.

57 Marie White, "Cultivating an interest in the past." *Sunday Republican Magazine*, Nov. 7, 1976.

58 "Rambles in Roxbury," *New Milford Gazette*, May 25, 1894.

59 Hurlbut, *Roxbury's Early Days,* 43; Ungeheuer, *Roxbury Remembered*, 57.

60 *Roxbury Town Meeting Minutes*, Dec. 20, 1978, 5: 70.

61 Bickford and Lamar, *Voices of the New Republic.* 1: 85.

62 *Ancient Woodbury Tercentenary,* 15; Humphrey, *Sketches,* 30.

63 Donald H. Westerberg, e-mail to author, Jan. 24, 2005.

64 Ungeheuer, *Roxbury Remembered*, 25; Swank, *History of the Manufacture of Iron in All Ages*, 4-5; http://www.reference.com/browse/Chalybians.

65 Cothren, *History of Ancient Woodbury,* 1872. 2: 852.

66 Ungeheuer, *Roxbury Remembered*, 6, 13; *Roxbury Cookery*, 247.

67 *Mail-A-Map Street Map of Washington & Roxbury*, 2007.

68 *Homes of Old Woodbury*, 258.

69 *Mail-A-Map Street Map of Washington & Roxbury*, 2007.

70 Ungeheuer, *Roxbury Remembered*, 3.

71 Cunningham, *Architectural Resource Survey,* 20, 28.

72 Evelyn Williams, e-mails to author, Jan. 10 and 11, 2005.

73 Cunningham, *Architectural Resource Survey*, 56.

74 *U. S. Federal Census*, 1860, 1870.

75 Cunningham, *Architectural Resource Survey*, 56.

76 *U. S. Federal Census*, 1910. There is some confusion in the records about whether George R. Crofut was married. According to *Architectural Resource Survey*, p. 56, he was unmarried. However, census records listed Josephen N. as his wife and indicate they had four children, though only Calvin H. was listed.

77 "Roxbury," *New Milford Gazette*, May 12, 1893; "Rambles in Roxbury," *New Milford Gazette*, May 11, 1894.

78 Cunningham, *Architectural Resource Survey*, 56.

79 Hughes and Allen, *Connecticut Place Names,* 707.

80 *Roxbury Land Records*, Index to Vols. 1-10, 460.

81 Cunningham, *Architectural Resource Survey,* 86.

82 Ibid., 133.

83 Ungeheuer, *Roxbury Remembered,* 218.

84 *Connecticut Town Marriage Records, pre-1870 (Barbour Collection).* http.//www.ancestry.com.

85 Cunningham, *Architectural Resource Survey*, 88.

86 *U. S. Federal Census*, 1850. *Homes of Old Woodbury*, 257.

87 Pepin, *Genealogy Information for the Town of Roxbury, CT*, 23.

88 Cunningham, *Architectural Resource Survey*, 88.

89 Bickford and Lamar, *Voices of the New Republic,* 2: 199.

90 Peter Hurlbut, conversation with author, Jan. 6, 2006.

91 Humphrey, *Sketches,* 5.

92 Peggy Crabtree, conversation with author, Aug. 23, 2006.

93 Timothy Beard, telephone conversation with author, Jan. 15, 2005.

94 Bee Warburton, editor, *The World of Irises* (Wichita, Kansas, American Iris Society, 1978), 44, 47.

95 U. S. Dept. of Agriculture Forest Service Web site. http://www.na.fs.fed.us/fhp/invasive_plants.

96 Tovah Martin. "All-Garden Alert! Aliens Have Landed," *New York Times*, Mar. 20, 2005, CT8.

97 State of Connecticut. http://www.ct.gov/.;Cathy Shufro, "It's tough diggin' to trace garnet mines," *News Times* Apr. 11, 1977.

98 Cathy Shufro, "It's tough diggin' to trace garnet mines," *News Times* Apr. 11, 1977.

99 Ungeheuer, *Roxbury Remembered*, 121-122.

100 "Rambles in Roxbury," *New Milford Gazette*, May 25, 1894.

101 *Roxbury Land Records*, Feb. 25, 1935. 23: 676.

102 *Homes of Old Woodbury*, 228.

103 Cathy Shufro, "It's tough diggin' to trace garnet mines," *News Times* Apr. 11, 1977.

104 Ibid.

105 Catherine S. Thompson, "Roxbury's Golden Harvest: Little Change in 8 Years," *Litchfield County Times*. July 24, 1992.

106 *U. S. Federal Census*, 1810; 1850-1880. The 1810 census for Roxbury listed John Woodruff and family and it is likely that Enoch Woodruff was a descendant.

107 Hurlbut, *Roxbury's Early Days,* 35; *American Civil War Soldiers*. http://www.ancestry.com.

108 Hurlbut, *Roxbury's Early Days,* 67.

109 del Po, *Was a Way of Life*, Chapter VII, unpaged.

110 Cothren, *History of Ancient Woodbury*, 1872. 2: 843.

111 Cothren, *History of Ancient Woodbury*, 1854. 1: 36.

112 Ibid., 1854. 1: 74; 1872. 2:849.

113 Jan Napier, e-mail to author, July 19, 2005.

114 Betty Blyn, letter to author, Feb. 2005.

115 Cunningham, *Architectural Resource Survey*, 96-97; *Roxbury Annual Report*, year ending Sept. 22, 1895, 3.

116 *Roxbury Town Meeting Minutes.* Nov. 14, 1974, 5:52.

117 Hughes and Allen, *Connecticut Place Names*, 490.

118 "Rambles in Roxbury," *New Milford Gazette*, May 25, 1894.

119   *Roxbury Grand List*, 1992, 44.

120   Mathews, *Philo Hodge (1756-1842)*, 51-53.

121   Ibid., 55-58; 91.

122   Ibid., 91-92.

123   Ibid., 111.

124   Ibid., 112-114.

125   Ibid., 132-135.

126   "Roxbury," *New Milford Gazette*, July 22, 1910.

127   Correspondence about the windmill is in the Roxbury Museum.

128   "Roxbury's Ranking Citizen, Liberal Donor to Town Needs," *Waterbury Republican*, May 17, 1936.

129   Mathews, *Philo Hodge (1756-1842)*, 114-115.

130   Worley, *Guide to New Milford Connecticut…,* 84.

131   "Resident Honored," *Voices*, Mar. 12, 2008; Tammy McVey-Camilleri. "Roxbury Volunteers Receive Recognition…," *Voices*, Sept. 17, 2008.

132   Francis Chamberlain. "Roxbury Scout numbers houses, now is New Eagle." *Republican-American* (Waterbury, Conn.), Feb. 4, 1993.

133   Cunningham, *Architectural Resource Survey,* 99-100.

134   James M. Scott, e-mails to author, Jan. 17, 2005; Feb. 2, 2005.

135   "Roxbury Voters Accept New Road." *New Milford Times*, Sept. 6, 1974.

136   Judd Family Web site. http://juddfamilytree.org/Deacon%20Thomas%20Judd%20Family.pdf.

137   *U. S. Federal Census*, 1830-1870.

138   *U. S. Federal Census*, 1860; Cothren, *History of Ancient Woodbury,* 1879. 3: 582.

139 University of Michigan. Litchfield County (Conn.). *Litchfield County Centennial Celebration, held at Litchfield, Conn., 13th and 14th of Aug., 1851.* Ann Arbor, Michigan Library, 2005, 20.

140 Hurlbut, *Roxbury's Early Days,* 33.

141 Worthington, *Roxbury in the Civil War,* 1, 5, 15; *American Civil War Soldiers.* http://www.ancestry.com.

142 *U. S. Federal Census,* 1870 and 1880.

143 Margot Judge, interview with author, Jan. 2005.

144 Margot Judge, conversation with author, Mar. 18, 2005.

145 *Roxbury Assessor Records,* Book 43, July 7, 1984, 162; Margot Judge, conversation with author, Mar. 18, 2005.

146 Chuck and Doris Farrell, e-mail to author, Dec. 9, 2004; *State Handbook & Guide.* http://www.shgresources.com/ct/.

147 Narendra P. Loomba, letters to author, Jan. 8 and 29, 2005.

148 *Annual Report,* year ending June 30, 1993, 6.

149 Fay, *Historical Sketch Roxbury Congregational Church, 1744-1944,* 22.

150 Cothren, *History of Ancient Woodbury,* 1854. 1: 153-155.

151 Cunningham, *Architectural Resource Survey,* 106.

152 Cothren, *History of Ancient Woodbury,* 1854. 2: 615-618.

153 *Homes of Old Woodbury,* 244; Cunningham, *Architectural Resource Survey,* 89.

154 Hurlbut, *Roxbury's Early Days,* 37.

155 Earle, *The Sabbath in Puritan New England,* 66-75.

156 Hurlbut, *Roxbury's Early Days,* 38.

157 Ibid., 52; *Litchfield Republican,* Sept. 18, 1820.

158 "Celebration at Roxbury," *Columbian Register,* July 19, 1817.

159 Bell and Mayerfeld. *Time and the Land,* 24. The authors describe the geology, ecology and history of Mine Hill, along with photos, maps and drawings.

160 Roxbury Land Trust, "Mine Hill, A National Historic Landmark," 2007; Chesson, Frederick W., "Yankee Steel, or The Rise and Fall of the American Silver Steel Company," 2000. This brochure describes the corporate ownership of Mine Hill and contains an extensive bibliography.

161 Roxbury Land Trust, "Mine Hill, A National Historic Landmark," 2007; Hurlbut, *Roxbury's Early Days,* 43-44.

162 Bell and Mayerfeld. *Time and the Land,* 22.

163 Cothren, *History of Ancient Woodbury*, 1854. 2: 642-657; Miner Family Web site. http://familytreemaker.genealogy.com/users/a/t/k/Patti-L-Atkinson/GENE4-0001.html.

164 Minor/Miner family Web site has a family tree and information on Thomas Minor's work in Stonington, Ct. where he is buried. http://alum.wpi.edu/~p_miner/Miner1.html#TM2.

165 For a condensed version of Minor's journey, see *Centennial Celebration at Roxbury, Connecticut July Fourth A. D. 1876.* For a detailed account, see Cothren, *History of Ancient Woodbury*, 3 vols. 1854 and 1872.

166 Cothren, *History of Ancient Woodbury*, 1854. 1: 30-31; *Homes of Old Woodbury,* 76, 115.

167 Humphrey, *Sketches,* 6; "Roxbury." *New Milford Gazette.* May 25, 1891.

168 Elizabeth Nourse, telephone conversation with author, Feb. 24, 2005.

169 Obituary. *Republican-American* (Waterbury, Conn.), Sept. 5, 1972, 2.

170 Ungeheuer, *Roxbury Remembered*, 3; Cunningham, *Architectural Resource Survey,* 116, 118 & 119.

171 *Milford Gazette*, Aug. 18, 1893; Mar. 30, 1894.

172 Paul A. Elwell, letter to author, Dec. 2004.

173 Humphrey. *Sketches,* 35; *Connecticut Journal,* May 5, 1807, 1.

174 Henrietta Johnson, telephone conversation with author, Dec. 9, 2004.

175 Stephen Zaleta, e-mail to author, Dec. 18, 2004.

176 Scott Oglesby's Web site. www.kurumi.com/roads/ct/.

177 *Roxbury Land Records*, Dec. 11, 1821. 6:3; Ungeheuer, *Roxbury Remembered*, 13.

178 Cothren, *History of Ancient Woodbury*, 1854. 1:282.

179 Cothren, *History of Ancient Woodbury*, 1854. 2: 795; Hurlbut, *Roxbury's Early Days*, 52.

180 *Census of Pensioners in 1835* and *A Census of Pensioners for Revolutionary or Military Services 1841*, 58. http:// www.ancestry.com.

181 Marian Skedgell, conversation, summer 2005.

182 Cunningham, *Architectural Resource Survey*, 130.

183 Tracey Andrews, letter to author, Jan. 2005.

184 *New York Passenger Lists, 1820-1957.* http:// www.ancestry.com; *U. S. Federal Census*, 1860.

185 Cunningham, *Architectural Resource Survey*, 78, 125.

186 *New York Passenger Lists, 1820-1957.* http:// www.ancestry.com.

187 *Roxbury Annual Report*, 1890, 1, item #3; Sept. 16, 1898 to Sept. 16, 1899, unpaged, item # 20 and # 57.

188 Deborah B. Donnelly, "Man's foresight produced notable tree," *Country Life*, Nov. 13, 2003.

189 Cunningham, *Architectural Resource Survey*, 39.

190 "Early Roxbury History Recalled," *Newtown Bee*, Sept. 16, 1962.

191 "Roxbury Station," *New Milford Gazette*, Mar.24, Nov. 11, Dec. 22, 1899.

192 Ibid.

193 Bell and Mayerfeld, *Time and the Land*, 28-29.

194 Roxbury Land Trust, "Mine Hill, A National Historic Landmark," 2007.

195 Cothren, *History of Ancient Woodbury*, 1854. 2:777; Hurlbut, *Roxbury's Early Days,* 32.

196 *U. S. Federal Census*, 1800. Note: Ranney's name is indexed as Hanney in this census.

197 Rawson, *From Here To Yender: Early Trails and Highway Life*, 13-14.

198 Elinor Hurlbut, "How Ranney Hill Was," *Roxbury Historical Society Newsletter*, spring 2002.

199 Desert USA. http://www.desertusa.com/mag99/oct/papr/raven. html; Web site on birds of Kaweah River Delta in Central California, http://kaweahoaks.com/html/raven.html.

200 Cothren, *History of Ancient Woodbury*, 1854. 2: 581.

201 Hurlbut family Web site. http://www.hurlbut.info/ght/np40.htm

202 Hurlbut family Web site. http://www.hurlbut.info/ght/np40. htm#iin1278

203 *Connecticut Town Marriage Records (pre-1870) (Barbour Collection).* http:// www.ancestry.com.

204 Douglas Forrest, "Bad Man from Bridgewater," *Lure of the Litchfield Hills*, Summer 1963.

205 Humphrey, *Sketches*, 7; Leroy W. Foote, "Caves in the Litchfield Hills," *Lure of the Litchfield Hills,* June 1951.

206 Roxbury Planning Commission Office, letter from Jack Gilpin, Jan. 8, 2004.

207 Gary Steinman, e-mail to author, Sept. 14, 2005.

208 Ungeheuer, *Roxbury Remembered,* 184.

209 Hurlbut, *Roxbury's Early Days,* 14; *Roxbury Cookery*, 290.

210 Cunningham, *Architectural Resource Survey,* 140.

211 Ungeheuer, *Roxbury Remembered,* 126; *U. S. Federal Census*, 1880. http:// www.ancestry.com.

212 Cunningham, *Architectural Resource Survey,*138; *Homes of Old Woodbury*, 234.

213 "Probate Notices," *Connecticut Herald*, May 30, 1809, 4.

214 Roger L. Payne. U. S. Board on Geographic Names, e-mail to author, Aug. 5, 2005; U. S. Board of Geographic Names. http://geonames.usgs.gov/domestic/quarterly_list.htm. *Quarterly Review List 381*, released Sept. 26, 2002. The U. S. Board on Geographic Names issued its final decision on spelling in the July 2005 minutes. http://geonames.usgs.gov/docs/minutes/DNCJul05Minutes.pdf .

215 Timothy Beard, telephone conversation with author, Jan. 15, 2005.

216 Ruth G. Torres, e-mails to author, Dec. 1, 2004; Feb. 19, 2005. Torres noted that Mahican and Mohegan are separate languages and should not be confused with one another.

217 Nora Costello, e-mail to author, May 23, 2005.

218 Stewart Kellerman, e-mail to author, Apr. 8, 2005.

219 Beers, *County Atlas of Litchfield Connecticut*, 67.

220 *Roxbury Annual Report*, year ending Sept. 13, 1930, 18.

221 Deborah B. Donnelly, "The last of the 1-room school…." *Country Life*, Mar. 2, 2000.

222 Cothren, *History of Ancient Woodbury*, 1854. 1: 46-47; Hurlbut, *Roxbury's Early Days,* 32.

223 Ungeheuer, *Roxbury Remembered*, 3; "Rambles in Roxbury," *New Milford Gazette*, May 11 & 25, 1894.

224 Hurlbut, *Roxbury's Early Days,* 50.

225 Ungeheuer, *Roxbury Remembered*, 3.

226 Kurumi Web site on Connecticut highway history. http://www.kurumi.com/roads/ct/ctx195.html#199.

227 Ibid.

228 Cunningham, *Architectural Resource Survey,* 170; University of
     Virginia Web site. http://xroads.virginia.edu/~HYPER/DETOC/
     TRANSPORT/how.html.

229 CT Dept of Transportation Web site. http://www.ct.gov/dot/site/
     default.asp; "Turnpikes," *Hartford Daily Courant (1840-1887);*
     Feb 12, 1885.

230 *U. S. Federal Census*, 1900.

231 Ibid.

232 *U. S. Federal Census*, 1930 and Death certificate in Roxbury Town
     Clerk's Office.

233 *U. S. World War I Draft Registration Cards, 1917-1918; U. S. World
     War II Draft Registration Cards*, 1942.
     http:// www.ancestry.com.

234 *U. S. Federal Census*, 1910, 1920, 1930; *Connecticut Death Index,
     1949-2001 Record.*

235 Ungeheuer, *Roxbury Remembered,* 115; Cunningham, *Architectural
     Resource Survey,* 166, 187.

236 "Obituary,"*Republican American*, Oct. 3, 1978, page 4, col. 1.; Bud
     Squire interview with Margot Judge and author, Mar. 14, 2005.

237 *Connecticut, A Guide To Its Roads, Lore And People*, 14; "Roxbury
     Trees Have Personality, Too," *Voices*, Nov. 12, 2003.

238 Webster, *Webster's Handy Dictionary,* 280; Cothren, *History of
     Ancient Woodbury,* 1872. 2: 852.

239 Mary Jonker, conversation with author, June 22, 2006; *The Oxford
     English Dictionary*, 18:252.

240 Marion Hawley, conversation with author, May 31, 2006; Merriam-
     Webster Online Dictionary. http://www.merriam-webster.com

241 *Bible*. 2 Kings 23:10; Isaiah 30:33; Jeremiah 7:31-32; Jeremiah
     19:6, 11-14.

242 Cothren, *History of Ancient Woodbury*, 1854. 1:159-161.

243   Cothren, *History of Ancient Woodbury*, 1854. 1:28.

244   "Roxbury Trees Have Personality, Too," *Voices*, Nov. 12, 2003.

245   Ungeheuer, *Roxbury Remembered,* 137.

246   *Colonial Connecticut Records, 1636-1776.* 3:80.

247   Cothren, *History of Ancient Woodbury*, 1854. 1:153-155.

248   One World Tree. http://trees.ancestry.com/owt/person.
      aspx?pid=31564527.

249   Hurlbut, *Roxbury's Early Days,* 33, 45; Cothren, *History of Ancient
      Woodbury*, 1854. 1:209.

250   Hurlbut. *Roxbury's Early Days,* 33; *Connecticut Revolutionary War
      Military Lists, 1775-83.* http:// www.ancestry.com.

251   Earle, *Home Life in Colonial Days,* 413.

252   Ibid, 401.

253   Beers, *County Atlas of Litchfield Connecticut,* 67.

254   Cothren, *History of Ancient Woodbury*, 1854. 2: 744-747.

255   Ungeheuer, *Roxbury Remembered*, 3; "Rambles in Roxbury," *New
      Milford Gazette*, May 11, 1894.

256   Humphrey, *Sketches*, 31; Cunningham, *Architectural Resource
      Survey,* 201.

257   Hurlbut, *Roxbury's Early Days*, 37.

258   Cunningham, *Architectural Resource Survey,* 63.

259   Cothren, *History of Ancient Woodbury,* 1854. 1: 283; Barber,
      Connecticut Historical Collections, 486.

260   *Architectural Resource Survey,* 204; *U. S. Federal Census*, 1850-1870.

261   *Homes of Old Woodbury*, 230; Cunningham, *Architectural Resource
      Survey,* 204.

262   *Connecticut Town Marriage Records, pre-1870 (Barbour Collection).*
      http:// www.ancestry.com.

263 *U. S. Federal Census*, 1850-1880; Cunningham, *Architectural Resource Survey,* 204.

264 Vaughn Gray, mapmaker. *Litchfield County Connecticut map*, 1975.

Selected Bibliography

American Revolution Bicentennial, 1776-1976 Woodbury, Old Woodbury in the Revolution: The Five Parishes and their Soldiers. Woodbury: Woodbury Bicentennial Committee, July 4, 1976.

Ancient Woodbury Tercentenary: Historical Souvenir and Official Program. Three Hundredth Anniversary of the First Exploration and the First Indian Deed, July 4 and 5, 1959. Woodbury: Ancient Woodbury Tercentenary Committee, 1959.

Barber, John Warner. *Connecticut Historical Collections….* 2nd edition. New Haven: Durrie & Peck and J. W. Barber, 1836.

Beers, F. W. *County Atlas of Litchfield Connecticut from Actual Surveys.* New York: F. W. Beers & Co., 1874.

Bell, Michael, and Diane B. Mayerfeld. *Time and the Land: the Story of Mine Hill.* n. p.: Roxbury Land Trust and Yale School of Forestry and Environmental Studies, 1982.

The Bicentennial Celebration Calendar, 1996-1997. Roxbury, 1997.

Bickford, Christopher P., and Howard Roberts Lamar, editors. *Voices of the New Republic: Connecticut Towns 1800-1832.* 2 vols. New Haven: Connecticut Academy of Arts and Sciences, 2003.

Booth Free School Journal. Centennial Edition. Roxbury, 1991.

Boyd, Edward S., and Helen S. Boyd. "Roxbury Inscriptions." n. p.:1910.

Centennial Celebration at Roxbury, Connecticut July Fourth A. D. 1876. Waterbury: Press of the Index Printing House, 1877.

Clark, Howard. *Saga of Pomperaug Plantation, 1673-1973.* Southbury, 1973.

Connecticut, A Guide to Its Roads, Lore, and People. Federal Writers' Project of the Works Progress Administration for the State of Connecticut. Boston: Houghton, Mifflin Company, 1938.

Cooper, Fletcher E. *The Shepaug Railroad, 1872-1948.* Litchfield, 2002.

Cothren, William. *History of Ancient Woodbury, Connecticut from the First Indian Deed in 1659 to 1854.* 3 vols. Waterbury: Bronson Brothers, 1854.

———. *History of Ancient Woodbury, Connecticut from the First Indian Deed in 1659 to 1872.* 2nd edition. Woodbury: William Cothren, 1872.

———. *History of Ancient Woodbury, Connecticut from the First Indian Deed in 1659 to 1879.* 2nd edition. Woodbury: William Cothren, 1879.

Cunningham, Jan. *Historical and Architectural Resource Survey of the Town of Roxbury, Connecticut.* [Cover title: *Roxbury, a Historic and Architectural Resource Survey*] Middletown: Cunningham Associates, Ltd., 1996-1997.

del Po, William J. *It Was a Way of Life.* unpublished. Woodbury, 1995.

Earle, Alice Morse. *Home Life in Colonial Days.* Stockbridge, Mass.: Berkshire Traveller Press, 1974. (written, 1898)

———. *The Sabbath in Puritan New England.* New York: Scribners, 1891.

Fay, Charles Edey. *Historical Sketch of the Roxbury Congregational Church 1744-1944.* Roxbury, 1944.

Francis, W. H. *History of the Hatting Trade in Danbury, Conn. from its commencement in 1780 to the present time….* Danbury: H. & L. Osborne Publishers, 1860.

Goodenough, Arthur. *The Clergy of Litchfield County.* n. p.: Litchfield Country University Club, 1909.

History of Litchfield County, Connecticut, with illustrations and biographical sketches of its prominent men and pioneers. Philadelphia: J. W. Lewis, 1881.

Homes of Old Woodbury: Tercentenary Celebration of Old Woodbury Connecticut. Woodbury: Old Woodbury Historical Society, 1959.

Hughes, Arthur H., and Morse S. Allen. *Connecticut Place Names.* n. p.: Connecticut Historical Society, 1976.

Hull, Daniel R. *Bewitched Mine Hill: the Silver-Lead-Iron Mine of Roxbury, Connecticut.* Southbury: Graphictype, 1966.

Humphrey, Helen Hunt W. *Sketches of Roxbury, Conn.* Reprint 1996. New Milford: Times Print Shop, 1924.

Hurlbut, Norman Henry. *Roxbury's Early Days.* n. p.,1996.

Larkin, Jack. *The Reshaping of Everyday Life, 1790-1840.* New York: Harper& Row, 1988.

Lenney, Christopher J. *Sightseeking, Clues to the Landscape History of New England.* Hanover: University of New Hampshire, 2003.

Mail-A-Map Street Maps. Madison: Harbor Publications, 2004-2009.

Mathews, Barbara Jean. *Philo Hodge (1756-1842) of Roxbury, Connecticut.* Baltimore: Gateway Press, Inc, 1992.

Mills, Lewis Sprague. *The Story of Connecticut.* New York: Charles Scribner's Sons, 1932.

The Oxford English Dictionary. 2nd edition, Oxford: Clarendon Press, 1989 (reprinted with corrections 1991), prepared by J. A. Simpson and E. S. C. Weiner.

Pepin, Linda Castle, comp. "Cemetery Inscriptions." unpublished paper. n. p.: n. d.

———. *Genealogy Information for the Town of Roxbury, CT.* n. p.: 1999?

Rawson, Marion Nicholl. *From Here To Yender: Early Trails and Highway Life.* New York: E. P. Dutton & Co., 1932.

Roxbury. *Annual Report of the Board of Selectmen.* Roxbury, various years.

Roxbury. *Town Meeting Minutes.* Roxbury, various years.

Roxbury Cookery, Favorite Recipes Collected by Members of the Roxbury Vol. Fire Dept. Womens Auxillary [sic]. Roxbury, 1974.

Roxbury Historic District Commission "Roxbury on the Move: The History of Roxbury's Many Traveling Buildings." n. p., 1999.

Roxbury Historical Society. *Roxbury Historical Society News.* Roxbury: Roxbury Historical Society. Spring 2002 and 2003.

Roxbury League of Women Voters, *Map of Town of Roxbury, Conn.*, n. p.: n. p.: May 1934.

Roxbury Past & Present: A Survey of the Evolution of Roxbury Center's Historic District and Walking Tour. n. p.: Roxbury Historic District Commission, 2007.

Roxbury Planning Commission. *Roxbury, 1999 Plan of Conservation & Development.* Avon: Planimetrics, 1999.

Rumford, Beatrix T., ed. *American Folk Portraits....* The Abby Aldrich Rockefeller Folk Art Center Series I. Boston: New York Graphic Society in association with the Colonial Williamsburg Foundation, 1981.

Sellers, Helen Earle. *Connecticut Town Origins: Their Names, Boundaries, Early Histories and First Families.* 2nd edition, Chester: Pequot Press, 1973.

Shepard, Odell. *Connecticut, Past and Present.* New York: A. Knopf, 1939.

Sloane, Eric. *Diary of an Early American Boy: Noah Blake 1805.* Reprint. New York: Ballantine Books, 1965.

Sterry, Iveagh Hunt, and William H. Garrigus. *They Found a Way: Connecticut's Restless People.* Brattleboro: Stephen Daye Press, 1938.

Stewart, George R. *American Place Names.* New York: Oxford University Press, 1970.

———. *Names on the Globe.* New York: Oxford University Press, 1975.

———. *Names on the Land.* Boston: Houghton Mifflin, 1967.

Swank, James M. *History of the Manufacture of Iron in All Ages….* Philadelphia, 1884.

U. S. Census Bureau. *Federal Census.* Washington, D. C.: U. S. Census Bureau, 1790-1930.

Ungeheuer, Frederick, Lewis Hurlbut, and Ethel Hurlbut. *Roxbury Remembered.* Oxford: Connecticut Heritage Press, 1989.

Vanderpoel, Emily Noyes, comp. *Chronicles of a pioneer school from 1782-1833 being the history of Miss Sarah Pierce….* Cambridge: University Press, 1903.

Webster, Noah. *A Handy Dictionary of the English Language….* compiled by Loomis J. Campbell. New York: American Book Co., 1877.

Whittlesey, Charles Barney. *Genealogy of the Whittlesey-Whittlesey Family.* 2nd edition. New York: McGraw Hill, 1941.

Worley, A. C., comp. *Guide to New Milford Connecticut and Its Environs*….New Milford: The Times Print Shop, 1928.

Worthington, Elmer. *History of the Roxbury Congregational Church (United Church of Christ) Roxbury, Connecticut, 1673-1974*. unpublished. Roxbury, 1973.

———. *Roxbury Cemeteries 1745-1934*. unpublished. Roxbury, 1976.

———. *Roxbury in the Civil War*. unpublished. Roxbury, 1963.

Index

Note that the following are grouped into categories: Bridges, Cemeteries, Churches, Historic houses, Indian languages and dialects, Indian tribes, Bridgewater and Roxbury Land Trust preserves, and Schools.

Y

Z